C-3720 CAREER EXAMINATION SERIES

This is your
PASSBOOK for...

General Clerical & Typing Careers Test

Test Preparation Study Guide
Questions & Answers

COPYRIGHT NOTICE

This book is SOLELY intended for, is sold ONLY to, and its use is RESTRICTED to individual, bona fide applicants or candidates who qualify by virtue of having seriously filed applications for appropriate license, certificate, professional and/or promotional advancement, higher school matriculation, scholarship, or other legitimate requirements of education and/or governmental authorities.

This book is NOT intended for use, class instruction, tutoring, training, duplication, copying, reprinting, excerption, or adaptation, etc., by:

1) Other publishers
2) Proprietors and/or Instructors of "Coaching" and/or Preparatory Courses
3) Personnel and/or Training Divisions of commercial, industrial, and governmental organizations
4) Schools, colleges, or universities and/or their departments and staffs, including teachers and other personnel
5) Testing Agencies or Bureaus
6) Study groups which seek by the purchase of a single volume to copy and/or duplicate and/or adapt this material for use by the group as a whole without having purchased individual volumes for each of the members of the group
7) Et al.

Such persons would be in violation of appropriate Federal and State statutes.

PROVISION OF LICENSING AGREEMENTS – Recognized educational, commercial, industrial, and governmental institutions and organizations, and others legitimately engaged in educational pursuits, including training, testing, and measurement activities, may address request for a licensing agreement to the copyright owners, who will determine whether, and under what conditions, including fees and charges, the materials in this book may be used them. In other words, a licensing facility exists for the legitimate use of the material in this book on other than an individual basis. However, it is asseverated and affirmed here that the material in this book CANNOT be used without the receipt of the express permission of such a licensing agreement from the Publishers. Inquiries re licensing should be addressed to the company, attention rights and permissions department.

All rights reserved, including the right of reproduction in whole or in part, in any form or by any means, electronic or mechanical, including photocopying, recording, or by any information storage and retrieval system, without permission in writing from the Publisher.

Copyright © 2025 by
National Learning Corporation

212 Michael Drive, Syosset, NY 11791
(516) 921-8888 • www.passbooks.com
E-mail: info@passbooks.com

PASSBOOK® SERIES

THE *PASSBOOK® SERIES* has been created to prepare applicants and candidates for the ultimate academic battlefield – the examination room.

At some time in our lives, each and every one of us may be required to take an examination – for validation, matriculation, admission, qualification, registration, certification, or licensure.

Based on the assumption that every applicant or candidate has met the basic formal educational standards, has taken the required number of courses, and read the necessary texts, the *PASSBOOK® SERIES* furnishes the one special preparation which may assure passing with confidence, instead of failing with insecurity. Examination questions – together with answers – are furnished as the basic vehicle for study so that the mysteries of the examination and its compounding difficulties may be eliminated or diminished by a sure method.

This book is meant to help you pass your examination provided that you qualify and are serious in your objective.

The entire field is reviewed through the huge store of content information which is succinctly presented through a provocative and challenging approach – the question-and-answer method.

A climate of success is established by furnishing the correct answers at the end of each test.

You soon learn to recognize types of questions, forms of questions, and patterns of questioning. You may even begin to anticipate expected outcomes.

You perceive that many questions are repeated or adapted so that you can gain acute insights, which may enable you to score many sure points.

You learn how to confront new questions, or types of questions, and to attack them confidently and work out the correct answers.

You note objectives and emphases, and recognize pitfalls and dangers, so that you may make positive educational adjustments.

Moreover, you are kept fully informed in relation to new concepts, methods, practices, and directions in the field.

You discover that you are actually taking the examination all the time: you are preparing for the examination by "taking" an examination, not by reading extraneous and/or supererogatory textbooks.

In short, this PASSBOOK®, used directedly, should be an important factor in helping you to pass your test.

GENERAL CLERICAL & TYPING CAREERS TEST
PREPARING FOR THE GENERAL CLERICAL & TYPING CAREERS TEST

What are these tests?

The General Clerical Exam is given to all applicants for non-supervisory clerical jobs.

The Typing Careers Test is the test given to applicants for clerical positions that require typing. The Typing Careers Test is made up of two parts: a typing skills test and a written exam.

You must pass both the typing test and the written exam to receive a passing grade. In order to pass the typing test, you must type at least 40 words per minute.

What kinds of questions are on these written tests?

The test measures the basic abilities common to all non-supervisory clerical jobs. The test questions cover these four main areas:

1. Public Contact – 10 questions

   These questions test your knowledge of how to work well with members of the public and with other workers. Each question describes a situation that might occur on the job. You are asked to choose the BEST way to handle the situation.

2. Reading Comprehension – 20 questions

   These questions test your ability to read and understand written information. All the information you need to answer a question in this section is contained in each item. You are encouraged to read each item as often as you wish.

3. English Usage – 25 questions

   These questions test your knowledge of grammar, punctuation, spelling and sentence structure. There are four types of questions in this section:
   - Spelling – pick the word that is INCORRECTLY spelled out of the four choices given in each question
   - Pick the best sentence – pick the sentence that represents the best use of English grammar, punctuation and sentence structure in each question
   - Fill in the blank – fill in the blank with the choice that gives the best example of correct English grammar
   - How many errors in line – determine how many errors in grammar, spelling and punctuation are contained in each line

4. Math – 20 questions

   These questions will test your knowledge of how to do numerical work (add, subtract, divide, multiply, percentages and averages). There are two types of questions in this section:
   - <u>Word Problems</u>: You will be expected to work the problems using your knowledge of how to do numerical work and to pick the correct answer from the choices given.
   - <u>Passage Problems</u>: You will be expected to work several problems from information provided in a passage. You are encouraged to read the passage as often as you wish in order to work each problem.

How do I use this booklet?

This booklet contains a sample test with examples of the different types of questions on the real test. None of the sample questions will actually be on the real test, but they are VERY similar to the real questions.

After the end of the sample test, you are given the correct answer to each question and told why it is the best choice. You should carefully study each sample question to become familiar with questions of the same type on the test.

Don't be discouraged if you are not able to answer some of the sample questions correctly. No one is expected to answer ALL the questions on the test correctly.

TIPS FOR TAKING THE TEST

1. To avoid the risk of arriving too late to be admitted to the test, allow extra time for traveling to the test center. Notify Civil Service in advance if you will require special testing accommodations due to a disability.

2. Pay close attention to the instructions given by the monitor at the beginning of the test session.

3. Read the instructions included in the actual test booklet carefully. These instructions are given to help you and should be followed very closely.

4. Use the clock or your watch to keep track of the time.

5. Read each question carefully. Then read ALL of the answers to each question before deciding which answer is correct.

6. If you are having a hard time answering a question, skip that one and come back to it later if you have time.

7. Try to answer each question even if you must guess. The final grade will be based only on the number of correct answers. There is no penalty for guessing.

8. Be sure you mark your answers properly on your answer sheet and NOT in the test booklet. You will only be given credit for answers you mark on the answer sheet.

SAMPLE QUESTIONS

Public Contact

1. If others are within hearing distance while you are taking a confidential phone message, the BEST way to verify that the message is correct is to
    A. read the message back to the caller
    B. ask the caller to call back later
    C. explain that you will call back when you are free
    D. ask the caller to repeat the message

    1._____

2. In order to complete a certain task, you need to ask a favor of a worker you don't know very well. The best way to do this would be to
    A. ask the worker, briefly stating your reasons
    B. convince the worker that it is for the good of the office
    C. tell the worker how greatly he or she can benefit if it is done
    D. offer to do something for the worker in return

    2._____

Reading Comprehension

DIRECTIONS: Answer the questions below based on the information that precedes them. Your answers should be based only on information contained in the paragraph or passage associated with the question.

3. Often additional copies are needed of letters received. When this occurs, it will be necessary to make a notation on the back of the letters quoting the number of copies needed. Place all letters to be Xeroxed in the folders designated for this purpose. Place a rubber band around the folder and place it in the messenger mail bin.

    Usually letters are sent out once a day, depending on the quantity of papers received that day.

    According to the above:
    A. a rubber band should be placed around all letters to be Xeroxed before placing them in the designated folder
    B. the number of copies needed of a letter should be noted on the front of the letter in the upper right-hand corner
    C. special folders are set aside in which to place letters that need to be Xeroxed
    D. generally, the messenger photocopies letters once a day, depending on the quantity of papers received that day

    3._____

4. To close out records of patients on the daily closure listing, follows these steps:
   a) Pull patient's orange appointment card and chart
   b) Indicate "closed" on the chart and date closed
   c) Update master card showing "closed" and date of closure. Write in red ink.
   d) Destroy orange appointment card
   e) File chart and master card in closed files

   According to the above:
   A. when a patient's records are closed, his or her chart and master card are retained in closed files, but the appointment card is destroyed
   B. once "closed" and date of closure are properly shown on patient's chart, master card and appointment card, the three documents should be filed in closed files
   C. "closed" and date of closure should be written in red ink on patient's master card and orange appointment card
   D. the orange appointment card should be destroyed after writing "closed" and the date of closure on it

4._____

English Usage

5. Choose the word listed below that is spelled incorrectly:
   A. errors
   B. department
   C. carefuly
   D. business

5._____

6. Fill in the blank with the choice that gives the best example of correct English usage:

   Neither Amy _____ I like to mop the floor.

   A. or
   B. and
   C. nor
   D. but

6._____

7. Pick the sentence that represents the best English usage:
   A. It was them who did the work.
   B. It was her who did the work.
   C. It was him who did the work.
   D. It was she who did the work.

7._____

8. Pick the sentence that represents the best English usage:
   A. I will give the message to the person which answers the phone.
   B. He didn't know hisself what he wanted to do.
   C. I didn't know she needed treatment so bad.
   D. Norma is the girl whose desk is nearest the window.

8._____

For questions 9 and 10, determine how many errors in grammar, spelling and punctuation it contains. Mark the appropriate answer by using the following key:

(A) if there is one error in the line
(B) if there are two errors in the line
(C) if there are three or more errors in the line
(D) if there are no errors in the line

9. We need to buy the following supplies; pencils and pens,   9._____

10. stapels and tape. The cost of this supplies are to much   10._____

Mathematics

11. The department's total budget is $345,000. Nineteen percent of the budget is for supplies, thirty-four percent for new equipment and the rest is for employee salaries. How much budget money is used for employee salaries?   11._____
    A. $65,550
    B. $117,300
    C. $162,150
    D. $182,850

12. In May, the average cost per claim for benefits was $578. A total of $35,836 was paid in benefits. How many claims were paid?   12._____
    A. 60.9
    B. 61
    C. 62
    D. 59.6

13. A state agency will reimburse employees for meals at times when the employee is traveling outside the city where he works. However, to collect, the employee must leave before designated times and return after certain times. The schedule of times and amounts to be paid is listed below: 13._____

    - Breakfast: $4.00 – when travel begins before 6:00 a.m. and extends beyond 10:00 a.m.
    - Lunch: $4.50 – when travel begins before 10:00 a.m. and extends beyond 3:00 p.m.
    - Dinner: $8.00 – when travel begins before 3:00 p.m. and extends beyond 7:30 p.m.

    Employee A lives in New Orleans. He left New Orleans at 8:00 a.m. to travel to Slidell, and returned at 4:30 p.m. the same day. How much should he be paid for meals?
    A. $4.00
    B. $4.50
    C. $8.50
    D. $16.50

Refer to the chart below to answer questions 14 and 15. The chart contains spaces that correspond to the questions. You are to figure the amount that should be entered in the space and mark the correct choice on your answer sheet.

CLIENT APPOINTMENTS FOR MAY

WORKER	INITIAL	REEVALUATION	MEDICAL	TOTAL
Smith	45	70	15	130
Jones	34	___	9	134
Austin	51	65	27	143
Piper	49	83	19	151
Total	179	309	70	___

14. How many reevaluations did Jones do during May?
    A. 71
    B. 81
    C. 91
    D. None of the above

14._____

15. What is the total of all types of client appointments?
    A. 448
    B. 558
    C. 668
    D. None of the above

15._____

ANSWERS AND EXPLANATIONS

1. Correct answer: D

    If the caller repeats the message to you, the other people in the room will not hear what he or she is saying and you will be able to check the facts in the message.

2. Correct answer: A

    Be businesslike and to the point when you ask a work-related favor from a fellow worker.

3. Correct answer: C

    Read the second sentence in question 3 to see why choice C is the correct answer. Choice A is incorrect. In the paragraph it states, "place a rubber band around the folder," not around all the letters. Choice B is incorrect, because the number of copies of a letter should be noted on the back of the letter, not the front. Choice D is incorrect because in the paragraph it does not state that the messenger photocopies letters.

4. Correct answer: A

    Statements (d) and (e) support choice A. Choice B is incorrect because the appointment card is NOT filed when a file is closed. Choice C is incorrect because "closed" and date of closure are written in red only on a patient's master card when a file is closed. See (c). Choice D is incorrect because nothing is written on the appointment card when the case is closed. The appointment card is destroyed.

5. Correct answer: C

    <u>Carefuly</u> should be spelled <u>carefully.</u> The rest of the words are spelled correctly.

6. Correct answer: C

    <u>Nor</u> fills in the blank with the answer giving the best example of correct English usage.

7. Correct answer: D

    Choice D is the sentence that represents the best English usage. The pronouns *them, her* and *him* are used incorrectly.

8. Correct answer: D

    Choice D is the sentence that represents the best English usage. Choice A is incorrect because <u>which</u> should be <u>who</u>. Choice B is incorrect because <u>hisself</u> should be <u>himself</u>. Choice C is incorrect because <u>bad</u> should be <u>badly</u>.

9. Correct answer: B

    There are two errors in the line. The semicolon (;) should be a colon (:). There should be a comma (,) instead of the word "and" between pencils and pens. The line without any errors should read: "We need to buy the following supplies: pencils, pens,"

10. Correct answer: C

There are four errors in the line. The word <u>stapels</u> is misspelled, and should be spelled <u>staples</u>. <u>This supplies</u> should be <u>these supplies</u>. The verb <u>are</u> should be <u>is</u>. The word <u>to</u> should be spelled <u>too</u>. The line without any errors should read: "staples and tape. The cost of these supplies is too much."

11. Correct answer: C

19% + 34% = 53%
Subtract 53% from 100% (100 − 53 = 47%)
Multiply $345,000 x 47% = $162,150

12. Correct answer: C

Divide $35,836 by 578 = 62

13. Correct answer: B

Since Employee A left his home after 6:00 a.m., he should not be paid for breakfast. Since he did leave before 10:00 a.m. and returned after 3:00 p.m., he should be paid for lunch. He returned before 7:30 p.m., so he should not be paid for dinner. Therefore, his total reimbursement should be $4.50.

14. Correct answer: C

Add Jones' initial appointments to his medical appointments (34 + 9 = 43) and subtract that sum from the total (134 − 43 = 91), OR add Smith's, Austin's and Piper's reevaluations (70 + 65 + 83 = 218) and subtract that sum from the total number of reevaluations (309 − 218 = 91).

15. Correct answer: B

Add all the numbers in the TOTAL column (130 + 134 + 143 + 151 = 558), OR (179 + 309 + 70 = 558).

HOW TO TAKE A TEST

I. YOU MUST PASS AN EXAMINATION

A. WHAT EVERY CANDIDATE SHOULD KNOW

Examination applicants often ask us for help in preparing for the written test. What can I study in advance? What kinds of questions will be asked? How will the test be given? How will the papers be graded?

As an applicant for a civil service examination, you may be wondering about some of these things. Our purpose here is to suggest effective methods of advance study and to describe civil service examinations.

Your chances for success on this examination can be increased if you know how to prepare. Those "pre-examination jitters" can be reduced if you know what to expect. You can even experience an adventure in good citizenship if you know why civil service exams are given.

B. WHY ARE CIVIL SERVICE EXAMINATIONS GIVEN?

Civil service examinations are important to you in two ways. As a citizen, you want public jobs filled by employees who know how to do their work. As a job seeker, you want a fair chance to compete for that job on an equal footing with other candidates. The best-known means of accomplishing this two-fold goal is the competitive examination.

Exams are widely publicized throughout the nation. They may be administered for jobs in federal, state, city, municipal, town or village governments or agencies.

Any citizen may apply, with some limitations, such as the age or residence of applicants. Your experience and education may be reviewed to see whether you meet the requirements for the particular examination. When these requirements exist, they are reasonable and applied consistently to all applicants. Thus, a competitive examination may cause you some uneasiness now, but it is your privilege and safeguard.

C. HOW ARE CIVIL SERVICE EXAMS DEVELOPED?

Examinations are carefully written by trained technicians who are specialists in the field known as "psychological measurement," in consultation with recognized authorities in the field of work that the test will cover. These experts recommend the subject matter areas or skills to be tested; only those knowledges or skills important to your success on the job are included. The most reliable books and source materials available are used as references. Together, the experts and technicians judge the difficulty level of the questions.

Test technicians know how to phrase questions so that the problem is clearly stated. Their ethics do not permit "trick" or "catch" questions. Questions may have been tried out on sample groups, or subjected to statistical analysis, to determine their usefulness.

Written tests are often used in combination with performance tests, ratings of training and experience, and oral interviews. All of these measures combine to form the best-known means of finding the right person for the right job.

II. HOW TO PASS THE WRITTEN TEST

A. NATURE OF THE EXAMINATION

To prepare intelligently for civil service examinations, you should know how they differ from school examinations you have taken. In school you were assigned certain definite pages to read or subjects to cover. The examination questions were quite detailed and usually emphasized memory. Civil service exams, on the other hand, try to discover your present ability to perform the duties of a position, plus your potentiality to learn these duties. In other words, a civil service exam attempts to predict how successful you will be. Questions cover such a broad area that they cannot be as minute and detailed as school exam questions.

In the public service similar kinds of work, or positions, are grouped together in one "class." This process is known as *position-classification*. All the positions in a class are paid according to the salary range for that class. One class title covers all of these positions, and they are all tested by the same examination.

B. FOUR BASIC STEPS

1) Study the announcement

How, then, can you know what subjects to study? Our best answer is: "Learn as much as possible about the class of positions for which you've applied." The exam will test the knowledge, skills and abilities needed to do the work.

Your most valuable source of information about the position you want is the official exam announcement. This announcement lists the training and experience qualifications. Check these standards and apply only if you come reasonably close to meeting them.

The brief description of the position in the examination announcement offers some clues to the subjects which will be tested. Think about the job itself. Review the duties in your mind. Can you perform them, or are there some in which you are rusty? Fill in the blank spots in your preparation.

Many jurisdictions preview the written test in the exam announcement by including a section called "Knowledge and Abilities Required," "Scope of the Examination," or some similar heading. Here you will find out specifically what fields will be tested.

2) Review your own background

Once you learn in general what the position is all about, and what you need to know to do the work, ask yourself which subjects you already know fairly well and which need improvement. You may wonder whether to concentrate on improving your strong areas or on building some background in your fields of weakness. When the announcement has specified "some knowledge" or "considerable knowledge," or has used adjectives like "beginning principles of…" or "advanced … methods," you can get a clue as to the number and difficulty of questions to be asked in any given field. More questions, and hence broader coverage, would be included for those subjects which are more important in the work. Now weigh your strengths and weaknesses against the job requirements and prepare accordingly.

3) Determine the level of the position

Another way to tell how intensively you should prepare is to understand the level of the job for which you are applying. Is it the entering level? In other words, is this the position in which beginners in a field of work are hired? Or is it an intermediate or advanced level? Sometimes this is indicated by such words as "Junior" or "Senior" in the class title. Other jurisdictions use Roman numerals to designate the level – Clerk I, Clerk II, for example. The word "Supervisor" sometimes appears in the title. If the level is not indicated by the title, check the description of duties. Will you be working under very close supervision, or will you have responsibility for independent decisions in this work?

4) Choose appropriate study materials

Now that you know the subjects to be examined and the relative amount of each subject to be covered, you can choose suitable study materials. For beginning level jobs, or even advanced ones, if you have a pronounced weakness in some aspect of your training, read a modern, standard textbook in that field. Be sure it is up to date and has general coverage. Such books are normally available at your library, and the librarian will be glad to help you locate one. For entry-level positions, questions of appropriate difficulty are chosen – neither highly advanced questions, nor those too simple. Such questions require careful thought but not advanced training.

If the position for which you are applying is technical or advanced, you will read more advanced, specialized material. If you are already familiar with the basic principles of your field, elementary textbooks would waste your time. Concentrate on advanced textbooks and technical periodicals. Think through the concepts and review difficult problems in your field.

These are all general sources. You can get more ideas on your own initiative, following these leads. For example, training manuals and publications of the government agency which employs workers in your field can be useful, particularly for technical and professional positions. A letter or visit to the government department involved may result in more specific study suggestions, and certainly will provide you with a more definite idea of the exact nature of the position you are seeking.

III. KINDS OF TESTS

Tests are used for purposes other than measuring knowledge and ability to perform specified duties. For some positions, it is equally important to test ability to make adjustments to new situations or to profit from training. In others, basic mental abilities not dependent on information are essential. Questions which test these things may not appear as pertinent to the duties of the position as those which test for knowledge and information. Yet they are often highly important parts of a fair examination. For very general questions, it is almost impossible to help you direct your study efforts. What we can do is to point out some of the more common of these general abilities needed in public service positions and describe some typical questions.

1) General information

Broad, general information has been found useful for predicting job success in some kinds of work. This is tested in a variety of ways, from vocabulary lists to questions about current events. Basic background in some field of work, such as sociology or economics, may be sampled in a group of questions. Often these are principles which have become familiar to most persons through exposure rather than through formal training. It is difficult to advise you how to study for these questions; being alert to the world around you is our best suggestion.

2) Verbal ability

An example of an ability needed in many positions is verbal or language ability. Verbal ability is, in brief, the ability to use and understand words. Vocabulary and grammar tests are typical measures of this ability. Reading comprehension or paragraph interpretation questions are common in many kinds of civil service tests. You are given a paragraph of written material and asked to find its central meaning.

3) Numerical ability

Number skills can be tested by the familiar arithmetic problem, by checking paired lists of numbers to see which are alike and which are different, or by interpreting charts and graphs. In the latter test, a graph may be printed in the test booklet which you are asked to use as the basis for answering questions.

4) Observation

A popular test for law-enforcement positions is the observation test. A picture is shown to you for several minutes, then taken away. Questions about the picture test your ability to observe both details and larger elements.

5) Following directions

In many positions in the public service, the employee must be able to carry out written instructions dependably and accurately. You may be given a chart with several columns, each column listing a variety of information. The questions require you to carry out directions involving the information given in the chart.

6) Skills and aptitudes

Performance tests effectively measure some manual skills and aptitudes. When the skill is one in which you are trained, such as typing or shorthand, you can practice. These tests are often very much like those given in business school or high school courses. For many of the other skills and aptitudes, however, no short-time preparation can be made. Skills and abilities natural to you or that you have developed throughout your lifetime are being tested.

Many of the general questions just described provide all the data needed to answer the questions and ask you to use your reasoning ability to find the answers. Your best preparation for these tests, as well as for tests of facts and ideas, is to be at your physical and mental best. You, no doubt, have your own methods of getting into an exam-taking mood and keeping "in shape." The next section lists some ideas on this subject.

IV. KINDS OF QUESTIONS

Only rarely is the "essay" question, which you answer in narrative form, used in civil service tests. Civil service tests are usually of the short-answer type. Full instructions for answering these questions will be given to you at the examination. But in case this is your first experience with short-answer questions and separate answer sheets, here is what you need to know:

1) **Multiple-choice Questions**

Most popular of the short-answer questions is the "multiple choice" or "best answer" question. It can be used, for example, to test for factual knowledge, ability to solve problems or judgment in meeting situations found at work.

A multiple-choice question is normally one of three types—
- It can begin with an incomplete statement followed by several possible endings. You are to find the one ending which *best* completes the statement, although some of the others may not be entirely wrong.
- It can also be a complete statement in the form of a question which is answered by choosing one of the statements listed.

- It can be in the form of a problem – again you select the best answer.

Here is an example of a multiple-choice question with a discussion which should give you some clues as to the method for choosing the right answer:

When an employee has a complaint about his assignment, the action which will *best* help him overcome his difficulty is to
- A. discuss his difficulty with his coworkers
- B. take the problem to the head of the organization
- C. take the problem to the person who gave him the assignment
- D. say nothing to anyone about his complaint

In answering this question, you should study each of the choices to find which is best. Consider choice "A" – Certainly an employee may discuss his complaint with fellow employees, but no change or improvement can result, and the complaint remains unresolved. Choice "B" is a poor choice since the head of the organization probably does not know what assignment you have been given, and taking your problem to him is known as "going over the head" of the supervisor. The supervisor, or person who made the assignment, is the person who can clarify it or correct any injustice. Choice "C" is, therefore, correct. To say nothing, as in choice "D," is unwise. Supervisors have and interest in knowing the problems employees are facing, and the employee is seeking a solution to his problem.

2) True/False Questions

The "true/false" or "right/wrong" form of question is sometimes used. Here a complete statement is given. Your job is to decide whether the statement is right or wrong.

SAMPLE: A roaming cell-phone call to a nearby city costs less than a non-roaming call to a distant city.

This statement is wrong, or false, since roaming calls are more expensive.

This is not a complete list of all possible question forms, although most of the others are variations of these common types. You will always get complete directions for answering questions. Be sure you understand *how* to mark your answers – ask questions until you do.

V. RECORDING YOUR ANSWERS

Computer terminals are used more and more today for many different kinds of exams.
For an examination with very few applicants, you may be told to record your answers in the test booklet itself. Separate answer sheets are much more common. If this separate answer sheet is to be scored by machine – and this is often the case – it is highly important that you mark your answers correctly in order to get credit.
An electronic scoring machine is often used in civil service offices because of the speed with which papers can be scored. Machine-scored answer sheets must be marked with a pencil, which will be given to you. This pencil has a high graphite content which responds to the electronic scoring machine. As a matter of fact, stray dots may register as answers, so do not let your pencil rest on the answer sheet while you are pondering the correct answer. Also, if your pencil lead breaks or is otherwise defective, ask for another.

Since the answer sheet will be dropped in a slot in the scoring machine, be careful not to bend the corners or get the paper crumpled.

The answer sheet normally has five vertical columns of numbers, with 30 numbers to a column. These numbers correspond to the question numbers in your test booklet. After each number, going across the page are four or five pairs of dotted lines. These short dotted lines have small letters or numbers above them. The first two pairs may also have a "T" or "F" above the letters. This indicates that the first two pairs only are to be used if the questions are of the true-false type. If the questions are multiple choice, disregard the "T" and "F" and pay attention only to the small letters or numbers.

Answer your questions in the manner of the sample that follows:

32. The largest city in the United States is
    A. Washington, D.C.
    B. New York City
    C. Chicago
    D. Detroit
    E. San Francisco

1) Choose the answer you think is best. (New York City is the largest, so "B" is correct.)
2) Find the row of dotted lines numbered the same as the question you are answering. (Find row number 32)
3) Find the pair of dotted lines corresponding to the answer. (Find the pair of lines under the mark "B.")
4) Make a solid black mark between the dotted lines.

VI. BEFORE THE TEST

Common sense will help you find procedures to follow to get ready for an examination. Too many of us, however, overlook these sensible measures. Indeed, nervousness and fatigue have been found to be the most serious reasons why applicants fail to do their best on civil service tests. Here is a list of reminders:

- Begin your preparation early – Don't wait until the last minute to go scurrying around for books and materials or to find out what the position is all about.
- Prepare continuously – An hour a night for a week is better than an all-night cram session. This has been definitely established. What is more, a night a week for a month will return better dividends than crowding your study into a shorter period of time.
- Locate the place of the exam – You have been sent a notice telling you when and where to report for the examination. If the location is in a different town or otherwise unfamiliar to you, it would be well to inquire the best route and learn something about the building.
- Relax the night before the test – Allow your mind to rest. Do not study at all that night. Plan some mild recreation or diversion; then go to bed early and get a good night's sleep.
- Get up early enough to make a leisurely trip to the place for the test – This way unforeseen events, traffic snarls, unfamiliar buildings, etc. will not upset you.
- Dress comfortably – A written test is not a fashion show. You will be known by number and not by name, so wear something comfortable.

- Leave excess paraphernalia at home – Shopping bags and odd bundles will get in your way. You need bring only the items mentioned in the official notice you received; usually everything you need is provided. Do not bring reference books to the exam. They will only confuse those last minutes and be taken away from you when in the test room.
- Arrive somewhat ahead of time – If because of transportation schedules you must get there very early, bring a newspaper or magazine to take your mind off yourself while waiting.
- Locate the examination room – When you have found the proper room, you will be directed to the seat or part of the room where you will sit. Sometimes you are given a sheet of instructions to read while you are waiting. Do not fill out any forms until you are told to do so; just read them and be prepared.
- Relax and prepare to listen to the instructions
- If you have any physical problem that may keep you from doing your best, be sure to tell the test administrator. If you are sick or in poor health, you really cannot do your best on the exam. You can come back and take the test some other time.

VII. AT THE TEST

The day of the test is here and you have the test booklet in your hand. The temptation to get going is very strong. Caution! There is more to success than knowing the right answers. You must know how to identify your papers and understand variations in the type of short-answer question used in this particular examination. Follow these suggestions for maximum results from your efforts:

1) Cooperate with the monitor

The test administrator has a duty to create a situation in which you can be as much at ease as possible. He will give instructions, tell you when to begin, check to see that you are marking your answer sheet correctly, and so on. He is not there to guard you, although he will see that your competitors do not take unfair advantage. He wants to help you do your best.

2) Listen to all instructions

Don't jump the gun! Wait until you understand all directions. In most civil service tests you get more time than you need to answer the questions. So don't be in a hurry. Read each word of instructions until you clearly understand the meaning. Study the examples, listen to all announcements and follow directions. Ask questions if you do not understand what to do.

3) Identify your papers

Civil service exams are usually identified by number only. You will be assigned a number; you must not put your name on your test papers. Be sure to copy your number correctly. Since more than one exam may be given, copy your exact examination title.

4) Plan your time

Unless you are told that a test is a "speed" or "rate of work" test, speed itself is usually not important. Time enough to answer all the questions will be provided, but this does not mean that you have all day. An overall time limit has been set. Divide the total time (in minutes) by the number of questions to determine the approximate time you have for each question.

5) Do not linger over difficult questions

If you come across a difficult question, mark it with a paper clip (useful to have along) and come back to it when you have been through the booklet. One caution if you do this – be sure to skip a number on your answer sheet as well. Check often to be sure that you have not lost your place and that you are marking in the row numbered the same as the question you are answering.

6) Read the questions

Be sure you know what the question asks! Many capable people are unsuccessful because they failed to *read* the questions correctly.

7) Answer all questions

Unless you have been instructed that a penalty will be deducted for incorrect answers, it is better to guess than to omit a question.

8) Speed tests

It is often better NOT to guess on speed tests. It has been found that on timed tests people are tempted to spend the last few seconds before time is called in marking answers at random – without even reading them – in the hope of picking up a few extra points. To discourage this practice, the instructions may warn you that your score will be "corrected" for guessing. That is, a penalty will be applied. The incorrect answers will be deducted from the correct ones, or some other penalty formula will be used.

9) Review your answers

If you finish before time is called, go back to the questions you guessed or omitted to give them further thought. Review other answers if you have time.

10) Return your test materials

If you are ready to leave before others have finished or time is called, take ALL your materials to the monitor and leave quietly. Never take any test material with you. The monitor can discover whose papers are not complete, and taking a test booklet may be grounds for disqualification.

VIII. EXAMINATION TECHNIQUES

1) Read the general instructions carefully. These are usually printed on the first page of the exam booklet. As a rule, these instructions refer to the timing of the examination; the fact that you should not start work until the signal and must stop work at a signal, etc. If there are any *special* instructions, such as a choice of questions to be answered, make sure that you note this instruction carefully.

2) When you are ready to start work on the examination, that is as soon as the signal has been given, read the instructions to each question booklet, underline any key words or phrases, such as *least, best, outline, describe* and the like. In this way you will tend to answer as requested rather than discover on reviewing your paper that you *listed without describing*, that you selected the *worst* choice rather than the *best* choice, etc.

3) If the examination is of the objective or multiple-choice type – that is, each question will also give a series of possible answers: A, B, C or D, and you are called upon to select the best answer and write the letter next to that answer on your answer paper – it is advisable to start answering each question in turn. There may be anywhere from 50 to 100 such questions in the three or four hours allotted and you can see how much time would be taken if you read through all the questions before beginning to answer any. Furthermore, if you come across a question or group of questions which you know would be difficult to answer, it would undoubtedly affect your handling of all the other questions.

4) If the examination is of the essay type and contains but a few questions, it is a moot point as to whether you should read all the questions before starting to answer any one. Of course, if you are given a choice – say five out of seven and the like – then it is essential to read all the questions so you can eliminate the two that are most difficult. If, however, you are asked to answer all the questions, there may be danger in trying to answer the easiest one first because you may find that you will spend too much time on it. The best technique is to answer the first question, then proceed to the second, etc.

5) Time your answers. Before the exam begins, write down the time it started, then add the time allowed for the examination and write down the time it must be completed, then divide the time available somewhat as follows:
    - If 3-1/2 hours are allowed, that would be 210 minutes. If you have 80 objective-type questions, that would be an average of 2-1/2 minutes per question. Allow yourself no more than 2 minutes per question, or a total of 160 minutes, which will permit about 50 minutes to review.
    - If for the time allotment of 210 minutes there are 7 essay questions to answer, that would average about 30 minutes a question. Give yourself only 25 minutes per question so that you have about 35 minutes to review.

6) The most important instruction is to *read each question* and make sure you know what is wanted. The second most important instruction is to *time yourself properly* so that you answer every question. The third most important instruction is to *answer every question*. Guess if you have to but include something for each question. Remember that you will receive no credit for a blank and will probably receive some credit if you write something in answer to an essay question. If you guess a letter – say "B" for a multiple-choice question – you may have guessed right. If you leave a blank as an answer to a multiple-choice question, the examiners may respect your feelings but it will not add a point to your score. Some exams may penalize you for wrong answers, so in such cases *only*, you may not want to guess unless you have some basis for your answer.

7) Suggestions
    a. Objective-type questions
        1. Examine the question booklet for proper sequence of pages and questions
        2. Read all instructions carefully
        3. Skip any question which seems too difficult; return to it after all other questions have been answered
        4. Apportion your time properly; do not spend too much time on any single question or group of questions

5. Note and underline key words – *all, most, fewest, least, best, worst, same, opposite*, etc.
6. Pay particular attention to negatives
7. Note unusual option, e.g., unduly long, short, complex, different or similar in content to the body of the question
8. Observe the use of "hedging" words – *probably, may, most likely*, etc.
9. Make sure that your answer is put next to the same number as the question
10. Do not second-guess unless you have good reason to believe the second answer is definitely more correct
11. Cross out original answer if you decide another answer is more accurate; do not erase until you are ready to hand your paper in
12. Answer all questions; guess unless instructed otherwise
13. Leave time for review

b. Essay questions
1. Read each question carefully
2. Determine exactly what is wanted. Underline key words or phrases.
3. Decide on outline or paragraph answer
4. Include many different points and elements unless asked to develop any one or two points or elements
5. Show impartiality by giving pros and cons unless directed to select one side only
6. Make and write down any assumptions you find necessary to answer the questions
7. Watch your English, grammar, punctuation and choice of words
8. Time your answers; don't crowd material

8) Answering the essay question

Most essay questions can be answered by framing the specific response around several key words or ideas. Here are a few such key words or ideas:

M's: manpower, materials, methods, money, management
P's: purpose, program, policy, plan, procedure, practice, problems, pitfalls, personnel, public relations

a. Six basic steps in handling problems:
1. Preliminary plan and background development
2. Collect information, data and facts
3. Analyze and interpret information, data and facts
4. Analyze and develop solutions as well as make recommendations
5. Prepare report and sell recommendations
6. Install recommendations and follow up effectiveness

b. Pitfalls to avoid
1. *Taking things for granted* – A statement of the situation does not necessarily imply that each of the elements is necessarily true; for example, a complaint may be invalid and biased so that all that can be taken for granted is that a complaint has been registered

2. *Considering only one side of a situation* – Wherever possible, indicate several alternatives and then point out the reasons you selected the best one
3. *Failing to indicate follow up* – Whenever your answer indicates action on your part, make certain that you will take proper follow-up action to see how successful your recommendations, procedures or actions turn out to be
4. *Taking too long in answering any single question* – Remember to time your answers properly

IX. AFTER THE TEST

Scoring procedures differ in detail among civil service jurisdictions although the general principles are the same. Whether the papers are hand-scored or graded by machine we have described, they are nearly always graded by number. That is, the person who marks the paper knows only the number – never the name – of the applicant. Not until all the papers have been graded will they be matched with names. If other tests, such as training and experience or oral interview ratings have been given, scores will be combined. Different parts of the examination usually have different weights. For example, the written test might count 60 percent of the final grade, and a rating of training and experience 40 percent. In many jurisdictions, veterans will have a certain number of points added to their grades.

After the final grade has been determined, the names are placed in grade order and an eligible list is established. There are various methods for resolving ties between those who get the same final grade – probably the most common is to place first the name of the person whose application was received first. Job offers are made from the eligible list in the order the names appear on it. You will be notified of your grade and your rank as soon as all these computations have been made. This will be done as rapidly as possible.

People who are found to meet the requirements in the announcement are called "eligibles." Their names are put on a list of eligible candidates. An eligible's chances of getting a job depend on how high he stands on this list and how fast agencies are filling jobs from the list.

When a job is to be filled from a list of eligibles, the agency asks for the names of people on the list of eligibles for that job. When the civil service commission receives this request, it sends to the agency the names of the three people highest on this list. Or, if the job to be filled has specialized requirements, the office sends the agency the names of the top three persons who meet these requirements from the general list.

The appointing officer makes a choice from among the three people whose names were sent to him. If the selected person accepts the appointment, the names of the others are put back on the list to be considered for future openings.

That is the rule in hiring from all kinds of eligible lists, whether they are for typist, carpenter, chemist, or something else. For every vacancy, the appointing officer has his choice of any one of the top three eligibles on the list. This explains why the person whose name is on top of the list sometimes does not get an appointment when some of the persons lower on the list do. If the appointing officer chooses the second or third eligible, the No. 1 eligible does not get a job at once, but stays on the list until he is appointed or the list is terminated.

X. HOW TO PASS THE INTERVIEW TEST

The examination for which you applied requires an oral interview test. You have already taken the written test and you are now being called for the interview test – the final part of the formal examination.

You may think that it is not possible to prepare for an interview test and that there are no procedures to follow during an interview. Our purpose is to point out some things you can do in advance that will help you and some good rules to follow and pitfalls to avoid while you are being interviewed.

What is an interview supposed to test?

The written examination is designed to test the technical knowledge and competence of the candidate; the oral is designed to evaluate intangible qualities, not readily measured otherwise, and to establish a list showing the relative fitness of each candidate – as measured against his competitors – for the position sought. Scoring is not on the basis of "right" and "wrong," but on a sliding scale of values ranging from "not passable" to "outstanding." As a matter of fact, it is possible to achieve a relatively low score without a single "incorrect" answer because of evident weakness in the qualities being measured.

Occasionally, an examination may consist entirely of an oral test – either an individual or a group oral. In such cases, information is sought concerning the technical knowledges and abilities of the candidate, since there has been no written examination for this purpose. More commonly, however, an oral test is used to supplement a written examination.

Who conducts interviews?

The composition of oral boards varies among different jurisdictions. In nearly all, a representative of the personnel department serves as chairman. One of the members of the board may be a representative of the department in which the candidate would work. In some cases, "outside experts" are used, and, frequently, a businessman or some other representative of the general public is asked to serve. Labor and management or other special groups may be represented. The aim is to secure the services of experts in the appropriate field.

However the board is composed, it is a good idea (and not at all improper or unethical) to ascertain in advance of the interview who the members are and what groups they represent. When you are introduced to them, you will have some idea of their backgrounds and interests, and at least you will not stutter and stammer over their names.

What should be done before the interview?

While knowledge about the board members is useful and takes some of the surprise element out of the interview, there is other preparation which is more substantive. It *is* possible to prepare for an oral interview – in several ways:

1) Keep a copy of your application and review it carefully before the interview

This may be the only document before the oral board, and the starting point of the interview. Know what education and experience you have listed there, and the sequence and dates of all of it. Sometimes the board will ask you to review the highlights of your experience for them; you should not have to hem and haw doing it.

2) Study the class specification and the examination announcement

Usually, the oral board has one or both of these to guide them. The qualities, characteristics or knowledges required by the position sought are stated in these documents. They offer valuable clues as to the nature of the oral interview. For example, if the job involves supervisory responsibilities, the announcement will usually indicate that knowledge of modern supervisory methods and the qualifications of the candidate as a supervisor will be tested. If so, you can expect such questions, frequently in the form of a hypothetical situation which you are expected to solve. NEVER go into an oral without knowledge of the duties and responsibilities of the job you seek.

3) Think through each qualification required

Try to visualize the kind of questions you would ask if you were a board member. How well could you answer them? Try especially to appraise your own knowledge and background in each area, *measured against the job sought*, and identify any areas in which you are weak. Be critical and realistic – do not flatter yourself.

4) Do some general reading in areas in which you feel you may be weak

For example, if the job involves supervision and your past experience has NOT, some general reading in supervisory methods and practices, particularly in the field of human relations, might be useful. Do NOT study agency procedures or detailed manuals. The oral board will be testing your understanding and capacity, not your memory.

5) Get a good night's sleep and watch your general health and mental attitude

You will want a clear head at the interview. Take care of a cold or any other minor ailment, and of course, no hangovers.

What should be done on the day of the interview?

Now comes the day of the interview itself. Give yourself plenty of time to get there. Plan to arrive somewhat ahead of the scheduled time, particularly if your appointment is in the fore part of the day. If a previous candidate fails to appear, the board might be ready for you a bit early. By early afternoon an oral board is almost invariably behind schedule if there are many candidates, and you may have to wait. Take along a book or magazine to read, or your application to review, but leave any extraneous material in the waiting room when you go in for your interview. In any event, relax and compose yourself.

The matter of dress is important. The board is forming impressions about you – from your experience, your manners, your attitude, and your appearance. Give your personal appearance careful attention. Dress your best, but not your flashiest. Choose conservative, appropriate clothing, and be sure it is immaculate. This is a business interview, and your appearance should indicate that you regard it as such. Besides, being well groomed and properly dressed will help boost your confidence.

Sooner or later, someone will call your name and escort you into the interview room. *This is it.* From here on you are on your own. It is too late for any more preparation. But remember, you asked for this opportunity to prove your fitness, and you are here because your request was granted.

What happens when you go in?

The usual sequence of events will be as follows: The clerk (who is often the board stenographer) will introduce you to the chairman of the oral board, who will introduce you to the other members of the board. Acknowledge the introductions before you sit down. Do not be surprised if you find a microphone facing you or a stenotypist sitting by. Oral interviews are usually recorded in the event of an appeal or other review.

Usually the chairman of the board will open the interview by reviewing the highlights of your education and work experience from your application – primarily for the benefit of the other members of the board, as well as to get the material into the record. Do not interrupt or comment unless there is an error or significant misinterpretation; if that is the case, do not hesitate. But do not quibble about insignificant matters. Also, he will usually ask you some question about your education, experience or your present job – partly to get you to start talking and to establish the interviewing "rapport." He may start the actual questioning, or turn it over to one of the other members. Frequently, each member undertakes the questioning on a particular area, one in which he is perhaps most competent, so you can expect each member to participate in the examination. Because time is limited, you may also expect some rather abrupt switches in the direction the questioning takes, so do not be upset by it. Normally, a board member will not pursue a single line of questioning unless he discovers a particular strength or weakness.

After each member has participated, the chairman will usually ask whether any member has any further questions, then will ask you if you have anything you wish to add. Unless you are expecting this question, it may floor you. Worse, it may start you off on an extended, extemporaneous speech. The board is not usually seeking more information. The question is principally to offer you a last opportunity to present further qualifications or to indicate that you have nothing to add. So, if you feel that a significant qualification or characteristic has been overlooked, it is proper to point it out in a sentence or so. Do not compliment the board on the thoroughness of their examination – they have been sketchy, and you know it. If you wish, merely say, "No thank you, I have nothing further to add." This is a point where you can "talk yourself out" of a good impression or fail to present an important bit of information. Remember, *you close the interview yourself.*

The chairman will then say, "That is all, Mr. _____, thank you." Do not be startled; the interview is over, and quicker than you think. Thank him, gather your belongings and take your leave. Save your sigh of relief for the other side of the door.

How to put your best foot forward

Throughout this entire process, you may feel that the board individually and collectively is trying to pierce your defenses, seek out your hidden weaknesses and embarrass and confuse you. Actually, this is not true. They are obliged to make an appraisal of your qualifications for the job you are seeking, and they want to see you in your best light. Remember, they must interview all candidates and a non-cooperative candidate may become a failure in spite of their best efforts to bring out his qualifications. Here are 15 suggestions that will help you:

1) Be natural – Keep your attitude confident, not cocky

If you are not confident that you can do the job, do not expect the board to be. Do not apologize for your weaknesses, try to bring out your strong points. The board is interested in a positive, not negative, presentation. Cockiness will antagonize any board member and make him wonder if you are covering up a weakness by a false show of strength.

2) Get comfortable, but don't lounge or sprawl

Sit erectly but not stiffly. A careless posture may lead the board to conclude that you are careless in other things, or at least that you are not impressed by the importance of the occasion. Either conclusion is natural, even if incorrect. Do not fuss with your clothing, a pencil or an ashtray. Your hands may occasionally be useful to emphasize a point; do not let them become a point of distraction.

3) Do not wisecrack or make small talk

This is a serious situation, and your attitude should show that you consider it as such. Further, the time of the board is limited – they do not want to waste it, and neither should you.

4) Do not exaggerate your experience or abilities

In the first place, from information in the application or other interviews and sources, the board may know more about you than you think. Secondly, you probably will not get away with it. An experienced board is rather adept at spotting such a situation, so do not take the chance.

5) If you know a board member, do not make a point of it, yet do not hide it

Certainly you are not fooling him, and probably not the other members of the board. Do not try to take advantage of your acquaintanceship – it will probably do you little good.

6) Do not dominate the interview

Let the board do that. They will give you the clues – do not assume that you have to do all the talking. Realize that the board has a number of questions to ask you, and do not try to take up all the interview time by showing off your extensive knowledge of the answer to the first one.

7) Be attentive

You only have 20 minutes or so, and you should keep your attention at its sharpest throughout. When a member is addressing a problem or question to you, give him your undivided attention. Address your reply principally to him, but do not exclude the other board members.

8) Do not interrupt

A board member may be stating a problem for you to analyze. He will ask you a question when the time comes. Let him state the problem, and wait for the question.

9) Make sure you understand the question

Do not try to answer until you are sure what the question is. If it is not clear, restate it in your own words or ask the board member to clarify it for you. However, do not haggle about minor elements.

10) Reply promptly but not hastily

A common entry on oral board rating sheets is "candidate responded readily," or "candidate hesitated in replies." Respond as promptly and quickly as you can, but do not jump to a hasty, ill-considered answer.

11) Do not be peremptory in your answers

A brief answer is proper – but do not fire your answer back. That is a losing game from your point of view. The board member can probably ask questions much faster than you can answer them.

12) Do not try to create the answer you think the board member wants

He is interested in what kind of mind you have and how it works – not in playing games. Furthermore, he can usually spot this practice and will actually grade you down on it.

13) Do not switch sides in your reply merely to agree with a board member

Frequently, a member will take a contrary position merely to draw you out and to see if you are willing and able to defend your point of view. Do not start a debate, yet do not surrender a good position. If a position is worth taking, it is worth defending.

14) Do not be afraid to admit an error in judgment if you are shown to be wrong

The board knows that you are forced to reply without any opportunity for careful consideration. Your answer may be demonstrably wrong. If so, admit it and get on with the interview.

15) Do not dwell at length on your present job

The opening question may relate to your present assignment. Answer the question but do not go into an extended discussion. You are being examined for a *new* job, not your present one. As a matter of fact, try to phrase ALL your answers in terms of the job for which you are being examined.

Basis of Rating

Probably you will forget most of these "do's" and "don'ts" when you walk into the oral interview room. Even remembering them all will not ensure you a passing grade. Perhaps you did not have the qualifications in the first place. But remembering them will help you to put your best foot forward, without treading on the toes of the board members.

Rumor and popular opinion to the contrary notwithstanding, an oral board wants you to make the best appearance possible. They know you are under pressure – but they also want to see how you respond to it as a guide to what your reaction would be under the pressures of the job you seek. They will be influenced by the degree of poise you display, the personal traits you show and the manner in which you respond.

ABOUT THIS BOOK

This book contains tests divided into Examination Sections. Go through each test, answering every question in the margin. We have also attached a sample answer sheet at the back of the book that can be removed and used. At the end of each test look at the answer key and check your answers. On the ones you got wrong, look at the right answer choice and learn. Do not fill in the answers first. Do not memorize the questions and answers, but understand the answer and principles involved. On your test, the questions will likely be different from the samples. Questions are changed and new ones added. If you understand these past questions you should have success with any changes that arise. Tests may consist of several types of questions. We have additional books on each subject should more study be advisable or necessary for you. Finally, the more you study, the better prepared you will be. This book is intended to be the last thing you study before you walk into the examination room. Prior study of relevant texts is also recommended. NLC publishes some of these in our Fundamental Series. Knowledge and good sense are important factors in passing your exam. Good luck also helps. So now study this Passbook, absorb the material contained within and take that knowledge into the examination. Then do your best to pass that exam.

EXAMINATION SECTION

EXAMINATION SECTION
TEST 1

DIRECTIONS: Each question or incomplete statement is followed by several suggested answers or completions. Select the one that BEST answers the question or completes the statement. *PRINT THE LETTER OF THE CORRECT ANSWER IN THE SPACE AT THE RIGHT.*

1. Good procedure in handling complaints from the public may be divided into the following four principal stages:
   I. Investigation of the complaint
   II. Receipt of the complaint
   III. Assignment of responsibility for investigation and correction
   IV. Notification of correction

   The ORDER in which these stages ordinarily come is:
   A. III, II, I, IV   B. II, III, I, IV   C. II, III, IV, I   D. II, IV, III, I

   1.____

2. The department may expect the MOST severe public criticism if
   A. it asks for an increase in its annual budget
   B. it purchases new and costly street cleaning equipment
   C. sanitation officers and men are reclassified to higher salary grades
   D. there is delay in cleaning streets of snow

   2.____

3. The MOST important function of public relations in the department should be to
   A. develop cooperation on the part of the public in keeping streets clean
   B. get stricter penalties enacted for health code violations
   C. recruit candidates for entrance positions who ca be developed into supervisors
   D. train career personnel so that they can advance in the department

   3.____

4. The one of the following which has MOST frequently elicited unfavorable public comment has been
   A. dirty sidewalks or streets   B. dumping on lot
   C. failure to curb dogs   D. overflowing garbage cans

   4.____

5. It has been suggested that, as a public relations measure, sections hold *open house* for the public.
   The MOST effective time for this would be
   A. during the summer when children are not in school and can accompany their parents
   B. during the winter when show is likely to fall and the public can see snow removal preparations
   C. immediately after a heavy snow storm when department snow removal operations are in full progress
   D. when street sanitation is receiving general attention as during *Keep City Clean* week

   5.____

6. When a public agency conducts a public relations program, it is MOST likely to find that each recipient of its message will
   A. disagree with the basic purpose of the message if the officials are not well known to him
   B. accept the message if it is presented by someone perceived as having a definite intention to persuade
   C. ignore the message unless it is presented in a literate and clever manner
   D. give greater attention to certain portions of the message as a result of his individual and cultural differences

7. Following are three statements about public relations and communications:
   I. A person who seeks to influence public opinion can speed up a trend
   II. Mass communications is the exposure of a mass audience to an idea
   III. All media are equally effective in reaching opinion leaders
   Which of the following choices CORRECTLY classifies the above statements into those which are correct and those which are not?
   A. I and II are correct, but III is not.
   B. II and III are correct, but I is not.
   C. I and III are correct, but II is not.
   D. III is correct, but I and II are not.

8. Public relations experts say that MAXIMUM effect for a message results from
   A. concentrating in one medium
   B. ignoring mass media and concentrating on *opinion makers*
   C. presenting only those factors which support a given position
   D. using a combination of two or more of the available media

9. To assure credibility and avoid hostility, the public relations man MUST
   A. make certain his message is truthful, not evasive or exaggerated
   B. make sure his message contains some dire consequence if ignored
   C. repeat the message often enough so that it cannot be ignored
   D. try to reach as many people and groups as possible

10. The public relations man MUST be prepared to assume that members of his audience
    A. may have developed attitudes toward his proposals—favorable, neutral, or unfavorable
    B. will be immediately hostile
    C. will consider his proposals with an open mind
    D. will invariably need an introduction to his subject

11. The one of the following statements that is CORRECT is:
    A. When a stupid question is asked of you by the public, it should be disregarded
    B. If you insist on formality between you and the public, the public will not be able to ask stupid questions that cannot be answered
    C. The public should be treated courteously, regardless of how stupid their questions may be
    D. You should explain to the public how stupid their questions are

12. With regard to public relations, the MOST important item which should be emphasized in an employee training program is that
    A. each inspector is a public relations agent
    B. an inspector should give the public all the information it asks for
    C. it is better to make mistakes and give erroneous information than to tell the public that you do not know the correct answer to their problem
    D. public relations is so specialized a field that only persons specially trained in it should consider it

13. Members of the public frequently ask about departmental procedures. Of the following, it is BEST to
    A. advise the public to put the question in writing so that he can get a proper formal reply
    B. refuse to answer because this is a confidential matter
    C. explain the procedure as briefly as possible
    D. attempt to avoid the issue by discussing other matters

14. The effectiveness of a public relations program in a public agency such as the authority is BEST indicated by the
    A. amount of mass media publicity favorable to the policies of the authority
    B. morale of those employees who directly serve the patrons of the authority
    C. public's understanding and support of the authority's program and policies
    D. number of complaint received by the authority from patrons using its facilities

15. In an attempt to improve public opinion about a certain idea, the BEST course of action for an agency to take would be to present the
    A. clearest statements of the idea even though the language is somewhat technical
    B. idea as the result of long-term studies
    C. idea in association with something familiar to most people
    D. idea as the viewpoint of the majority leaders

16. The fundamental factor in any agency's community relations program is
    A. an outline of the objectives
    B. relations with the media
    C. the everyday actions of the employees
    D. a well-planned supervisory program

17. The FUNDAMENTAL factor in the success of a community relations program is
    A. true commitment by the community
    B. true commitment by the administration
    C. a well-planned, systematic approach
    D. the actions of individuals in their contacts with the public

18. The statement below which is LEAST correct is: 18.____
    A. Because of selection standards, the supervisor frequently encounters problems resulting from subordinates' inability to express themselves in the language of the profession.
    B. Distortion of the meaning of a communication is usually brought about by a failure to use language that has a precise meaning to others.
    C. The term *filtering* is the distortion or dilution of content of a communication that occurs as information is passed from individual to individual.
    D. The complexity of the *communications net* will directly affect.

19. Consider the following three statements that may or may not be CORRECT: 19.____
    I. In order to prevent the stifling of communications flow, supervisors should insist that employees use the formal communications network.
    II. Two-way communications are faster and more accurate than one-way communications.
    III. There is a direct correlation between the effectiveness of communications and the total setting in which they occur.
    The choice below which MOST accurately describes the above statement is:
    A. All three are correct.
    B. All three are incorrect.
    C. More than one statement is correct.
    D. Only one of the statements is correct.

20. The statement below which is MOST inaccurate is: 20.____
    A. The supervisor's most important tool in learning whether or not he is communicating well is feedback.
    B. Follow-up is essential if useful feedback is to be obtained.
    C. Subordinates are entitled, as a matter of right, to explanations from management concerning the reasons for orders or directives.
    D. A skilled supervisor is often able to use the grapevine to good advantage.

21. *Since concurrence by those affected is not sought, this kind of communication can be issued with relative ease.* 21.____
    The kind of communication being referred to in this quotation is
    A. autocratic   B. democratic   C. directive   D. free-rein

22. The statement below which is LEAST correct is: 22.____
    A. Clarity is more important in oral communicating than in written since the readers of a written communication can read it over again.
    B. Excessive use of abbreviations in written communications should be avoided.
    C. Short sentences with simple words are preferred over complex sentences and difficult words in a written communication.
    D. The *newspaper* style of writing ordinarily simplifies expression and facilitates understanding.

23. Which one of the following is the MOST important factor for the department to consider in building a good public image?
    A. A good working relationship with the news media
    B. An efficient community relations program
    C. An efficient system for handling citizen complaints
    D. The proper maintenance of facilities and equipment
    E. The behavior of individuals in their contacts with the public.

24. It has been said that the ability to communicate clearly and concisely is the MOST important single skill of the supervisor.
    Consider the following statements:
    I. The adage, *Actions speak louder than words*, has NO application in superior/subordinate communications since good communications are accomplished with words.
    II. The environment in which a communication takes place will *rarely* determine its effect.
    III. Words are symbolic representations which must be associated with past experience or else they are meaningless.
    The choice below which MOST accurately describes the above statements is:
    A. I, II, and III are correct.
    B. I and II are correct, but III is not.
    C. I and III are correct, but II is not.
    D. III is correct, but I and II are not.
    E. I, II, and III are incorrect.

25. According to expert opinion, the effectiveness of an organization is very dependent upon good upward, downward, and lateral communications. Lateral communications are most important to the activity of coordinating the efforts of organizational units. Before real communication can take place at any level, barriers to communication must be recognized, understood, and removed.
    Consider the following three statements:
    I. The *principal* barrier to good communications is a failure to establish empathy between sender and receiver.
    II. The difference in status or rank between the sender and receiver of a communication may be a communications barrier.
    III. Communications are easier if they travel upward from subordinate to superior
    The choice below which MOST accurately describes the above statements is:
    A. I, II and III are incorrect.   B. I and II are incorrect.
    C. I, II, and III are correct.   D. I and II are correct.
    E. I and III are incorrect.

KEY (CORRECT ANSWERS)

1.	B		11.	C
2.	D		12.	A
3.	A		13.	C
4.	A		14.	C
5.	D		15.	C
6.	D		16.	C
7.	A		17.	D
8.	D		18.	A
9.	A		19.	D
10.	A		20.	C

21. A
22. A
23. E
24. D
25. E

EXAMINATION SECTION
TEST 1

DIRECTIONS: Each question or incomplete statement is followed by several suggested answers or completions. Select the one that BEST answers the question or completes the statement. *PRINT THE LETTER OF THE CORRECT ANSWER IN THE SPACE AT THE RIGHT.*

1. If you open a personal letter by mistake, the one of the following actions which it would generally be BEST for you to take is to

    A. ignore your error, attach the envelope to the letter, and distribute in the usual manner
    B. personally give the addressee the letter without any explanation
    C. place the letter inside the envelope, indicate under your initials that it was opened in error, and give to the addressee
    D. reseal the envelope or place the contents in another envelope and pass on to addressee

    1.____

2. If you receive a telephone call regarding a matter which your office does not handle, you should FIRST

    A. give the caller the telephone number of the proper office so that he can dial again
    B. offer to transfer the caller to the proper office
    C. suggest that the caller re-dial since he probably dialed incorrectly
    D. tell the caller he has reached the wrong office and then hang up

    2.____

3. When you answer the telephone, the MOST important reason for identifying yourself and your organization is to

    A. give the caller time to collect his or her thoughts
    B. impress the caller with your courtesy
    C. inform the caller that he or she has reached the right number
    D. set a business-like tone at the beginning of the conversation

    3.____

4. The one of the following cases in which you would NOT place a special notation in the left margin of a letter that you have typed is when

    A. one of the copies is intended for someone other than the addressee of the letter
    B. you enclose a flyer with the letter
    C. you sign your superior's name to the letter, at his or her request
    D. the letter refers to something being sent under separate cover

    4.____

5. Suppose that you accidentally cut a letter or enclosure as you are opening an envelope with a paper knife.
   The one of the following that you should do FIRST is to

    A. determine whether the document is important
    B. clip or staple the pieces together and process as usual
    C. mend the cut document with transparent tape
    D. notify the sender that the communication was damaged and request another copy

    5.____

6. As soon as you pick up the phone, a very angry caller begins immediately to complain about city agencies and *red tape*. He says that he has been shifted to two or three different offices. It turns out that he is seeking information which is not immediately available to you. You believe you know, however, where it can be found.
Which of the following actions is the BEST one for you to take?

   A. To eliminate all confusion, suggest that the caller write the mayor stating explicitly what he wants.
   B. Apologize by telling the caller how busy city agencies now are, but also tell him directly that you do not have the information he needs.
   C. Ask for the caller's telephone number, and assure him you will call back after you have checked further.
   D. Give the caller the name and telephone number of the person who might be able to help, but explain that you are not positive he will get results.

7. Suppose that one of your duties is to dictate responses to routine requests from the public for information. A letter writer asks for information which, as expressed in a one-sentence, explicit agency rule, cannot be given out to the public.
Of the following ways of answering the letter, which is the MOST efficient?

   A. Quote verbatim that section of the agency rules which prohibits giving this information to the public.
   B. Without quoting the rule, explain why you cannot accede to the request and suggest alternative sources.
   C. Describe how carefully the request was considered before classifying it as subject to the rule forbidding the issuance of such information.
   D. Acknowledge receipt of the letter and advise that the requested information is not released to the public.

8. Suppose you assist in supervising a staff which has rather high morale, and your own supervisor asks you to poll the staff to find out who will be able to work overtime this particular evening to help complete emergency work.
Which of the following approaches would be MOST likely to win their cooperation while maintaining their morale?

   A. Tell them that the better assignments will be given only to those who work overtime.
   B. Tell them that occasional overtime is a job requirement.
   C. Assure them they'll be doing you a personal favor.
   D. Let them know clearly why the overtime is needed.

9. Suppose that you have been asked to write and to prepare for reproduction new departmental vacation leave regulations.
After you have written the new regulations, all of which fit on two pages, which one of the following would be the BEST method of reproducing 1,000 copies?

   A. An outside private printer because you can best maintain confidentiality using this technique
   B. Photocopying because the copies will have the best possible appearance
   C. Sending the file to all department employees as printable PDFs
   D. Printing and collating on the office high-volume printer

10. You are in charge of verifying employees' qualifications. This involves telephoning previous employers and schools. One of the applications which you are reviewing contains information which you are almost certain is correct on the basis of what the employee has told you.
    The BEST thing to do is to

    A. check the information again with the employer
    B. perform the required verification procedures
    C. accept the information as valid
    D. ask a superior to verify the information

11. The practice of immediately identifying oneself and one's place of employment when contacting persons on the telephone is

    A. *good* because the receiver of the call can quickly identify the caller and establish a frame of reference
    B. *good* because it helps to set the caller at ease with the other party
    C. *poor* because it is not necessary to divulge that information when making general calls
    D. *poor* because it takes longer to arrive at the topic to be discussed

12. Which one of the following should be the MOST important overall consideration when preparing a recommendation to automate a large-scale office activity?
    The

    A. number of models of automated equipment available
    B. benefits and costs of automation
    C. fears and resistance of affected employees
    D. experience of offices which have automated similar activities

13. A tickler file is MOST appropriate for filing materials

    A. chronologically according to date they were received
    B. alphabetically by name
    C. alphabetically by subject
    D. chronologically according to date they should be followed up

14. Which of the following is the BEST reason for decentralizing rather then centralizing the use of duplicating machines?

    A. Developing and retaining efficient duplicating machine operators
    B. Facilitating supervision of duplicating services
    C. Motivating employees to produce legible duplicated copies
    D. Placing the duplicating machines where they are most convenient and most frequently used

15. Window envelopes are sometimes considered preferable to individually addressed envelopes PRIMARILY because

    A. window envelopes are available in standard sizes for all purposes
    B. window envelopes are more attractive and official-looking
    C. the use of window envelopes eliminates the risk of inserting a letter in the wrong envelope
    D. the use of window envelopes requires neater typing

16. In planning the layout of a new office, the utilization of space and the arrangement of staff, furnishings, and equipment should usually be MOST influenced by the

    A. gross square footage
    B. status differences in the chain of command
    C. framework of informal relationships among employees
    D. activities to be performed

17. Office forms sometimes consist of several copies, each of a different color. The MAIN reason for using different colors is to

    A. make a favorable impression on the users of the form
    B. distinguish each copy from the others
    C. facilitate the preparation of legible carbon copies
    D. reduce cost, since using colored stock permits recycling of paper

18. Which of the following is the BEST justification for obtaining a photocopying machine for the office?

    A. A photocopying machine can produce an unlimited number of copies at a low fixed cost per copy.
    B. Employees need little training in operating a photocopying machine.
    C. Office costs will be reduced and efficiency increased.
    D. The legibility of a photocopy generally is superior to copy produced by any other office duplicating device.

19. An administrative officer in charge of a small fund for buying office supplies has just written a check to Charles Laird, a supplier, and has sent the check by messenger to him. A half-hour later, the messenger telephones the administrative officer. He has lost the check.
    Which of the following is the MOST important action for the administrative officer to take under these circumstances?

    A. Ask the messenger to return and write a report describing the loss of the check.
    B. Make a note on the performance record of the messenger who lost the check.
    C. Take the necessary steps to have payment stopped on the check.
    D. Refrain from doing anything since the check may be found shortly.

20. A petty cash fund is set up PRIMARILY to

    A. take care of small investments that must be made from time to time
    B. take care of small expenses that arise from time to time
    C. provide a fund to be used as the office wants to use it with little need to maintain records
    D. take care of expenses that develop during emergencies such as machine breakdowns and fires

21. Your superior has asked you to send a package from your agency to a government agency in another city. He has written out the message and has indicated the name of the government agency.
    When you prepare the package for mailing, which of the following items that your superior has not mentioned must you be sure to include?

A. Today's date
B. The full address of the government agency
C. A polite opening such as *Dear Sirs*
D. A final sentence such as *We would appreciate hearing from your agency in reply as soon as is convenient for you*

22. In addition to the original piece of correspondence, one should USUALLY also have typed

    A. a single copy
    B. as many copies as can be typed at one time
    C. no more copies than are needed
    D. two copies

22._____

23. The one of the following which is the BEST procedure to follow when making a short insert in a completed dictation is to

    A. label the insert with a letter and indicate the position of the insert in the text by writing the identifying letter in the proper place
    B. squeeze the insert into its proper place within the main text of the dictation
    C. take down the insert and check the placement with the person who dictated when you are ready to transcribe your notes
    D. transcribe the dictation into longhand, including the insert in its proper position

23._____

24. The one of the following procedures which will be MOST efficient in helping you to quickly open your dictation notebook to a clean sheet is to

    A. clip or place a rubberband around the used portion of the notebook
    B. leave the book out and open to a clean page when not in use
    C. transcribe each dictation after it is given and rip out the used pages
    D. use a book marker to indicate which portion of the notebook has been used

24._____

25. The purpose of dating your dictation notebooks is GENERALLY to

    A. enable you to easily refer to your notes at a later date
    B. ensure that you transcribe your notes in the order in which they were dictated
    C. set up a precise record-keeping procedure
    D. show your employer that you pay attention to detail

25._____

KEY (CORRECT ANSWERS)

1.	C	11.	A
2.	B	12.	B
3.	C	13.	D
4.	C	14.	D
5.	C	15.	C
6.	C	16.	D
7.	A	17.	B
8.	D	18.	C
9.	D	19.	C
10.	B	20.	B

21. B
22. C
23. A
24. A
25. A

TEST 2

DIRECTIONS: Each question or incomplete statement is followed by several suggested answers or completions. Select the one that BEST answers the question or completes the statement. *PRINT THE LETTER OF THE CORRECT ANSWER IN THE SPACE AT THE RIGHT.*

1. With regard to typed correspondence received by most offices, which of the following is the GREATEST problem?   1.____

    A. Verbosity
    B. Illegibility
    C. Improper folding
    D. Excessive copies

2. Of the following, the GREATEST advantage of flash drives over rewritable CD storage is that they   2.____

    A. are portable
    B. are both smaller and lighter
    C. contain more storage space
    D. allow files to be deleted to free space

3. Suppose that a large quantity of information is in the files which are located a good distance from your desk. Almost every worker in your office must use these files constantly. Your duties in particular require that you daily refer to about 25 of the same items. They are short, one-page items distributed throughout the files. In this situation, your BEST course would be to   3.____

    A. take the items that you use daily from the files and keep them on your desk, inserting *out cards* in their place
    B. go to the files each time you need the information so that the items will be there when other workers need them
    C. make xerox copies of the information you use most frequently and keep them in your desk for ready reference
    D. label the items you use most often with different colored tabs for immediate identification

4. Of the following, the MOST important advantage of preparing manuals of office procedures in loose-leaf form is that this form   4.____

    A. permits several employees to use different sections simultaneously
    B. facilitates the addition of new material and the removal of obsolete material
    C. is more readily arranged in alphabetical order
    D. reduces the need for cross-references to locate material carried under several headings

5. Suppose that you establish a new clerical procedure for the unit you supervise. Your keeping a close check on the time required by your staff to handle the new procedure is WISE mainly because such a check will find out   5.____

    A. whether your subordinates know how to handle the new procedure
    B. whether a revision of the unit's work schedule will be necessary as a result of the new procedure
    C. what attitude your employees have toward the new procedure
    D. what alterations in job descriptions will be necessitated by the new procedure

6. The numbered statements below relate to the stenographic skill of taking dictation. According to authorities on secretarial practices, which of these are generally recommended guides to development of efficient stenographic skills?

STATEMENTS
1. A stenographer should date her notebook daily to facilitate locating certain notes at a later time.
2. A stenographer should make corrections of grammatical mistakes while her boss is dictating to her.
3. A stenographer should draw a line through the dictated matter in her notebook after she has transcribed it.
4. A stenographer should write in longhand unfamiliar names and addresses dictated to her.

The CORRECT answer is:

A. Only Statements 1, 2, and 3 are generally recommended guides.
B. Only Statements 2, 3, and 4 are generally recommended guides.
C. Only Statements 1, 3, and 4 are generally recommended guides.
D. All four statements are generally recommended guides.

7. According to generally recognized rules of filing in an alphabetic filing system, the one of the following names which normally should be filed LAST is

A. Department of Education, New York State
B. F.B.I.
C. Police Department of New York City
D. P.S. 81 of New York City

8. Which one of the following forms for the typed name of the dictator in the closing lines of a letter is generally MOST acceptable in the United States?

A. (Dr.) James F. Fenton
B. Dr. James F. Fenton
C. Mr. James F. Fenton, Ph.D.
D. James F. Fenton

9. Which of the following is, MOST generally, a rule to be followed when typing a rough draft?

A. The copy should be single spaced.
B. The copy should be triple spaced.
C. There is no need for including footnotes.
D. Errors must be neatly corrected.

10. An office assistant needs a synonym.
Of the following, the book which she would find MOST useful is

A. a world atlas
B. BARTLETT'S FAMILIAR QUOTATIONS
C. a manual of style
D. a thesaurus

11. Of the following examples of footnotes, the one that is expressed in the MOST generally accepted standard form is:

    A. Johnson, T.F. (Dr.), <u>English for Everyone</u>, 3rd or 4th edition; New York City Linton Publishing Company, p. 467
    B. Frank Taylor, <u>English for Today</u> (New York: Rayton Publishing Company, 1971), p. 156
    C. Ralph Wilden, <u>English for Tomorrow,</u> Reynolds Publishing Company, England, p. 451
    D. Quinn, David, Yesterday's English (New York: Baldwin Publishing Company, 1972), p. 431

12. Standard procedures are used in offices PRIMARILY because

    A. an office is a happier place if everyone is doing the tasks in the same manner
    B. particular ways of doing jobs are considered more efficient than other ways
    C. it is good discipline for workers to follow standard procedures approved by the supervisor
    D. supervisors generally don't want workers to be creative in planning their work

13. Assume that an office assistant has the responsibility for compiling, typing, and mailing a preliminary announcement of Spring term course offerings. The announcement will go to approximately 900 currently enrolled students. Assuming that the following equipment is available for use, the MOST EFFECTIVE method for distributing the announcement to all 900 students is to

    A. e-mail it as a text document using the electronic student mailing list
    B. post the announcement as a PDF document for download on the department website
    C. send it by fax
    D. post the announcement and leave copies in buildings around campus

14. *Justified typing* is a term that refers MOST specifically to typewriting copy

    A. that has been edited and for which final copy is being prepared
    B. in a form that allows for an even right-hand margin
    C. with a predetermined vertical placement for each alternate line
    D. that has been approved by the supervisor and his superior

15. Which one of the following is the BEST form for the address in a letter?

    A. Mr. John Jones
       Vice President, The Universal Printing Company
       1220 Fifth Avenue
       New York, 10023 New York
    B. Mr. John Jones, Vice President
       The Universal Printing Company
       1220 Fifth Avenue
       New York, New York 10023
    C. Mr. John Jones, Vice President, The Universal Printing Company
       1220 Fifth Avenue
       New York, New York 10023

D. Mr. John Jones Vice President,
The Universal Printing Company
1220 Fifth Avenue
New York, 10023 New York

16. Of the following, the CHIEF advantage of the use of window envelopes over ordinary envelopes is that window envelopes

    A. eliminate the need for addressing envelopes
    B. protect the confidential nature of enclosed material
    C. cost less to buy than ordinary envelopes
    D. reduce the danger of the address becoming illegible

17. In the complimentary close of a business letter, the FIRST letter of _____ should be capitalized.

    A. all the words
    B. none of the words
    C. only the first word
    D. only the last word

18. Assume that one of your duties is to procure needed office supplies from the supply room. You are permitted to draw supplies every two weeks.
    The one of the following which would be the MOST desirable practice for you to follow in obtaining supplies is to

    A. obtain a quantity of supplies sufficient to last for several months to make certain that enough supplies are always on hand
    B. determine the minimum supply necessary to keep on hand for the various items and obtain an additional quantity as soon as possible after the supply on hand has been reduced to this minimum
    C. review the supplies once a month to determine what items have been exhausted and obtain an additional quantity as soon as possible
    D. obtain a supply of an item as soon after it has been exhausted as is possible

19. Some offices that keep carbon copies of letters use several different colors of carbon paper for making carbon copies.
    Of the following, the CHIEF reason for using different colors of carbon paper is to

    A. facilitate identification of different types of letters in the files
    B. relieve the monotony of typing and filing carbon copies
    C. reduce the costs of preparing carbon copies
    D. utilize both sides of the carbon paper for typing

20. Your supervisor asks you to post an online ad for freelance designers interested in submitting samples for a new company logo. Prospective workers should be proficient in which of the following software?

    A. Microsoft Word
    B. Adobe Acrobat Pro
    C. Adobe Illustrator
    D. Microsoft PowerPoint

21. Gary Thompson is applying for a position with the firm of Gray and Williams.
    Which letter should be filed in top position in the *Application* folder?

    A. A letter of recommendation written on September 18 by Johnson & Smith
    B. Williams' letter of October 8 requesting further details regarding Thompson's experience

C. Thompson's letter of September 8 making application for a position as sales manager
   D. Letter of September 20 from Alfred Jackson recommending Thompson for the job

22. The USUAL arrangement in indexing the names of the First National Bank, Toledo, is

   A. First National Bank, Toledo, Ohio
   B. Ohio, First National Bank, Toledo
   C. Toledo, First National Bank, Ohio
   D. Ohio, Toledo, First National Bank

23. A single line through typed text indicating that it's incorrect or invalid is known as a(n)

   A. underline
   B. strikethrough
   C. line font
   D. eraser

24. A typical e-mail with an attachment should contain all of the following for successful transmittal EXCEPT

   A. recipient's address
   B. file attachment
   C. body text
   D. description of attachment

25. The subject line in a letter is USUALLY typed a _____ space below the _____.

   A. single; inside address
   B. single; salutation
   C. double; inside address
   D. double; salutation

KEY (CORRECT ANSWERS)

1.	A	11.	B
2.	C	12.	B
3.	C	13.	A
4.	B	14.	B
5.	B	15.	B
6.	C	16.	A
7.	D	17.	C
8.	D	18.	B
9.	B	19.	A
10.	D	20.	C

21. B
22. A
23. B
24. D
25. D

EXAMINATION SECTION
TEST 1

DIRECTIONS: Each question or incomplete statement is followed by several suggested answers or completions. Select the one that BEST answers the question or completes the statement. *PRINT THE LETTER OF THE CORRECT ANSWER IN THE SPACE AT THE RIGHT.*

1. Assume that a few co-workers meet near your desk and talk about personal matters during working hours. Lately, this practice has interfered with your work. In order to stop this practice, the BEST action for you to take FIRST is to
   A. ask your supervisor to put a stop to the co-workers' meeting near your desk
   B. discontinue any friendship with this group
   C. ask your co-workers not to meet near your desk
   D. request that your desk be moved to another location

   1.____

2. In order to maintain office coverage during working hours, your supervisor has scheduled your lunch hour from 1 P.M. to 2 P.M. and your co-workers' lunch hour from 12 P.M. to 1 P.M. Lately, your co-worker has been returning late from lunch each day. As a result, you don't get a full hour since you must return to the office by 2 P.M.
   Of the following, the BEST action for you to take FIRST is to
   A. explain to your co-worker in a courteous manner that his lateness is interfering with your right to a full hour for lunch
   B. tell your co-worker that his lateness must stop or you will report him to your supervisor
   C. report your co-worker's lateness to your supervisor
   D. leave at 1 P.M. for lunch, whether your co-worker has returned or not

   2.____

3. Assume that, as an office worker, one of your jobs is to open mail sent to your unit, read the mail for content, and send the mail to the appropriate person to handle. You accidentally open and begin to read a letter marked *personal* to a co-worker.
   Of the following, the BEST action for you to take is to
   A. report to your supervisor that your co-worker is receiving personal mail at the office
   B. destroy the letter so that your co-worker does not know you saw it
   C. reseal the letter and place it on the co-worker's desk without saying anything
   D. bring the letter to your co-worker and explain that you opened it by accident

   3.____

4. Suppose that in evaluating your work, your supervisor gives you an overall rating, but states that you sometimes turn in work with careless errors.
   The BEST action for you to take would be to
   A. ask a co-worker who is good at details to proofread your work
   B. take time to do a careful job, paying more attention to detail
   C. continue working as usual since occasional errors are to be expected
   D. ask your supervisor if she would mind correcting your errors

5. Assume that you are taking a telephone message for a co-worker who is not in the office at the time.
   Of the following, the LEAST important item to write on the message is the
   A. length of the call   B. name of the caller
   C. time of the call   D. telephone number of the caller

Questions 6-13.

DIRECTIONS: Questions 6 through 13 each consist of a sentence which may or may not be an example of good English. The underlined parts of each sentence may be correct or incorrect. Examine each sentence, considering grammar, punctuation, spelling, and capitalization. If the English usage in the underlined parts of the sentence given is better than any of the changes in the underlined words suggested in Options B, C, or D, choose Option A. If the changes in the underlined words suggested in Options B, C, or D would make the sentence correct, choose the correct option. Do not choose an option that will change the meaning of the sentence.

6. This Fall, the office will be closed on Columbus Day, October 9th.
   A. Correct as is   B. fall...Columbus Day, October
   C. Fall...Columbus day, October D. fall...Columbus Day, october

7. This manual discribes the duties performed by an Office Aide.
   A. Correct as is   B. describe the duties performed
   C. discribe the duties performed D. describes the duties performed

8. There weren't no paper in the supply closet.
   A. Correct as is   B. weren't any
   C. wasn't any   D. wasn't no

9. The new employees left there office to attend a meeting.
   A. Correct as is   B. they're
   C. their   D. thier

10. The office worker started working at 8:30 a.m.
    A. Correct as is   B. 8:30 a.m.
    C. 8;30 a,m.   D. 8:30 am.

11. The alphabet, or A to Z sequence are the basis of most filing systems.
    A. Correct as is   B. alphabet, or A to Z sequence, is
    C. alphabet, or A to Z sequence are D. alphabet, or A too Z sequence, is

12. <u>Those</u> file cabinets are five <u>feet</u> tall. 12.____
 A. Correct as is B. Them…feet
 C. Those…foot D. Them…foot

13. The Office Aide checked the <u>register and finding</u> the date of the meeting. 13.____
 A. Correct as is B. regaster and finding
 C. register and found D. regaster and found

Questions 14-21.

DIRECTIONS: Each of Questions 14 through 21 has two lists of numbers. Each list contains three sets of numbers. Check each of the three sets in the list on the right to see if they are the same as the corresponding set in the list on the left. Mark your answers
 A. if none of the sets in the right list are the same as those in the left list
 B. if only one of the sets in the right list are the same as those in the left list
 C. if only two of the sets in the right list are the same as those in the left list
 D. if all three sets in the right list are the same as those in the left list

14. 7354183476   7354983476   14.____
    4474747744   4474747774
    57914302311   57914302311

15. 7143592185   7143892185   15.____
    8344517699   8344518699
    9178531263   9178531263

16. 2572114731   257214731   16.____
    8806835476   8806835476
    8255831246   8255831246

17. 331476853821   331476858621   17.____
    6976658532996   6976655832996
    3766042113715   3766042113745

18. 8806663315   8806663315   18.____
    74477138449   74477138449
    211756663666   211756663666

19. 990006966996   99000696996   19.____
    53022219743   53022219843
    4171171117717   4171171177717

20. 24400222433004   24400222433004   20.____
    5300030055000355   5300030055500355
    20000075532002022   20000075532002022

4 (#1)

21. 6111666406600001116   61116664066001116   21._____
     7111300117001100733   7111300117001100733
     26666446664476518   26666446664476518

Questions 22-25.

DIRECTIONS: Each of Questions 22 through 25 has two lists of names and addresses. Each list contains three sets of names and addresses. Check each of the three sets in the list on the right to see if they are the same as the corresponding set in the list on the left. Mark your answers
    A. if none of the sets in the right list are the same as those in the left list
    B. if only one of the sets in the right list are the same as those in the left list
    C. if only two of the sets in the right list are the same as those in the left list
    D. if all three sets in the right list are the same as those in the left list

22. Mary T. Berlinger   Mary T. Berlinger   22._____
     2351 Hampton St.   2351 Hampton St.
     Monsey, N.Y. 20117   Monsey, N.Y. 20117

     Eduardo Benes   Eduardo Benes
     473 Kingston Avenue   473 Kingston Avenue
     Central Islip, N.Y. 11734   Central Islip, N.Y. 11734

     Alan Carrington Fuchs   Alan Carrington Fuchs
     17 Gnarled Hollow Road   17 Gnarled Hollow Road
     Los Angeles, CA 91635   Los Angeles, CA 91685

23. David John Jacobson   David John Jacobson   23._____
     178 35 St. Apt. 4C   178 53 St. Apt. 4C
     New York, N.Y. 00927   New York, N.Y. 00927

     Ann-Marie Calonella   Ann-Marie Calonella
     7243 South Ridge Blvd.   7243 South Ridge Blvd.
     Bakersfield, CA 96714   Bakersfield, CA 96714

     Pauline M. Thompson   Pauline M. Thomson
     872 Linden Ave.   872 Linden Ave.
     Houston, Texas 70321   Houston, Texas 70321

24. Chester LeRoy Masterton   Chester LeRoy Masterson   24._____
     152 Lacy Rd.   152 Lacy Rd.
     Kankakee, Ill. 54532   Kankakee, Ill. 54532

     William Maloney   William Maloney
     S. LaCrosse Pla.   S. LaCross Pla.
     Wausau, Wisconsin 52146   Wausau, Wisconsin 52146

5 (#1)

Cynthia V. Barnes
16 Pines Rd.
Greenpoint, Miss. 20376

Cynthia V. Barnes
16 Pines Rd.
Greenpoint, Miss. 20376

25. Marcel Jean Frontenac
6 Burton On The Water
Calender, Me. 01471

Marcel Jean Frontenac
6 Burton On The Water
Calender, Me. 01471

25.____

J. Scott Marsden
174 S. Tipton St.
Cleveland, Ohio

J. Scott Marsden
174 Tipton St.
Cleveland, Ohio

Lawrence T. Haney
171 McDonough St.
Decatur, Ga. 31304

Lawrence T. Haney
171 McDonough St.
Decatur, Ga. 31304

KEY (CORRECT ANSWERS)

1. C
2. A
3. D
4. B
5. A

6. B
7. D
8. C
9. C
10. B

11. B
12. A
13. C
14. B
15. B

16. C
17. A
18. D
19. A
20. C

21. C
22. C
23. B
24. B
25. C

TEST 2

DIRECTIONS: Each question or incomplete statement is followed by several suggested answers or completions. Select the one that BEST answers the question or completes the statement. *PRINT THE LETTER OF THE CORRECT ANSWER IN THE SPACE AT THE RIGHT.*

Questions 1-6.

DIRECTIONS: Questions 1 through 6 are to be answered SOLELY on the basis of the information contained in the following passage.

Duplicating is the process of making a number of identical copies of letters, document, etc. from an original. Some duplicating processes make copies directly from the original document. Other duplicating processes require the preparation of a special master, and copies are then made from the master. Four of the most common duplicating processes are stencil, fluid, offset, and xerox.

In the stencil process, the typewriter is used to cut the words into a master called a stencil. Drawings, charts, or graphs can be cut into the stencil using a stylus. As many as 3,500 good-quality copies can be reproduced from one stencil. Various grades of finished paper from inexpensive mimeograph to expensive bond can be used.

The fluid process is a good method of copying from 50 to 125 good-quality copies from a master, which is prepared with a special dye. The master is placed on the duplicator, and special paper with a hard finish is moistened and then passed through the duplicator. Some of the dye on the master is dissolved, creating an impression on the paper. The impression becomes lighter as more copies are made; and once the dye on the master is used up, a new master must be made.

The offset process is the most adaptable office duplicating process because this process can be used for making a few copies or many copies. Masters can be made on paper or plastic for a few hundred copies, or on metal plates for as many as 75,000 copies. By using a special technique called photo-offset, charts, photographs, illustrations, or graphs can be reproduced on the master plate. The offset process is capable of producing large quantities of fine, top-quality copies on all types of finished paper.

The xerox process reproduces an exact duplicate from an original. It is the fastest duplicating method because the original material is placed directly on the duplicator, eliminating the need to make a special master. Any kind of paper can be used. The xerox process is the most expensive duplicating process; however, it is the best method of reproducing small quantities of good-quality copies of reports, letters, official documents, memos, or contracts.

1. Of the following, the MOST efficient method of reproducing 5,000 copies of a graph is 1.____
   A. stencil   B. fluid   C. offset   D. xerox

2. The offset process is the MOST adaptable office duplicating process because
    A. it is the quickest duplicating method
    B. it is the least expensive duplicating method
    C. it can produce a small number or large number of copies
    D. a softer master can be used over and over again

3. Which one of the following duplicating processes uses moistened paper?
    A. Stencil   B. Fluid   C. Offset   D. Xerox

4. The fluid process would be the BEST process to use for reproducing
    A. five copies of a school transcript
    B. fifty copies of a memo
    C. five hundred copies of a form letter
    D. five thousand copies of a chart

5. Which one of the following duplicating processes does NOT require a special master?
    A. Fluid   B. Xerox   C. Offset   D. Stencil

6. Xerox is NOT used for all duplicating jobs because
    A. it produces poor-quality copies
    B. the process is too expensive
    C. preparing the master is too time-consuming
    D. it cannot produce written reports

7. Assume a city agency has 775 office workers.
    If 2 out of 25 office workers were absent on a particular day, how many office workers reported to work on that day?
    A. 713   B. 744   C. 750   D. 773

Questions 8-11,

DIRECTIONS: In Questions 8 through 11, select the choice that is CLOSEST in meaning to the underlined word.

SAMPLE: This division reviews the fiscal reports of the agency.
In this sentence, the word *fiscal* means MOST NEARLY
A. financial   B. critical   C. basic   D. personnel

The correct answer is A, financial, because financial is closest to *fiscal*.

8. A central file eliminates the need to retain duplicate material.
    The word *retain* means MOST NEARLY
    A. keep   B. change   C. locate   D. process

9. Filing is a routine office task.
    Routine means MOST NEARLY
    A. proper   B. regular   C. simple   D. difficult

10. Sometimes a word, phrase, or sentence must be <u>deleted</u> to correct an error. *Deleted* means MOST NEARLY
    A. removed   B. added   C. expanded   D. improved

11. Your supervisor will <u>evaluate</u> your work. *Evaluate* means MOST NEARLY
    A. judge   B. list   C. assign   D. explain

Questions 12-19.

DIRECTIONS: The code table below shows 10 letters with matching numbers. For each Question 12 through 19, there are three sets of letters. Each set of letters is followed by a set of numbers which may or may not match their correct letter according to the code table. For each question, check all three sets of letters and numbers and mark your answer
   A. if no pairs are correctly matched
   B. if only one pair is correctly matched
   C. if only two pairs are correctly matched
   D. if all three pairs are correctly matched

CODE TABLE

T	M	V	D	S	P	R	G	B	H
1	2	3	4	5	6	7	8	9	0

SAMPLE QUESTION: TMVDSP   123456
                    RGBHTM   789011
                    DSPRGB   256789

In the sample question above, the first set of numbers correctly matches its set of letters. But the second and third pairs contain mistakes. In the second pair, M is incorrectly matched with number 1. According to the code table, letter M should be correctly matched with number 2. In the third pair, the letter D is incorrectly matched with number 2. According to the code table, letter D should be correctly matched with number 4. Since only one of the pairs is correctly matched, the answer to this sample question is B.

12. RSBMRM   759262
    GDSRVH   845730
    VDBRTM   349713

13. TGVSDR   183247
    SMHRDP   520647
    TRMHSR   172057

14. DSPRGM   456782
    MVDBHT   234902
    HPMDBT   062491

15. BVPTRD   936184   15._____
    GDPHMB   807029
    GMRHMV   827032

16. MGVRSH   283750   16._____
    TRDMBS   174295
    SPRMGV   567283

17. SGBSDM   489542   17._____
    MGHPTM   290612
    MPBMHT   269301

18. TDPBHM   146902   18._____
    VPBMRS   369275
    GDMBHM   842902

19. MVPTBV   236194   19._____
    PDRTMB   647128
    BGTMSM   981232

Questions 20-25.

DIRECTIONS: In each of Questions 20 through 25, the names of four people are given. For each question, choose as your answer the one of the four names given which should be filed FIRST according to the usual system of alphabetical filing of names, as described in the following paragraph.

In filing names, you must start with the last name. Names are filed in order of the first letter of the last name, then the second letter, etc. Therefore, BAILY would be filed before BROWN, which would be filed before COLT. A name with fewer letters of the same type comes first; i.e., Smith before Smithe. If the last names are the same, the names are filed alphabetically by the first name. If the first name is an initial, a name with an initial would come before a first name that starts with the same letter as the initial. Therefore, I. BROWN would come before IRA BROWN. Finally, if both last name and first name are the same, the name would be filed alphabetically by the middle name, one again an initial coming before a middle name which starts with the same letter as the initial. If there is no middle name at all, the name would come before those with middle initials or names.

    SAMPLE QUESTION: A. Lester Daniels
                                   B. William Dancer
                                   C. Nathan Danzig
                                   D. Dan Lester

The last names beginning with D are filed before the last name beginning with L. Since DANIELS, DANCER, and DANZIG all begin with the same three letters, you must look at the fourth letter of the last name to determine which name should be filed first. C comes before I or Z in the alphabet, so DANCER is filed before DANIELS or DANZIG. Therefore, the answer to the above sample question is B.

20. A. Scott Biala B. Mary Byala 20._____
    C. Martin Baylor D. Francis Bauer

21. A. Howard J. Black B. Howard Black 21._____
    C. J. Howard Black D. John H. Black

22. A. Theodora Garth Kingston B. Theadore Barth Kingston 22._____
    C. Thomas Kingston D. Thomas T. Kingston

23. A. Paulette Mary Huerta B. Paul M. Huerta 23._____
    C. Paulette L. Huerta D. Peter A. Huerta

24. A. Martha Hunt Morgan B. Martin Hunt Morgan 24._____
    C. Mary H. Morgan D. Martine H. Morgan

25. A. James T. Meerschaum B. James M. Mershum 25._____
    C. James F. Mearshaum D. James N. Meshum

KEY (CORRECT ANSWERS)

1.	C	11.	A
2.	C	12.	B
3.	B	13.	B
4.	B	14.	C
5.	B	15.	A
6.	B	16.	D
7.	A	17.	A
8.	A	18.	D
9.	B	19.	A
10.	A	20.	D

21. B
22. B
23. B
24. A
25. C

TEST 3

DIRECTIONS: Each question or incomplete statement is followed by several suggested answers or completions. Select the one that BEST answers the question or completes the statement. *PRINT THE LETTER OF THE CORRECT ANSWER IN THE SPACE AT THE RIGHT.*

1. Which one of the following statements about proper telephone usage is NOT always correct?
   When answering the telephone, you should
   A. know whom you are speaking to
   B. give the caller your undivided attention
   C. identify yourself to the caller
   D. obtain the information the caller wishes before you do your other work

   1.____

2. Assume that, as a member of a worker's safety committee in your agency, you are responsible for encouraging other employees to follow correct safety practices. While you are working on your regular assignment, you observe an employee violating a safety rule.
   Of the following, the BEST action for you to take FIRST is to
   A. speak to the employee about safety practices and order him to stop violating the safety rule
   B. speak to the employee about safety practices and point out the safety rule he is violating
   C. bring the matter up in the next committee meeting
   D. report this violation of the safety rule to the employee's supervisor

   2.____

3. Assume that you have been temporarily assigned by your supervisor to do a job which you do not want to do.
   The BEST action for you to take is to
   A. discuss the job with your supervisor, explaining why you do not want to do it
   B. discuss the job with your supervisor and tell her that you will not do it
   C. ask a co-worker to take your place on this job
   D. do some other job that you like; your supervisor may give the job you do not like to someone else

   3.____

4. Assume that you keep the confidential personnel files of employees in your unit. A friend asks you to obtain some information from the file of one of your co-workers.
   The BEST action to take is to _____ to your friend.
   A. ask the co-worker if you can give the information
   B. ask your supervisor if you can give the information
   C. give the information
   D. refuse to give the information

   4.____

29

Questions 5-8.

DIRECTIONS: Questions 5 through 8 are to be answered SOLELY on the basis of the information contained in the following passage.

City government is committed to providing a safe and healthy work environment for all city employees. An effective agency safety program reduces accidents by educating employees about the types of careless acts which can cause accidents. Even in an office, accidents can happen. If each employee is aware of possible safety hazards, the number of accidents on the job can be reduced.

Careless use of office equipment can cause accidents and injuries. For example, file cabinet drawers which are filled with papers can be so heavy that the entire cabinet could tip over from the weight of one open drawer.

The bottom drawers of desks and file cabinets should never be left open since employees can easily trip over open drawers and injure themselves.

When reaching for objects on a high shelf, an employee should use a strong, sturdy object such as a stepstool to stand on. Makeshift platforms made out of books, papers, or boxes can easily collapse. Even chairs can slide out from under foot, causing serious injury.

Even at an employee's desk, safety hazards can occur. Frayed or cut wires should be repaired or replaced immediately. Computers which are not firmly anchored to the desk or table could fall, causing injury.

Smoking is one of the major causes of fires in the office. A lighted match or improperly extinguished cigarette thrown into a wastebasket filled with paper could cause a major fire with possible loss of life. Where smoking is permitted, ashtrays should be used. Smoking is particularly dangerous in offices were flammable chemicals are used.

5. The goal of an effective safety program is to
   A. reduce office accidents
   B. stop employees from smoking on the job
   C. encourage employees to continue their education
   D. eliminate high shelves in offices

6. Desks and file cabinets can become safety hazards when
   A. their drawers are left open
   B. they are used as wastebaskets
   C. they are makeshift
   D. they are not anchored securely to the floor

7. Smoking is especially hazardous when it occurs
   A. near exposed wires
   B. in a crowded office
   C. in an area where flammable chemicals are used
   D. where books and papers are stored

8. Accidents are likely to occur when
   A. employees' desks are cluttered with books and papers
   B. employees are not aware of safety hazards
   C. employees close desk drawers
   D. stepstools are used to reach high objects

9. Assume that part of your job as a worker in the accounting division of a city agency is to answer the telephone.
   When you first answer the telephone, it is LEAST important to tell the caller
   A. your title
   B. your name
   C. the name of your unit
   D. the name of your agency

10. Assume that you are assigned to work as a receptionist, and your duties are to answer phones, greet visitors, and do other general office work. You are busy with a routine job when several visitors approach your desk.
    The BEST action to take is to
    A. ask the visitors to have a seat and assist them after your work is completed
    B. tell the visitors that you are busy and they should return at a more convenient time
    C. stop working long enough to assist the visitors
    D. continue working and wait for the visitors to ask you for assistance

11. Assume that your supervisor has chosen you to take a special course during hours to learn a new payroll procedure. Although you know that you were chosen because of your good work record, a co-worker, who feels that he should have been chosen, has been telling everyone in your unit that the choice was unfair.
    Of the following, the BEST way to handle this situation FIRST is to
    A. suggest to the co-worker that everything in life is unfair
    B. contact your union representative in case your co-worker presents a formal grievance
    C. tell your supervisor about your co-worker's complaints and let her handle the situation
    D. tell the co-worker that you were chosen because of your superior work record

12. Assume that while you are working on an assignment which must be completed quickly, a supervisor from another unit asks you to obtain information for her.
    Of the following, the BEST way to respond to her request is to
    A. tell her to return in an hour since you are busy
    B. give her the names of some people in her own unit who could help her
    C. tell her you are busy and refer her to a co-worker
    D. tell her that you are busy and ask her if she could wait until you finish your assignment

13. A co-worker in your unit is often off from work because of illness. Your supervisor assigns the co-worker's work to you when she is not there. Lately, doing her work has interfered with your own job.
    The BEST action for you to take FIRST is to
    A. discuss the problem with your supervisor
    B. complete your own work before starting your co-worker's work
    C. ask other workers in your unit to assist you
    D. work late in order to get the jobs done

14. During the month of June, 40,587 people attended a city-owned swimming pool. In July, 13,014 more people attended the swimming pool than the number that had attended in June. In August, 39,655 people attended the swimming pool. The TOTAL number of people who attended the swimming pool during the months of June, July, and August was 14.____
  A. 80,242 B. 93,256 C. 133,843 D. 210,382

Questions 15-22.

DIRECTIONS: Questions 15 through 22 test how well you understand what you read. It will be necessary for you to read carefully because your answers to these questions must be based ONLY on the information in the following paragraphs.

  The telephone directory is made up of two books. The first book consists of the introductory section and the alphabetical listing of names section. The second book is the classified directory (also known as the yellow pages). Many people who are familiar with one book do not realize how useful the other can be. The efficient office worker should become familiar with both books in order to make the best use of this important source of information.
  The introductory section gives general instructions for finding numbers in the alphabetical listing and classified directory. This section also explains how to use the telephone company's many services, including the operator and information services, gives examples of charges for local and long-distance calls, and lists area codes for the entire country. In addition, this section provides a useful zip code map.
  The alphabetical listing of names section lists the names, addresses, and telephone numbers of subscribers in an area. Guide names, or *telltales*, are on the top corner of each page. These guide names indicate the first and last name to be found on that page. *Telltales* help locate any particular name quickly. A cross-reference spelling is also given to help locate names which are spelled several different ways. City, state, and federal government agencies are listed under the major government heading. For example, an agency of the federal government would be listed under *United States Government*.
  The classified directory, or yellow pages, is a separate book. In this section are advertising services, public transportation line maps, shopping guides, and listings of businesses arranged by the type of product or services they offer. This book is most useful when looking for the name or phone number of a business when all that is known is the type of product offered and the address, or when trying to locate a particular type of business in an area. Businesses listed in the classified directory can usually be found in the alphabetical listing of names section. When the name of the business is known, you will find the address or phone number more quickly in the alphabetical listing of names section.

15. The introductory section provides 15.____
  A. shopping guides B. government listings
  C. business listings D. information services

16. Advertising services would be found in the 16.____
  A. introductory section B. alphabetical listing of names section\
  C. classified directory D. information services

17. According to the information in the above passage for locating government agencies, the Information Office of the Department of Consumer Affairs of New York City government would be alphabetically listed FIRST under
    A. *I* for Information Offices
    B. *D* for Department of Consumer Affairs
    C. *N* for New York City
    D. *G* for government

17.____

18. When the name of a business is known, the QUICKEST way to find the phone number is to look in the
    A. classified directory
    B. introductory section
    C. alphabetical listing of name section
    D. advertising service section

18.____

19. The QUICKEST way to find the phone number of a business when the type of service a business offers and its address is known is to look in the
    A. classified directory
    B. alphabetical listing of names section
    C. introductory section
    D. information service

19.____

20. What is a *telltale*?
    A. An alphabetical listing
    B. A guide name
    C. A map
    D. A cross-reference listing

20.____

21. The BEST way to find a postal zip code is to look in the
    A. classified directory
    B. introductory section
    C. alphabetical listing of names section
    D. government heading

21.____

22. To help find names which have several different spellings, the telephone directory provides
    A. cross-reference spelling
    B. *telltales*
    C. spelling guides
    D. advertising services

22.____

23. Assume that your agency has been given $2,025 to purchase file cabinets. If each file cabinet costs $135, how many file cabinet can your agency purchase?
    A. 8   B. 10   C. 15   D. 16

23.____

24. Assume that your unit ordered 14 staplers at a total cost of $30.20 and each stapler cost the same.
    The cost of one stapler was MOST NEARLY
    A. $1.02   B. $1.61   C. $2.16   D. $2.26

24.____

25. Assume that you are responsible for counting and recording licensing fees collected by your department. On a particular day, your department collected in fees 40 checks in the amount of $6 each, 80 checks in the amount of $4 each, 45 twenty dollar bills, 30 ten dollar bills, 42 five dollar bills, and 186 one dollar bills.
The TOTAL amount in fees collected on that day was
   A. $1,406   B. $1,706   C. $2,156   D. $2,356

26. Assume that you are responsible for your agency's petty cash fund. During the month of February, you pay out 7 $2.00 subway fares and one taxi fare for $10.85. You pay out nothing else from the fund. At the end of February, you count the money left in the fund and find 3 one dollar bills, 4 quarters, 5 dimes, and 4 nickels.
The amount of money you had available in the petty cash fund at the BEGINNING of February was
   A. $4.70   B. $16.35   C. $24.85   D. $29.55

27. You overhear your supervisor criticize a co-worker for handling equipment in an unsafe way. You feel that the criticism may be unfair.
Of the following, it would be BEST for you to
   A. take your co-worker aside and tell her how you feel about your supervisor's comments
   B. interrupt the discussion and defend your co-worker to your supervisor
   C. continue working as if you had not overheard the discussion
   D. make a list of other workers who have violated safety rules and give it to your supervisor

28. Assume that you have been assigned to work on a long-term project with an employee who is known for being uncooperative.
In beginning to work with this employee, it would be LEAST desirable for you to
   A. understand why the person is uncooperative
   B. act in a calm manner rather than an emotional manner
   C. be appreciative of the co-worker's work
   D. report the co-worker's lack of cooperation to your supervisor

29. Assume that you are assigned to sell tickets at a city-owned ice skating rink. An adult ticket costs $4.50, and a children's ticket costs $2.25. At the end of a day, you find that you have sold 36 adult tickets and 80 children's tickets.
The TOTAL amount of money you collected for that day was
   A. $244.80   B. $318.00   C. $342.00   D. $348.00

30. If each office worker files 487 index cards in one hour, how many card can 26 office workers file in one hour?
   A. 10,662   B. 12,175   C. 12,662   D. 14,266

KEY (CORRECT ANSWERS)

1.	D	11.	C	21.	B
2.	B	12.	D	22.	A
3.	A	13.	A	23.	C
4.	D	14.	C	24.	C
5.	A	15.	D	25.	C
6.	A	16.	C	26.	D
7.	C	17.	C	27.	C
8.	B	18.	C	28.	D
9.	A	19.	A	29.	C
10.	C	20.	B	30.	C

EXAMINATION SECTION
TEST 1

DIRECTIONS: Each question or incomplete statement is followed by several suggested answers or completions. Select the one that BEST answers the question or completes the statement. *PRINT THE LETTER OF THE CORRECT ANSWER IN THE SPACE AT THE RIGHT.*

1. A multi-line telephone with buttons for eight separate lines, plus a *hold* button, is often used when an office requires more than one outside line.
 If you are talking on one line of this type of office phone when another call comes in, what is the procedure to follow if you want to answer the second call but keep the first call on the line?
 Push the
    A. *hold* button at the same time as you push the *pickup* button of the ringing line
    B. *hold* button and then push the *pickup* button of the ringing line
    C. *pickup* button of the ringing line and then push the *hold* button
    D. *pickup* button of the ringing line and push the *hold* button when you return to the original line

    1.____

2. Suppose that you are asked to prepare a petty cash statement for March. The original and one copy are to go to the personnel office. One copy is to go to the fiscal office, and another copy is to go to your supervisor. The last copy is for your files.
 In preparing the statement and the copies, how many sheets of copy paper should you use?
    A. 3   B. 4   C. 5   D. 8

    2.____

3. Which one of the following is the LEAST important advantage of putting the subject of a letter in the heading to the right of the address? It
    A. makes filing of the copy easier
    B. makes more space available in the body of the letter
    C. simplifies distribution of letters
    D. simplifies determination of the subject of the letter

    3.____

4. Of the following, the MOST efficient way to put 100 copies of a one-page letter into 9½" x 4⅛" envelopes for mailing is to fold _____ into an envelope.
    A. each letter and insert it immediately after folding
    B. each letter separately until all 100 are folded; then insert each one
    C. the 100 letters two at a time, then separate them and insert each one
    D. two letters together, slip them apart, and insert each one

    4.____

5. When preparing papers for filing, it is NOT desirable to
   A. smooth papers that are wrinkled
   B. use paper clips to keep related papers together in the files
   C. arrange the papers in the order in which they will be filed
   D. mend torn papers with cellophane tape

6. Of the following, the BEST reason for a clerical unit to have its own duplicating machine is that the unit
   A. uses many forms which it must reproduce internally
   B. must make two copies of each piece of incoming mail for a special file
   C. must make seven copies of each piece of outgoing mail
   D. must type 200 envelopes each month for distribution to the same offices

7. Several offices use the same photocopying machine.
   If each office must pay its share of the cost of running this machine, the BEST way of determining how much of this cost should be charged to each of these offices is to
   A. determine the monthly number of photocopies made by each office
   B. determine the monthly number of originals submitted for photocopying by each office
   C. determine the number of times per day each office uses the photocopying machine
   D. divide the total cost of running the photocopy machine by the total number of offices using the machine

8. Which one of the following would it be BEST to use to indicate that a file folder has been removed from the files for temporary use in another office?
   A(n)
   A. cross-reference card   B. tickler file marker
   C. aperture card   D. out guide

9. Which one of the following is the MOST important objective of filing?
   A. Giving a secretary something to do in her spare time
   B. Making it possible to locate information quickly
   C. Providing a place to store unneeded documents
   D. Keeping extra papers from accumulating on workers' desks

10. If a check has been made out for an incorrect amount, the BEST action for the writer of the check to take is to
    A. erase the original amount and enter the correct amount
    B. cross out the original amount with a single line and enter the correct amount above it
    C. black out the original amount so that it cannot be read and enter the correct amount above it
    D. write a new check

11. Which one of the following BEST describes the usual arrangement of a tickler file?
    A. Alphabetical
    B. Chronological
    C. Numerical
    D. Geographical

    11.____

12. Which one of the following is the LEAST desirable filing practice?
    A. Using staples to keep papers together
    B. Filing all material without regard to date
    C. Keeping a record of all materials removed from the files
    D. Writing filing instructions on each paper prior to filing

    12.____

13. Assume that one of your duties is to keep records of the office supplies used by your unit for the purpose of ordering new supplies when the old supplies run out.
    The information that will be of MOST help in letting you know when to reorder supplies is the
    A. quantity issued
    B. quantity received
    C. quantity on hand
    D. stock number

    13.____

Questions 14-19.

DIRECTIONS: Questions 14 through 19 consist of sets of names and addresses. In each question, the name and address in Column II should be an exact copy of the name and address in Column I. If there is
a mistake *only* in the name, mark your answer A;
a mistake *only* in the address, mark your answer B;
a mistake in *both* name and address, mark your answer C;
no mistake in either name or address, mark your answer D.

SAMPLE QUESTION

Column I	Column II
Michael Filbert	Michael Filbert
456 Reade Street	645 Reade Street
New York, N.Y. 10013	New York, N.Y. 10013

Since there is a mistake only in the address (the street number should be 456 instead of 645), the answer to the sample question is B.

COLUMN I	COLUMN II	
14. Esta Wong 141 West 68 St. New York, N.Y. 10023	Esta Wang 141 West 68 St. New York,, N.Y. 10023	14.____
15. Dr. Alberto Grosso 3475 12th Avenue Brooklyn, N.Y. 11218	Dr. Alberto Grosso 3475 12th Avenue Brooklyn, N.Y. 11218	15.____

	Column I	Column II	

16. Mrs. Ruth Bortlas
    482 Theresa Ct.
    Far Rockaway, N.Y. 11691

    Ms. Ruth Bortlas
    482 Theresa Ct.
    Far Rockaway, N.Y. 11169   16.____

17. Mr. and Mrs. Howard Fox
    2301 Sedgwick Avenue
    Bronx, N.Y. 10468

    Mr. and Mrs. Howard Fox
    231 Sedgwick Ave.
    Bronx, N.Y. 10458   17.____

18. Miss Marjorie Black
    223 East 23 Street
    New York, N.Y. 10010

    Miss Margorie Black
    223 East 23 Street
    New York, N.Y. 10010   18.____

19. Michelle Herman
    806 Valley Rd.
    Old Tappan, N.J. 07675

    Michelle Hermann
    806 Valley Dr.
    Old Tappan, N.J. 07675   19.____

Questions 20-25.

DIRECTIONS: Questions 20 through 25 are to be answered SOLELY on the basis of the information in the following passage.

Basic to every office is the need for proper lighting. Inadequate lighting is a familiar cause of fatigue and serves to create a somewhat dismal atmosphere in the office. One requirement of proper lighting is that it be of an appropriate intensity. Intensity is measured in foot-candles. According to the Illuminating Engineering Society of New York, for casual seeing tasks such as in reception rooms, inactive file rooms, and other service areas, it is recommended that the amount of light be 30 foot-candles. For ordinary seeing tasks such as reading and work in active file rooms and in mail rooms, the recommended lighting is 100 foot-candles. For very difficult seeing tasks such as accounting, transcribing, and business machine use, the recommended lighting is 150 foot-candles.

Lighting intensity is only one requirement. Shadows and glare are to be avoided. For example, the larger the proportion of a ceiling filled with lighting units, the more glare-free and comfortable the lighting will be. Natural lighting from windows is not too dependable because on dark wintry days, windows yield little usable light, and on sunny afternoons, the glare from windows may be very distracting. Desks should not face the windows. Finally, the main lighting source ought to be overhead and to the left of the user.

20. According to the above passage, insufficient light in the office may cause   20.____
    A. glare   B. shadows   C. tiredness   D. distraction

21. Based on the above passage, which of the following must be considered when   21.____
    planning lighting arrangements?
    The
    A. amount of natural light present
    B. amount of work to be done
    C. level of difficulty of work to be done
    D. type of activity to be carried out

22. It can be inferred from the above passage that a well-coordinated lighting scheme is LIKELY to result in
    A. greater employee productivity
    B. elimination of light reflection
    C. lower lighting cost
    D. more use of natural light

23. Of the following, the BEST title for the above passage is
    A. Characteristics of Light
    B. Light Measurement Devices
    C. Factors to Consider When Planning Lighting Systems
    D. Comfort vs. Cost When Devising Lighting Arrangements

24. According to the above passage, a foot-candle is a measurement of the
    A. number of bulbs used
    B. strength of the light
    C. contrast between glare and shadow
    D. proportion of the ceiling filled with lighting units

25. According to the above passage, the number of foot-candles of light that would be needed to copy figures onto a payroll is _____ foot-candles.
    A. less than 30   B. 30   C. 100   D. 150

KEY (CORRECT ANSWERS)

1.	B		11.	B
2.	B		12.	B
3.	B		13.	C
4.	A		14.	A
5.	B		15.	D
6.	A		16.	C
7.	A		17.	B
8.	D		18.	A
9.	B		19.	C
10.	D		20.	C

21. D
22. A
23. C
24. B
25. D

TEST 2

DIRECTIONS: Each question or incomplete statement is followed by several suggested answers or completions. Select the one that BEST answers the question or completes the statement. *PRINT THE LETTER OF THE CORRECT ANSWER IN THE SPACE AT THE RIGHT.*

1. Assume that a supervisor has three subordinates who perform clerical tasks. One of the employees retires and is replaced by someone who is transferred from another unit in the agency. The transferred employee tells the supervisor that she has worked as a clerical employee for two years and understands clerical operations quite well. The supervisor then assigns the transferred employee to a desk, tells the employee to begin working, and returns to his own desk.
The supervisor's action in this situation is
   A. *proper;* experienced clerical employees do not require training when they are transferred to new assignments
   B. *improper;* before the supervisor returns to his desk, he should tell the other two subordinates to watch the transferred employee perform the work
   C. *proper;* if the transferred employee makes any mistakes, she will bring them to the supervisor's attention
   D. *improper;* the supervisor should find out what clerical tasks the transferred employee has performed and give her instruction in those which are new or different

1.____

2. Assume that you are falling behind in completing your work assignments and you believe that your workload is too heavy.
Of the following, the BEST course of action for you to take FIRST is to
   A. discuss the problem with your supervisor
   B. decide which of your assignments can be postponed
   C. try to get some of your co-workers to help you out
   D. plan to take some of the work home with you in order to catch up

2.____

3. Suppose that one of the clerks under your supervision is filling in monthly personnel forms. She asks you to explain a particular personnel regulation which is related to various items on the forms. You are not thoroughly familiar with the regulation.
Of the following responses you may make, the one which will gain the MOST respect from the clerk and which is generally the MOST advisable is to
   A. tell the clerk to do the best she can and that you will check her work later
   B. inform the clerk that you are not sure of a correct explanation but suggest a procedure for her to follow
   C. give the clerk a suitable interpretation so that she will think you are familiar with all regulations
   D. tell the clerk that you will have to read the regulation more thoroughly before you can give her an explanation

3.____

4. Charging out records until a specified due date, with prompt follow-up if they are not returned, is a   4._____
   A. *good* idea; it may prevent the records from being kept needlessly on someone's desk for long periods of time
   B. *good* idea; it will indicate the extent of your authority to other departments
   C. *poor* idea; the person borrowing the material may make an error because of the pressure put upon him to return the records
   D. *poor* idea; other departments will feel that you do not trust them with the records and they will be resentful

Questions 5-9.

DIRECTIONS: Questions 5 through 9 consist of three lines of code letters and numbers. The numbers on each line should correspond with the code letters on the same line in accordance with the table below.

Code Letter	P	L	I	J	B	O	H	U	C	G
Corresponding Letter	0	1	2	3	4	5	6	7	8	9

On some of the lines, an error exists in the coding. Compare the letters and numbers in each question carefully. If you find an error or errors on
only one of the lines in the question, mark your answer A;
any two lines in the question, mark your answer B;
all three lines in the question, mark your answer C;
none of the lines in the question, mark your answer D.

SAMPLE QUESTION
JHOILCP   3652180
BICLGUP   4286970
UCIBHLJ   5824613

In the above sample, the first line is correct since each code letter listed has the correct corresponding number. On the second line, an error exists because code letter L should have the number 1 instead of the number 6. On the third line, an error exists because the code letter U should have the number 7 instead of the number 5. Since there are errors on two of the three lines, the correct answer is B.

5. BULJCIP   4713920   5._____
   HIGPOUL   6290571
   OCUHJJBI   5876342

6. CUBLOIJ   8741023   6._____
   LCLGCLB   1818914
   JPUHIOC   3076158

7. OIJGCBPO   52398405   7._____
   UHPBLIOP   76041250
   CLUIPGPC   81720908

8. BPCOUOJI   40875732
    UOHCIPLB   75682014
    GLHUUCBJ   92677843

9. HOIOHJLH   65256361
    IOJJHHBP   25536640
    OJHBJOPI   53642502

Questions 10-13.

DIRECTIONS: Questions 10 through 13 are to be answered SOLELY on the basis of the information given in the following passage.

The mental attitude of the employee toward safety is exceedingly important in preventing accidents. All efforts designed to keep safety on the employee's mind and to keep accident prevention a live subject in the office will help substantially in a safety program. Although it may seem strange, it is common for people to be careless. Therefore, safety education is a continuous process.

Safety rules should be explained, and the reasons for their rigid enforcement should be given to employees. Telling employees to be careful or giving similar general safety warnings and slogans is probably of little value. Employees should be informed of basic safety fundamentals. This can be done through staff meetings, informal suggestions to employees, movies, and safety instruction cards. Safety instruction cards provide the employees with specific suggestions about safety and serve as a series of timely reminder helping to keep safety on the minds of employees. Pictures, posters, and cartoon sketches on bulletin boards that are located in areas continually used by employees arouse the employees' interest in safety. It is usually good to supplement this type of safety promotion with intensive individual follow-up.

10. The above passage implies that the LEAST effective of the following safety measures is
    A. rigid enforcement of safety rules
    B. getting employees to think in terms of safety
    C. elimination of unsafe conditions in the office
    D. telling employees to stay alert at all times

11. The reason given by the passage for maintaining ongoing safety education is that
    A. people are often careless
    B. office tasks are often dangerous
    C. the value of safety slogans increases with repetition
    D. safety rules change frequently

12. Which one of the following safety aids is MOST likely to be preferred by the passage? A
    A. cartoon of a man tripping over a carton and yelling, *Keep aisles clear!*
    B. poster with a large number one and a caption saying, *Safety First*

C. photograph of a very neatly arranged office
D. large sign with the word *THINK* in capital letters

13. Of the following, the BEST title for the above passage is 13.____
    A. Basic Safety Fundamentals
    B. Enforcing Safety Among Careless Employees
    C. Attitudes Toward Safety
    D. Making Employees Aware of Safety

Questions 14-21.

DIRECTIONS: Questions 14 through 21 are to be answered SOLELY on the basis of the information and chart given below.

The following chart shows expenses in five selected categories for a one-year period, expressed as percentages of these same expenses during the previous year. The chart compares two different offices. In Office T (represented by ▓▓▓▓), a cost reduction program has been tested for the past year. The other office, Office Q (represented by ▨▨▨▨), served as a control, in that no special effort was made to reduce costs during the past year.

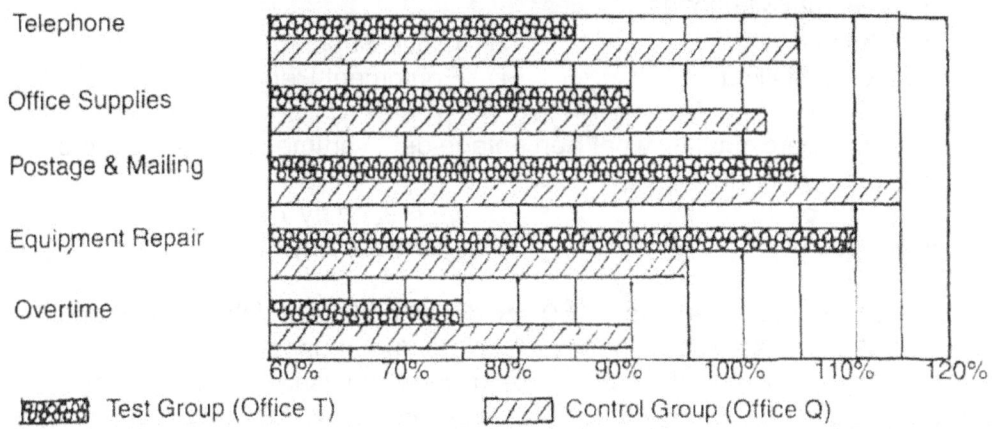

RESULTS OF OFFICE COST REDUCTION PROGRAM
Expenses of Test and Control Groups for 2020
Expressed as Percentages of Same Expenses for 2019

14. In Office T, which category of expense showed the greatest percentage REDUCTION from 2019 to 2020? 14.____
    A. Telephone   B. Office Supplies
    C. Postage & Mailing   D. Overtime

15. In which expense category did Office T show the BEST results in percentage terms when compared to Office Q? 15.____
    A. Telephone   B. Office Supplies
    C. Postage & Mailing   D. Overtime

16. According to the above chart, the cost reduction program was LEAST effective for the expense category of
    A. Office Supplies
    B. Postage & Mailing
    C. Equipment Repair
    D. Overtime

17. Office T's telephone costs went down during 2020 by approximately how many percentage points?
    A. 15   B. 20   C. 85   D. 104

18. Which of the following changes occurred in expenses for Office Supplies in Office Q in the year 2020 as compared with the year 2019?
    They
    A. increased by more than 100%
    B. remained the same
    C. decreased by a few percentage points
    D. increased by a few percentage points

19. For which of the following expense categories do the results in Office T and the results in Office Q differ MOST NEARLYY by 10 percentage points?
    A. Telephone
    B. Postage & Mailing
    C. Equipment Repair
    D. Overtime

20. In which expense category did Office Q's costs show the GREATEST percentage increase in 2020?
    A. Telephone
    B. Office Supplies
    C. Postage & Mailing
    D. Equipment Repair

21. In Office T, by approximately what percentage did overtime expense change during the past year? It
    A. *increased* by 15%
    B. *increased* by 75%
    C. *decreased* by 10%
    D. *decreased* by 25%

22. In a particular agency, there were 160 accidents in 2017. Of these accidents, 75% were due to unsafe acts and the rest were due to unsafe conditions. In the following year, a special safety program was established. The number of accidents in 2019 due to unsafe acts was reduced to 35% of what it had been in 2017.
    How many accidents due to unsafe acts were there in 2019?
    A. 20   B. 36   C. 42   D. 56

23. At the end of every month, the petty cash fund of Agency A is reimbursed for payments made from the fund during the month. During the month of February, the amounts paid from the fund were entered on receipts as follows: 10 bus fares of $3.50 each and one taxi fare of $35.00. At the end of the month, the money left in the fund was in the following denominations: 15 ten-dollar bills, 10 one-dollar bills, 40 quarters, and 100 dimes.
    If the petty cash fund is reduced by 20% for the following month, how much money will there be available in the petty cash fund for March?
    A. $110.00   B. $200.00   C. $215.00   D. $250.00

24. The one of the following records which it would be MOST advisable to keep in alphabetical order is a
    A. continuous listing of phone messages, including time and caller, for your supervisor
    B. listing of individuals currently employed by your agency in a particular title
    C. record of purchases paid for by the petty cash fund
    D. dated record of employees who have borrowed material from the files in your office

25. Assume that you have been asked to copy by hand a column of numbers with two decimal places from one record to another. Each number consists of three, four, and five digits.
    In order to copy them quickly and accurately, you should copy
    A. each number exactly, making sure that the column of digits farthest to the right is in a straight line and all other columns are lined up
    B. the column of digits farthest to the right and then copy the next column of digits moving from right to left
    C. the column of digits farthest to the left and then copy the next column of digits moving from left to right
    D. the digits to the right of each decimal point and then copy the digits to the left of each decimal point

KEY (CORRECT ANSWERS)

1. D
2. A
3. D
4. A
5. A

6. C
7. D
8. B
9. C
10. D

11. A
12. A
13. D
14. D
15. A

16. C
17. A
18. D
19. B
20. C

21. D
22. C
23. B
24. B
25. A

EXAMINATION SECTION
TEST 1

DIRECTIONS: Each question or incomplete statement is followed by several suggested answers or completions. Select the one that BEST answers the question or completes the statement. *PRINT THE LETTER OF THE CORRECT ANSWER IN THE SPACE AT THE RIGHT.*

1. The ∧ or caret symbol is a proofreader's mark which means that a
    A. space should have been left between two words
    B. new paragraph should be indicated
    C. word, phrase, or punctuation mark should be inserted
    D. word that is abbreviated should be spelled out

   1.____

2. Of the following items, the one which should NOT be omitted from a typed inter-office memorandum is the
    A. salutation
    B. complementary closing
    C. formal signature
    D. names of those to receive copies

   2.____

3. A typed rough draft should be double-spaced and should have wide margins PRIMARILY in order to
    A. save time in making typing corrections
    B. provide room for making insertions and corrections
    C. insure that the report is well-organized
    D. permit faster typing of the draft

   3.____

4. In tabular reports, when a main heading, secondary heading, and single line of columnar headings are used, a triple space (2 blank lines) would be used after the _____ heading(s).
    A. main
    B. secondary
    C. columnar
    D. main and secondary

   4.____

5. You have been requested to type a letter to Mr. Brown, a district attorney of a small town.
   Of the following, the CORRECT salutation to use is Dear
    A. District Attorney Brown:
    B. Mr. District Attorney:
    C. Mr. Brown:
    D. Honorable Brown:

   5.____

6. A form letter that is sent to the public can be made to look more personal in appearance by doing all of the following EXCEPT
    A. using a meter stamp on the envelope of the letter
    B. having the letter signed with pen and ink
    C. using a good quality of paper for the letter
    D. matching the type used in the letter with that used for fill-ins

   6.____

7. A senior typist opens a word-processing application to instruct a typist to create a table that contains three column headings. Under each column heading are three items.
   Of the following, which sequence should the senior typist tell the typist to use when creating this table?
   A. First type the headings, and then type the items under them, a column at a time
   B. type each heading with its column of items under it, one column at a time
   C. first type the column of items, then center the headings above them
   D. type the headings and items across the page line by line

8. When a letter is addressed to an agency and a particular person should see it, an *attention line* is used.
   This attention line is USUALLY found
   A. on the envelope only
   B. above the address
   C. below the address
   D. after the agency named in the address

9. The typing technique of *justifying* is used to
   A. decide how wide margins of different sized letters should be
   B. make all the lines of copy end evenly on the right-hand margin
   C. center headings above columns on tabular typed material
   D. condense the amount of space that is needed to make a manuscript look presentable

10. The date line on a letter is typed correctly when the date is ALL on one line
    A. with the month written out
    B. with slashes between the numbers
    C. and the month is abbreviated
    D. with a period at the end

11. When considering how wide to make a column when typing a table, the BASIC rule to follow is that the column should be as wide as the longest
    A. item in the body of the column
    B. heading of all of the columns
    C. item in the body or heading of that column
    D. heading or the longest item in the body of any column on that page

12. When a lengthy quotation is included in a letter or a report, it must be indicated that it is quoted material. This may be done by
    A. enclosing the quotation in parentheses
    B. placing an exclamation point at the end of the quotation
    C. using the apostrophe marks
    D. indenting from the regular margins on the left and right

13. In order to reach the highest rate of speed and the greatest degree of accuracy while typing, it is LEAST important to
    A. maintain good posture
    B. keep the hands and arms at a comfortable level
    C. strike the keys evenly
    D. keep the typing action in the wrists

14. It has been shown that the rate of typing and dictation drops when the secretary is not familiar with the language or topic of the copy.
    A practice that a supervisor might BEST advise to improve the knowledge and therefore increase the rate of typing dictation for such material would be for the secretary to
    A. plan a conference with her supervisor to discuss the subject matter
    B. read and review correspondence and related technical journals that come into the office
    C. recopy or retype previously transcribed material as practice
    D. withdraw sample materials from the files to take home for study

15. The one of the following in which the tab key is NOT generally used is the
    A. placement of the complimentary close and signature line
    B. indentation of paragraphs
    C. placement of the date line
    D. centering of title headings

16. In order for a business letter to be effective, it is LEAST important that it
    A. say what is meant simply and directly
    B. be written in formal language
    C. include all information the receiver needs to know
    D. be courteously written

17. If you are momentarily called away from your desk while typing a report of a confidential nature, you should cover or turn the copy over and
    A. remove the page being typed from the computer and file the report
    B. ask someone to watch your desk for you
    C. close the document so that the page is not visible
    D. spread a folder over the computer screen to conceal it

18. When typing a table that contains a column of figures and a column of words, the PROPER alignment of the column of figures and the column of words should be an even _____ the column of words.
    A. right-hand edge for the column of numbers and an even left-hand edge for
    B. right-hand edge for both the column of numbers and
    C. left-hand edge for the column of numbers and an even right-hand edge for
    D. left-hand edge for both the column of numbers and

19. The word *re*, when used in a memorandum, refers to the information that is   19.____
    on the _____ line.
    A. identification   B. subject   C. attention   D. reference

20. Of the following uses of the period, the one which requires NO spacing after   20.____
    it when it is typed is when the period
    A. follows an abbreviation or an initial
    B. follows a figure or letter at the beginning of a line in a list of items
    C. comes between the initials that make up a single abbreviation
    D. comes at the end of a sentence

21. This <u>mark</u> is a proofreader's mark meaning the word   21.____
    A. is misspelled   B. should be underlined
    C. should be bold   D. should be capitalized

22. When typing a report that is double-spaced, the STANDARD recommended   22.____
    practice for indicating the start of new paragraphs is to
    A. double-space between paragraphs and indent the first word at least five spaces
    B. triple-space between paragraphs and indent the first word at least five spaces
    C. triple-space between paragraphs and type block style at the margin
    D. double-space between paragraphs and type block style at the margin

23. In order to center a heading on a sheet of paper once the center of the paper   23.____
    has been found, the EASIEST and MOST efficient method to use is
    A. note the scale at each end of the heading to be centered and divide by two
    B. backspace from the center of the paper one space for every two letters and spaces in the heading
    C. arrange the heading around the middle number on the computer
    D. use a ruler to mark off the amount of space from both sides of the center of the paper that should be taken up by the heading

24. You are about to type a single-spaced letter from a typewritten draft.   24.____
    In order to center this letter from top to bottom, your FIRST step should be to
    A. determine the number of spaces needed for the top and bottom margins
    B. determine the number of spaces needed for the left and right margins
    C. count the number of lines, including blank ones, which will be used for the letter
    D. subtract from the number of writing lines on the sheet of paper the number of lines that will not be used for the letter

25. When typing a table which lists several amounts of money and the total in a   25.____
    column, the dollar sign should be placed in front of the
    A. first dollar amount only
    B. total dollar amount only
    C. first and total dollar amounts only
    D. all of the amounts of money in the column

26. If a legal document is being prepared and requires necessary information to be typed into blank areas on preprinted legal forms, the margins for a line of typewritten material should be determined PRIMARILY by
    A. counting the total number of words to be typed
    B. the margins set for the pre-printed matter
    C. spacing backwards from the right margin rule
    D. the estimated width and height of the material to be entered

26.____

27. When checking for errors in material you've typed, it is BEST to
    A. proofread the material and use the spell-check function in combination
    B. give the material to someone else to review
    C. run the spell-check function and auto-correct all found errors
    D. proofread the material then e-mail it to another typist for final approval

27.____

28. Assume that Mr. Frank Foran is an acting official. In a letter written to him, the word *acting* would
    A. be used with the title in the address and in the salutation
    B. not be used with the title in the address
    C. be used with the title in the address but not in the salutation
    D. not be used with the title in the address or in the salutation

28.____

29. The software program that requires proficiency in typing in order to best utilize its MOST important features is
    A. Microsoft Excel   B. Adobe Reader
    C. Microsoft Word   D. Intuit QuickBooks

29.____

30. The MAIN reason for keeping a careful record of incoming mail is that
    A. greater speed and accuracy is obtained for answering outgoing mail
    B. this record is legal evidence
    C. it develops the efficiency of the office clerks
    D. the information may be useful some day

30.____

KEY (CORRECT ANSWERS)

1.	C	11.	C	21.	D
2.	D	12.	D	22.	A
3.	B	13.	D	23.	B
4.	B	14.	B	24.	C
5.	C	15.	D	25.	C
6.	A	16.	B	26.	B
7.	D	17.	C	27.	A
8.	C	18.	A	28.	C
9.	B	19.	B	29.	C
10.	A	20.	C	30.	A

TEST 2

DIRECTIONS: Each question or incomplete statement is followed by several suggested answers or completions. Select the one that BEST answers the question or completes the statement. *PRINT THE LETTER OF THE CORRECT ANSWER IN THE SPACE AT THE RIGHT.*

Questions 1-4.

DIRECTIONS: Questions 1 through 4 are to be answered SOLELY on the basis of the information contained in the following passage which is taken from a typing test.

Modern office methods, geared to ever higher speeds and aimed at ever greater efficiency, are largely the result of the typewriter. The typewriter is a substitute for handwriting; and, in the hands of a skilled typist, not only turns out letters and other documents at least three times faster than a penman can do the work, but turns out the greater volume more uniformly and legibly. With the use of carbon paper and onionskin paper, identical copies can be made at the same time.

The typewriter, besides its effect on the conduct of business and government, has had a very important effect on the position of women. The typewriter has done much to bring women into business and government, and today there are vastly more women than men typists. Many women have used the keys of the typewriter to climb the ladder to responsible managerial positions.

The typewriter, as its name implies, employs type to make an ink impression on paper. For many years, the manual typewriter was the standard machine used. Today, the electric typewriter is dominant, with electronic typewriters, word processors, and computers coming into wider use.

The mechanism of the office manual typewriter includes a set of keys arranged systematically in rows; a semicircular frame of type, connected to the keys by levers; the carriage or paper carrier; a rubber roller called a platen, against which the type strikes; and an inked ribbon which makes the impression of the type character when the key strikes it. This machine, once omnipresent, is an antique today.

1. The above passage mentions a number of good features of the combination of a skilled typist and a typewriter.
   Of the following, the feature which is NOT mentioned in the passage is
   A. speed   B. uniformity   C. reliability   D. legibility

   1._____

2. According to the above passage, a skilled typist can
   A. turn out at least five carbon copies of typed matter
   B. type at least three times faster than a penman can write
   C. type more than 80 words a minute
   D. readily move into a managerial position

   2._____

55

3. According to the above passage, which of the following is NOT part of the mechanism of a manual typewriter?
   A. Carbon paper
   B. Paper carrier
   C. Platen
   D. Inked ribbon

3._____

4. According to the above passage, the typewriter has helped
   A. men more than women in business
   B. women in career advancement into management
   C. men and women equally, but women have taken better advantage of it
   D. more women than men, because men generally dislike routine typing work

4._____

5. Standard rules for typing spacing have developed through usage. According to these rules, two spaces are left after a(n)
   A. colon
   B. comma
   C. hyphen
   D. opening parenthesis

5._____

6. Assume that you have to type the heading CENTERING TYPED HEADINGS on a piece of paper which extends from 0 to 100 on the typewriter scale. You want the heading to be perfectly centered on the paper.
   In order to find the proper point on the typewriter scale at which to begin typing, you should determine the paper's center point on the typewriter scale and then _____ the number of letters and spaces in the heading.
   A. add
   B. add one-half
   C. subtract
   D. subtract one-half

6._____

7. While typing from a rough draft, the practice of reading a line ahead of what you are now typing is considered to be a
   A. *good* practice; it may prepare your fingers for the words which you will be typing
   B. *good* practice; it may help you to review the subject matter contained in the material
   C. *poor* practice; it may increase your typing speed so that your accuracy is decreased
   D. *poor* practice; it may cause you to lose your concentration and make errors in the words you are presently typing

7._____

8. Assume that you are transcribing a letter and you are not sure how to divide a word at the end of a line you are typing.
   The BEST way to determine where to divide the word is by
   A. asking your supervisor
   B. asking the person who dictated the letter
   C. checking with other stenographers
   D. looking up the word in a dictionary

8._____

9. When taking proper care of a typewriter, it is NOT a desirable action to
   A. clean the feed rolls with a cloth
   B. dust the exterior surface of the machine
   C. oil the rubber parts of the machine
   D. use a type-cleaning brush to clean the keys

10. Of the following, the LEAST desirable action to take when typing a rough draft of a report is to
    A. cross out typing errors instead of erasing them
    B. double or triple space between lines
    C. provide large margins on all sides of the typing paper
    D. use letterhead or onionskin paper

11. The date line of every business letter should indicate the month, the day of the month, and the year.
    The MOST common practice when typing a date line is to type it as
    A. Jan. 12, 2018
    B. January 12, 2018
    C. 1-12-18
    D. 1/12/18

Questions 12-16.

DIRECTIONS: Questions 12 through 16 are to be answered SOLELY on the basis of the information provided in the following passage.

A written report is a communication of information from one person to another. It is an account of some matter especially investigated, however routine that matter may be. The ultimate basis of any good written report is facts, which became known through observation and verification. Good written reports may seem to be no more than general ideas and opinions. However, in such cases, the facts leading to these opinions were gathered, verified, and reported earlier, and the opinions are dependent upon these facts. Good style, proper form, and emphasis cannot make a good written report out of unreliable information and bad judgments but on the other hand, solid investigation and brilliant thinking are not likely to become very useful until they are effectively communicated to others. If a person's work calls for written reports, then his work is often no better than his written reports.

12. Based on the information in the above passage, it can be concluded that opinions expressed in a report should be
    A. based on facts which are gathered and reported
    B. emphasized repeatedly when they result from a special investigation
    C. kept to a minimum
    D. separated from the body of the report

13. In the above passage, the one of the following which is mentioned as a way of establishing facts is
    A. authority
    B. communication
    C. reporting
    D. verification

14. According to the above passage, the characteristic shared by ALL written reports is that they are
    A. accounts of routine matters
    B. transmissions of information
    C. reliable and logical
    D. written in proper form

14.____

15. Which of the following conclusions can LOGICALLY be drawn from the information given in the above passage?
    A. Brilliant thinking can make up for unreliable information in a report.
    B. One method of judging an individual's work is the quality of the written reports he is required to submit.
    C. Proper form and emphasis can make a good report out of unreliable information.
    D. Good written reports that seem to be no more than general ideas should be rewritten.

15.____

16. Which of the following suggested titles would be MOST appropriate for this passage?
    A. GATHERING AND ORGANIZING FACTS
    B. TECHNIQUES OF OBSERVATION
    C. NATURE AND PURPOSE OF REPORTS
    D. REPORTS AND OPINIONS: DIFFERENCES AND SIMILARITIES

16.____

Questions 17-25

DIRECTIONS: Each of Questions 17 through 25 consists of a sentence which may or may not be an example of good English usage. Examine each sentence, considering grammar, punctuation, spelling, capitalization, and awkwardness. Then choose the correct statement about it from the four choices below it. If the English usage in the sentence given is better than any of the changes suggested in Choices B, C, or D, pick choice A. Do NOT pick a choice that will change the meaning of the sentence.

17. We attended a staff conference on Wednesday the new safety and fire rules were discussed.
    A. This is an example of acceptable writing.
    B. The words *safety*, *fire*, and *rules* should begin with capital letters.
    C. There should be a comma after the word *Wednesday*.
    D. There should be a period after the word *Wednesday*, and the word *the* should begin with a capital letter.

17.____

18. Neither the dictionary or the telephone directory could be found in the office library.
    A. This is an example of acceptable writing.
    B. The word *or* should be changed to *nor*.
    C. The word *library* should be spelled *libery*.
    D. The word *neither* should be changed to *either*.

18.____

19. The report would have been typed correctly if the typist cold read the draft.   19.____
    A. This is an example of acceptable writing.
    B. The word *would* should be removed.
    C. The word *have* should be inserted after the word *could*.
    D. The word *correctly* should be changed to *correct*.

20. The supervisor brought the reports and forms to an employees desk.   20.____
    A. This is an example of acceptable writing.
    B. The word *brought* should be changed to *took*.
    C. There should be a comma after the word *reports* and a comma after the word *forms*.
    D. The word *employees* should be spelled *employee's*.

21. It's important for all the office personnel to submit their vacation schedules on time.   21.____
    A. This is an example of acceptable writing.
    B. The word *It's* should be spelled *Its*.
    C. The word *their* should be spelled *they're*.
    D. The word *personnel* should be spelled *personal*.

22. The supervisor wants that all staff members report to the office at 9:00 A.M.   22.____
    A. This is an example of acceptable writing.
    B. The word *that* should be removed and the word *to* should be inserted after the word *members*.
    C. There should be a comma after the word *wants* and a comma after the word *office*.
    D. The word *wants* should be changed to *want* and the word *shall* should be inserted after the word *members*.

23. Every morning the clerk opens the office mail and distributes it.   23.____
    A. This is an example of acceptable writing.
    B. The word *opens* should be changed to *open*.
    C. The word *mail* should be changed to *letters*.
    D. The word *it* should be changed to *them*.

24. The secretary typed more fast on an electric typewriter than on a manual typewriter.   24.____
    A. This is an example of acceptable writing.
    B. The words *more fast* should be changed to *faster*.
    C. There should be a comma after the words *electric typewriter*.
    D. The word *than* should be changed to *then*.

25. The new stenographer needed a desk a typewriter, a chair and a blotter.   25.____
    A. This is an example of acceptable writing.
    B. The word *blotter* should be spelled *blodder*.
    C. The word *stenographer* should begin with a capital letter.
    D. There should be a comma after the word *desk*.

KEY (CORRECT ANSWERS)

1.	C		11.	B
2.	B		12	A
3.	A		13.	D
4.	B		14.	B
5.	A		15.	B
6.	D		16.	C
7.	D		17.	D
8.	D		18.	B
9.	C		19.	C
10.	D		20.	D

21. A
22. B
23. A
24. B
25. D

READING COMPREHENSION
UNDERSTANDING AND INTERPRETING WRITTEN MATERIAL
EXAMINATION SECTION

This exam section includes some passages and questions related to functions of the first computerized offices, which consisted of typewriters and other such manual office equipment.

TEST 1

DIRECTIONS: Each question or incomplete statement is followed by several suggested answers or completions. Select the one that BEST answers the question or completes the statement. *PRINT THE LETTER OF THE CORRECT ANSWER IN THE SPACE AT THE RIGHT.*

Questions 1-2.

DIRECTIONS: Questions 1 and 2 are to be answered SOLELY on the basis of the following passage.

The employees in a unit or division of a government agency may be referred to as a work group. Within a government agency which has existed for some time, the work groups will have evolved traditions of their own. The persons in these work groups acquire these traditions as part of the process of work adjustment within their groups. Usually, a work group in a large organization will contain *oldtimers*, *newcomers*, and *in-betweeners*. Like the supervisor of a group, who is not necessarily an oldtimer or the oldest member, oldtimers usually have great influence. They can recall events unknown to others and are a storehouse of information and advice about current problems in the light of past experience. They pass along the traditions of the group to the others who, in turn, become oldtimers themselves. Thus, the traditions of the group which have been honored and revered by long acceptance are continued.

1. According to the above passage, the traditions of a work group within a government agency are developed
   A. at the time the group is established
   B. over a considerable period of time
   C. in order to give recognition to oldtimers
   D. for the group before it is established

2. According to the above passage, the oldtimers within a work group
   A. are the means by which long accepted practices and customs are perpetuated
   B. would best be able to settle current problems that arise
   C. are honored because of the changes they have made in the traditions
   D. have demonstrated that they have learned to do their work well

Questions 3-4.

DIRECTIONS: Questions 3 and 4 are to be answered SOLELY on the following passage.

In public agencies, the success of a person assigned to perform first-line supervisory duties depends in large part upon the personal relations between him and his subordinate employees. The goal of supervising effort is something more than to obtain compliance with procedures established by some central office. The major objective is work accomplishment. In order for this goal to be attained, employees must want to attain it and must exercise initiative in their work. Only if employees are generally satisfied with the type of supervision which exists in an organization will they put forth their best efforts.

3. According to the above passage, in order for employees to try to do their work as well as they can, it is essential that
    A. they participate in determining their working conditions and rates of pay
    B. their supervisors support the employees' viewpoints in meetings with higher management
    C. they are content with the supervisory practices which are being used
    D. their supervisors make the changes in working procedures that the employees request

3._____

4. It can be inferred from the above passage that the goals of a unit in a public agency will not be reached unless the employees in the unit
    A. wish to reach them and are given the opportunity to make individual contributions to the work
    B. understand the relationship between the goals of the unit and goals of the agency
    C. have satisfactory personal relationships with employees of other units in the agency
    D. carefully follow the directions issued by higher authorities

4._____

Questions 5-9.

DIRECTIONS: Questions 5 through 9 are to be answered SOLELY on the basis of the following passage.

In an employee thinks he can save money, time, or material for the city or has an idea about how to do something better than it is being done, he shouldn't keep it to himself. He should send his ideas to the Employees' Suggestion Program, using the special form which is kept on hand in all departments. An employee may send in as many ideas as he wishes. To make sure that each idea is judged fairly, the name of the suggester is not made known until an award is made. The awards are certificate of merit or cash prizes ranging from $10 to $500.

5. According to the above passage, an employee who knows how to do a job in a better way should
    A. be sure it saves enough time to be worthwhile
    B. get paid the money he saves for the city
    C. keep it to himself to avoid being accused of causing a speed-up
    D. send his idea to the Employees' Suggestion Program

5._____

6. In order to send his idea to the Employees' Suggestion Program, an employee should
   A. ask the Department of Personnel for a special form
   B. get the special form in his own department
   C. mail the idea using Special Delivery
   D. send it on plain, white letter-size paper

7. An employee may send to the Employees' Suggestion Program
   A. as many ideas as he can think of
   B. no more than one idea each week
   C. no more than ten ideas in a month
   D. only one idea on each part of the job

8. The reason the name of an employee who makes a suggestion is not made known at first is to
   A. give the employee a larger award
   B. help the judges give more awards
   C. insure fairness in judging
   D. only one idea on each part of the job

9. An employee whose suggestion receives an award may be given a
   A. bonus once a year
   B. certificate for $10
   C. cash prize of up to $500
   D. salary increase of $500

Questions 10-12.

DIRECTIONS: Questions 10 through 12 are to be answered SOLELY on the basis of the following passage.

According to the rules of the Department of Personnel, the work of every permanent city employee is reviewed and rated by his supervisor at least once a year. The civil service rating system gives the employee and his supervisor a chance to talk about the progress made during the past year as well as about those parts of the job in which the employee needs to do better. In order to receive a pay increase each year, the employee must have a satisfactory service rating. Service ratings also count toward an employee's final mark on a promotion examination.

10. According to the above passage, a permanent city employee is rated AT LEAST once
    A. before his work is reviewed
    B. every six months
    C. yearly by his supervisor
    D. yearly by the Department of Personnel

11. According to the above passage, under the rating system the supervisor and the employee can discuss how
    A. much more work needs to be done next year
    B. the employee did his work last year
    C. the work can be made easier next year
    D. the work of the Department can be increased

12. According to the above passage, a permanent city employee will NOT receive a yearly pay increase
    A. if he received a pay increase the year before
    B. if he used his service rating for his mark on a promotion examination
    C. if his service rating is unsatisfactory
    D. unless he got some kind of a service rating

12.____

Questions 13-16.

DIRECTIONS: Questions 13 through 16 are to be answered SOLELY on the basis of the following passage.

It is an accepted fact that the rank and file employee can frequently advance worthwhile suggestions toward increasing efficiency. For this reason, an Employees' Suggestion System has been developed and put into operation. Suitable means have been provided at each departmental location for the confidential submission of suggestions. Numerous suggestions have been received thus far and, after study, about five percent of the ideas submitted are being translated into action. It is planned to set up, eventually, monetary awards for all worthwhile suggestions.

13. According to the above passage, a MAJOR reason why an Employees' Suggestion System was established is that
    A. an organized program of improvement is better than a haphazard one
    B. employees can often give good suggestions to increase efficiency
    C. once a fact is accepted, it is better to act on it than to do nothing
    D. the suggestions of rank and file employees were being neglected

13.____

14. According to the above passage, under the Employees' Suggestion System,
    A. a file of worthwhile suggestions will eventually be set up at each departmental location
    B. it is possible for employees to turn in suggestions without fellow employees knowing of it
    C. means have been provided for the regular and frequent collection of suggestions submitted
    D. provision has been made for the judging of worthwhile suggestions by an Employees' Suggestion Committee

14.____

15. According to the above passage, it is reasonable to assume that
    A. all suggestions must be turned in at a central office
    B. employees who make worthwhile suggestions will be promoted
    C. not all the prizes offered will be monetary ones
    D. prizes of money will be given for the best suggestions

15.____

16. According to the above passage, of the many suggestions made,
    A. all are first tested   B. a small part are put into use
    C. most are very worthwhile D. samples are studied

16.____

Questions 17-20.

DIRECTIONS: Questions 17 through 20 are to be answered SOLELY on the basis of the following passage.

Employees may be granted leaves of absence without pay at the discretion of the Personnel Officer. Such a leave without pay shall begin on the first working day on which the employee does not report for duty and shall continue to the first day on which the employee returns to duty. The Personnel Division may vary the dates of the leave for the record so as to conform with payroll periods, but in no case shall an employee be off the payroll for a different number of calendar days than would have been the case if the actual dates mentioned above had been used. An employee who has vacation or overtime to his credit, which is available for normal use, may take time off immediately prior to beginning a leave of absence without pay, chargeable against all or part of such vacation or overtime.

17. According to the above passage, the Personnel Officer must
    A. decide if a leave of absence without pay should be granted
    B. require that a leave end on the last working day of a payroll period
    C. see to it that a leave of absence to conform with a payroll period
    D. vary the dates of a leave of absence to conform with a payroll period

18. According to the above passage, the exact dates of a leave of absence without pay may be varied provided that the
    A. calendar days an employee is off the payroll equal the actual leave granted
    B. leave conforms to an even number of payroll periods
    C. leave when granted made provision for variance to simplify payroll records
    D. Personnel Officer approves the variation

19. According to the above passage, a leave of absence without pay must extend from the
    A. first day of a calendar period to the first day the employee resumes work
    B. first day of a payroll period to the last calendar day of the leave
    C. first working day missed to the first day on which the employee resumes work
    D. last day on which an employee works through the first day he returns to work

20. According to the above passage, an employee may take extra time off just before the start of a leave of absence without pay if
    A. he charges this extra time against his leave
    B. he has a favorable balance of vacation or overtime which has been frozen
    C. the vacation or overtime that he would normally use for a leave without pay has not been charged in this way before
    D. there is time to his credit which he may use

Question 21.

DIRECTIONS: Question 21 is to be answered SOLELY on the basis of the following passage.

In considering those things which are motivators and incentives to work, it might be just as erroneous not to give sufficient weight to money as an incentive as it is to give too much weight. It is not a problem of establishing a rank-order of importance, but one of knowing that motivation is a blend or mixture rather than a pure element. It is simple to say that cultural factors count more than financial considerations, but this leads only to the conclusion that our society is financial-oriented.

21. Based on the above passage, in our society, cultural and social motivations to work are
    A. things which cannot be avoided
    B. melded to financial incentives
    C. of less consideration than high pay
    D. not balanced equally with economic or financial considerations

21.____

Question 22.

DIRECTIONS: Question 22 is to be answered SOLELY on the basis of the following passage.

A general principle of training and learning with respect to people is that they learn more readily if they receive *feedback*. Essential to maintaining proper motivational levels is knowledge of results which indicate level of progress. Feedback also assists the learning process by identifying mistakes. If this kind of information were not given to the learner, then improper or inappropriate job performance may be instilled.

22. Based on the above passage, which of the following is MOST accurate?
    A. Learning will not take place without feedback.
    B. In the absence of feedback, improper or inappropriate job performance will be learned.
    C. To properly motivate a learner, the learner must have his progress made known to him.
    D. Trainees should be told exactly what to do if they are to learn properly

22.____

Questions 23.

DIRECTIONS: Question 23 is to be answered SOLELY on the basis of the following passage.

In a democracy, the obligation of public officials is twofold. They must not only do an efficient and satisfactory job of administration, but also they must persuade the public that it is an efficient and satisfactory job. It is a burden which, if properly assumed, will make democracy work and perpetuate reform government.

23. The above passage means that
    A. public officials should try to please everybody

23.____

B. public opinion is instrumental if determining the policy of public officials
C. satisfactory performance of the job of administration will eliminate opposition to its work
D. frank and open procedure in a public agency will aid in maintaining progressive government

Question 24.

DIRECTIONS: Question 24 is to be answered SOLELY on the basis of the following passage.

Upon retirement for service, a member shall receive a retirement allowance which shall consist of an annuity which shall be the actuarial equivalent of his accumulated deductions at the time of his retirement and a pension, in addition to his annuity, which shall be equal to one service-fraction of his final compensation, multiplied by the number of years of service since he last became a member credited to him, and a pension which is the actuarial equivalent of the reserve-for-increased-take-home-pay to which he may then be entitled, if any.

24. According to the above passage, a retirement allowance shall consist of a(n) 24.____
    A. annuity, plus a pension, plus an actuarial equivalent
    B. annuity, plus a pension, plus reserve-for-increased-take-home-pay, if any
    C. annuity, plus reserve-for-increased-take-home-pay, if any, plus final compensation
    D. pension, plus reserve-for-increased-take-home-pay, if any, plus accumulated deductions

Question 25.

DIRECTIONS: Question 25 is to be answered SOLELY on the basis of the following passage.

Membership in the retirement system shall cease upon the occurrence of any one of the following conditions: when the time out of service of any member who has total service of less than 25 years, shall aggregate more than 5 years; when the time out of service of any member who has total service of 25 years or more, shall aggregate more than 10 years; when any member shall have withdrawn more than 50% of his accumulated deductions; or when any member shall have withdrawn the cash benefit provided by Section B3.35.0 of the Administrative Code.

25. According to the information in the above passage, membership in the 25.____
    retirement system shall cease when an employee
    A. with 17 years of service has been on a leave of absence for 3 years
    B. withdraws 50% of his accumulated deductions
    C. with 28 years of service has been out of service for 10 years
    D. withdraws his cash benefits

KEY (CORRECT ANSWERS)

1.	B	11.	B
2.	A	12.	C
3.	C	13.	B
4.	A	14.	B
5.	D	15.	D
6.	B	16.	B
7.	A	17.	A
8.	C	18.	A
9.	B	19.	C
10.	C	20.	D

21. B
22. C
23. D
24. B
25. D

TEST 2

DIRECTIONS: Each question or incomplete statement is followed by several suggested answers or completions. Select the one that BEST answers the question or completes the statement. *PRINT THE LETTER OF THE CORRECT ANSWER IN THE SPACE AT THE RIGHT.*

Questions 1-6.

DIRECTIONS: Questions 1 through 6 are to be answered SOLELY on the basis of the following passage.

    Since almost every office has some contact with data-processed records, a stenographer should have some understanding of the basic operations of data processing. Data processing systems now handle a vast majority of all office paperwork. On coded forms and other specialized media, data are recorded before being fed into the computer for processing. The data written on the source document is converted in highly advanced ways in order to make the information accessible to the user. After data has been converted, it must be verified to guarantee absolute accuracy. In this manner, data becomes a permanent record which can be read by computers that compare, store, compute, and otherwise process data at high speeds.

    One key person in a computer installation is a programmer, the man or woman who puts business and scientific problems into special symbolic languages that can be read by the computer. Jobs done by the computer range all the way from payroll operations to chemical process control, but most computer applications are directed toward management data. Most programmers employed by business come to their positions with college degrees; the rest are promoted to their positions from within the organization on the basis of demonstrated ability without regard to education.

1. Of the following, the BEST title for the above passage is
   A. The Stenographer As Data Processor
   B. The Relation of Data Input to Stenography
   C. Understanding Data Processing
   D. Permanent Office Records

2. According to the above passage, a stenographer should understand the basic operations of data processing because
   A. almost every office today has contact with data processed by computer
   B. any office worker may be asked to verify the accuracy of data
   C. most offices are involved in the production of permanent records
   D. data may be converted into computer language by specialized media

3. According to the above passage, data accuracy is reviewed during the _____ stage.
   A. processing
   B. verification
   C. programming
   D. stenographic

1.____

2.____

3.____

4. According to the above passage, computers are used MOST often to handle
   A. management data
   B. problems of higher education
   C. the control of chemical processes
   D. payroll operations

5. Computer programming is taught in many colleges and business schools. The above passage implies that programmers in industry
   A. must have professional training
   B. need professional training to advance
   C. must have at least a college education to do adequate programming tasks
   D. do not necessarily need college education to do programming work

6. According to the above passage, data to be processed by computer should be
   A. recent   B. basic   C. complete   D. verified

Questions 7-10.

DIRECTIONS: Questions 7 through 10 are to be answered SOLELY on the basis of the following passage.

There is nothing that will take the place of good sense on the part of the stenographer. You may be perfect in transcribing exactly what the dictator says and your speed may be adequate, but without an understanding of the dictator's intent as well as his words, you are likely to be a mediocre secretary.

A serious error that is made when taking dictation is putting down something that does not make sense. Most people who dictate material would rather be asked to repeat and explain than to receive transcribed material which has errors due to inattention or doubt. Many dictators request that their grammar be corrected by their secretaries, but unless specifically asked to do so, secretaries should not do it without first checking with the dictator. Secretaries should be aware that, in some cases, dictators may use incorrect grammar or slang expressions to create a particular effect.

Some people dictate commas, periods, and paragraphs, while others expect the stenographer to know when, where, and how to punctuate. A well-trained secretary should be able to indicate the proper punctuation by listening to the pauses and tones of the dictator's voice.

A stenographer who has taken dictation from the same person for a period of time should be able to understand him under most conditions. By increasing her tack, alertness, and efficiency, a secretary can become more competent.

7. According to the above passage, which of the following statements concerning the dictation of punctuation is CORRECT?
   A. Dictator may use incorrect punctuation to create a desired style.
   B. Dictator should indicate all punctuation.

C. Stenographer should know how to punctuate based on the pauses and tones of the dictator.
D. Stenographer should not type any punctuation if it has not been dictated to her.

8. According to the above passage, how should secretaries handle grammatical errors in a dictation?
Secretaries should
   A. *not correct* grammatical errors unless the dictator is aware that this is being done
   B. *correct* grammatical errors by having the dictator repeat the line with proper pauses
   C. *correct* grammatical errors if they have checked the correctness in a grammar book
   D. *correct* grammatical errors based on their own good sense

8.____

9. If a stenographer is confused about the method of spacing and indenting of a report which has just been dictated to her, she GENERALLY should
   A. do the best she can
   B. ask the dictator to explain what she should do
   C. try to improve her ability to understand dictated material
   D. accept the fact that her stenographic ability is not adequate

9.____

10. In the last line of the first paragraph, the word *mediocre* means MOST NEARLY
    A. superior   B. respected   C. disregarded   D. second-rate

10.____

Questions 11-12.

DIRECTIONS: Questions 11 and 12 are to be answered SOLELY on the basis of the following passage.

The number of legible carbon copies required to be produced determines the weight of the carbon paper to be used. When only one copy is made, heavy carbon paper is satisfactory. Most typists, however, use medium-weight carbon paper and find it serviceable for up to three or four copies. If five or more copies are to be made, it is wise to use light carbon paper. On the other hand, the finish of carbon paper to be used depends largely on the stroke of the typist and, in lesser degree, on the number of copies to be made and on whether the typewriter has pica or elite type. A soft-finish carbon paper should be used if the typist's touch is light or if a noiseless machine is used. It is desirable for the average typist to use medium-finish carbon paper for ordinary work, when only a few carbon copies are required. Elite type requires a harder carbon finish than pica type for the same number of copies.

11. According to the above passage, the lighter the carbon paper used, the
    A. softer the finish of the carbon paper will be
    B. greater the number of legible carbon copies that can be made
    C. greater the number of times the carbon paper can be used
    D. lighter the typist's touch should be

11.____

12. According to the above passage, the MOST important factor which determines whether the finish of carbon paper to be used in typing should be hard, medium, or soft is
    A. the touch of the typist
    B. the number of carbon copies required
    C. whether the type in the typewriter is pica or elite
    D. whether a machine with pica type will produce the same number of carbon copies as a machine with elite type

12.____

Questions 13-16.

DIRECTIONS: Questions 13 through 16 are to be answered SOLELY on the basis of the following passage.

Looking back at past developments in office work, advances were made at higher speeds and at greater efficiency thanks largely to the typewriter. The typewriter was a substitute for handwriting and, in the hands of a skilled typist, not only turned out letters and other documents at least three times faster than a penman, but turned out the greater volume more uniformly and legibly. With the use of carbon paper and onionskin paper, identical copies could be made at the same time.

The typewriter, besides its effect on the conduct of business and government, had a very important effect on the position of women. The typewriter did much to bring women into business and government, and in a short time span, women far outnumbered men as typists. Many women used the keys of the typewriter to climb the ladder to professional managerial positions.

The typewriter, as its name implies, employs type to make an ink impression on paper. For many years, the manual typewriter was the standard machine used. Eventually, the electric typewriter became dominant, leading to innovations in and widespread use of completely automatic electronic typewriters.

The mechanism of the office manual typewriter includes a set of keys arranged systematically in rows; a semicircular frame of type, connected to the keys by levers; the carriage, or paper carrier; a rubber roller, called a platen, against which the type strikes; and an inked ribbon which makes the impression of the type character when the key strikes it.

13. The above passage mentions a number of good features of the combination of a skilled typist and a typewriter.
    Of the following the feature which is NOT mentioned in the passage is
    A. speed   B. reliability   C. uniformity   D. legibility

13.____

14. According to the above passage, a skilled typist can
    A. turn out at least five carbon copies of typed matter
    B. type at least three times faster than a penman can write
    C. type more than 80 words in a minute
    D. readily move into a managerial position

14.____

15. According to the above passage, which of the following is NOT part of the mechanism of a manual typewriter?   15._____
    A. Carbon paper   B. Platen
    C. Paper carrier   D. Inked ribbon

16. According to the above passage, the typewriter helped   16._____
    A. men more than women in business
    B. women in career advancement into management
    C. men and women equally, but women have taken better advantage of it
    D. more women than men, because men generally dislike routine typing work

Questions 17-21.

DIRECTIONS: Questions 17 through 21 are to be answered SOLELY on the basis of the following passage.

The recipient gains an impression of a typewritten letter before he begins to read the message. Factors which provide for a good first impression include margins and spacing that are visually pleasing, formal parts of the letter which are correctly placed according to the style of the letter, copy which is free of obvious erasures and over-strikes, and transcript that is even and clear. The problem for the typist is that of how to produce that first, positive impression of her work.

There are several general rules which a typist can follow when she wishes to prepare a properly spaced letter on a sheet of letterhead. Ordinarily, the width of a letter should not be less than four inches nor more than six inches. The side margins should also have a desirable relation to the bottom margin and the space between the letterhead and the body of the letter. Usually the most appealing arrangement is when the side margins are even and the bottom margin is slightly wider than the side margins. In some offices, however, standard line length is used for all business letter, and the secretary then varies the spacing between the date line and the inside address according to the length of the letter.

17. The BEST title for the above passage would be   17._____
    A. Writing Office Letters
    B. Making Good First Impressions
    C. Judging Well-Typed Letters
    D. Good Placing and Spacing for Office Letters

18. According to the above passage, which of the following might be considered the way in which people very quickly judge the quality of work which has been typed? By   18._____
    A. measuring the margins to see if they are correct
    B. looking at the spacing and cleanliness of the typescript
    C. scanning the body of the letter for meaning
    D. reading the date line and address for errors

19. What, according to the above passage, would be definitely UNDESIRABLE as the average line length of a typed letter?   19._____
    A. 4"   B. 6"   C. 5"   D. 7"

20. According to the above passage, when the line length is kept standard, the secretary   20._____
    A. does not have to vary the spacing at all since this also is standard
    B. adjusts the spacing between the date line and inside address for different lengths of letters
    C. uses the longest line as a guidance for spacing between the date line and inside address
    D. varies the number of spaces between the lines

21. According to the above passage, side margins are MOST pleasing when they   21._____
    A. are even and somewhat smaller than the bottom margin
    B. are slightly wider than the bottom margin
    C. vary with the length of the letter
    D. are figured independently from the letterhead and the body of the letter

Questions 22-25.

DIRECTIONS: Questions 22 through 25 are to be answered SOLELY on the basis of the following passage.

Typed pages can reflect the simplicity of modern art in a machine age. Lightness and evenness can be achieved by proper layout and balance of typed lines and white space. Instead of solid, cramped masses of uneven, crowded typing, there should be a pleasing balance up and down as well as horizontal.

To have real balance, your page must have a center. The eyes see the center of the sheet slightly above the real center. This is the way both you and the reader see it. Try imagining a line down the center of the page that divides the paper in equal halves. On either side of your paper, white space and blocks of typing need to be similar in size and shape. Although left and right margins should be equal, top and bottom margins need not be as exact. It looks better to hold a bottom border wider than a top margin, so that your typing rests upon a cushion of white space. To add interest to the appearance of the page, try making one paragraph between one-half and two-thirds the size of an adjacent paragraph.

Thus, by taking full advantage of your typewriter, the pages that you type will not only be accurate but will also be attractive.

22. It can be inferred from the above passage that the basic importance of proper balancing on a typed page is that proper balancing   22._____
    A. makes a typed page a work of modern art
    B. provides exercise in proper positioning of a typewriter
    C. increases the amount of typed copy on the paper
    D. draws greater attention and interest to the page

23. A reader will tend to see the center of a typed page 23.____
    A. somewhat higher than the true center
    B. somewhat lower than the true center
    C. on either side of the true center
    D. about two-thirds of an inch above the true center

24. Which of the following suggestions is NOT given by the above passage? 24.____
    A. Bottom margins may be wider than top borders.
    B. Keep all paragraphs approximately the same size.
    C. Divide your page with an imaginary line down the middle.
    D. Side margins should be equalized.

25. Of the following, the BEST title for the above passage is 25.____
    A. Increasing the Accuracy of the Typed Page
    B. Determination of Margins for Typed Copy
    C. Layout and Balance of the Typed Page
    D. How to Take Full Advantage of the Typewriter

KEY (CORRECT ANSWERS)

1.	C		11.	B
2.	A		12.	A
3.	B		13.	B
4.	A		14.	B
5.	D		15.	A
6.	D		16.	B
7.	C		17.	D
8.	A		18.	B
9.	B		19.	D
10.	D		20.	B

21. A
22. D
23. A
24. B
25. C

TEST 3

DIRECTIONS: Each question or incomplete statement is followed by several suggested answers or completions. Select the one that BEST answers the question or completes the statement. *PRINT THE LETTER OF THE CORRECT ANSWER IN THE SPACE AT THE RIGHT.*

Questions 1-5.

DIRECTIONS: Questions 1 through 5 are to be answered SOLELY on the basis of the following passage.

    A written report is a communication of information from one person to another. It is an account of some matter especially investigated, however routine that matter may be. The ultimate basis of any good written report is facts, which become known through observation and verification. Good written reports may seem to be no more than general ideas and opinions. However, in such cases, the facts leading too these opinions were gathered, verified, and reported earlier, and the opinions are dependent upon these facts. Good style, proper form, and emphasis cannot make a good written report out of unreliable information and bad judgment; but on the other hand, solid investigation and brilliant thinking are not likely to become very useful until they are effectively communicated to others. If a person's work calls for written reports, then his work is often no better than his written reports.

1. Based on the information in the above passage, it can be concluded that opinions expressed in a report should be
   A. based on facts which are gathered and reported
   B. emphasized repeatedly when they result from a special investigation
   C. kept to a minimum
   D. separated from the body of the report

   1.____

2. In the above passage, the one of the following which is mentioned as a way of establishing facts is
   A. authority
   B. reporting
   C. communication
   D. verification

   2.____

3. According to the above passage, the characteristic shared by ALL written reports is that they are
   A. accounts of routine matters
   B. transmissions of information
   C. reliable and logical
   D. written in proper form

   3.____

4. Which of the following conclusions can logically be drawn from the information given in the above passage?
   A. Brilliant thinking can make up for unreliable information in a report.
   B. One method of judging an individual's work is the quality of the written reports he is required to submit.
   C. Proper form and emphasis can make a good report out of unreliable information.
   D. Good written reports that seem to be no more than general ideas should be rewritten.

   4.____

76

5. Which of the following suggested titles would be MOST appropriate for the above passage?
   A. Gathering and Organizing Facts
   B. Techniques of Observation
   C. Nature and Purpose of Reports
   D. Reports and Opinions: Differences and Similarities

Questions 6-8.

DIRECTIONS: Questions 6 through 8 are to be answered SOLELY on the basis of the following passage.

The most important unit of the mimeograph machine is a perforated metal drum over which is stretched a cloth ink pad. A reservoir inside the drum contains the ink which flows through the perforations and saturates the ink pad. To operate the machine, the operator first removes from the machine the protective sheet, which keeps the ink from drying while the machine is not in use. He then hooks the stencil face down on the drum, draws the stencil smoothly over the drum, and fastens the stencil at the bottom. The speed with which the drum turns determines the blackness of the copies printed. Slow turning gives heavy, black copies; fast turning gives light, clear-cut reproductions. If reproductions are run on other than porous paper, slip-sheeting is necessary to prevent smearing. Often, the printed copy fails to drop readily as it comes from the machine. This may be due to static electricity. To remedy this difficulty, the operator fastens a strip of tinsel from side to side near the impression roller so that the printed copy just touches the soft stems of the tinsel as it is ejected from the machine, thus grounding the static electricity to the frame of the machine.

6. According to the above passage,
   A. turning the drum fast produces light copies
   B. stencils should be placed face up on the drum
   C. ink pads should be changed daily
   D. slip-sheeting is necessary when porous paper is being used

7. According to the above passage, when a mimeograph machine is not in use, the
   A. ink should be drained from the drum
   B. ink pad should be removed
   C. machine should be covered with a protective sheet
   D. counter should be set at zero

8. According to the above passage, static electricity is grounded to the frame of the mimeograph machine by means of
   A. a slip-sheeting device
   B. a strip of tinsel
   C. an impression roller
   D. hooks located at the top of the drum

Questions 9-10.

DIRECTIONS: Questions 9 and 10 are to be answered SOLELY on the basis of the following passage.

The proofreading of material typed from copy is performed more accurately and more speedily when two persons perform this work as a team. The person who did not do the typing should read aloud the original copy while the person who did the typing should check the reading against the typed copy. The reader should speak very slowly and repeat the figures, using a different grouping of number when repeating the figures. For example, in reading 1967, the reader may say *one-nine-six-seven* on first reading the figure and *nineteen-sixty-seven* on repeating the figure. The reader should read all punctuation marks, taking nothing for granted. Since mistakes can occur anywhere, everything typed should be proofread. To avoid confusion, the proofreading team should use the standard proofreading marks, which are given in most dictionaries.

9. According to the above passage, the
   A. person who holds the typed copy is called the reader
   B. two members of a proofreading team should take turns in reading the typed copy aloud
   C. typed copy should be checked by the person who did the typing
   D. person who did not do the typing should read aloud from the typed copy

10. According to the above passage,
    A. it is unnecessary to read the period at the end of a sentence
    B. typographical errors should be noted on the original copy
    C. each person should develop his own set of proofreading marks
    D. figures should be read twice

Questions 11-16.

DIRECTIONS: Questions 11 through 16 are to be answered SOLELY on the basis of the following passage.

Basic to every office is the need for proper lighting. Inadequate lighting is a familiar cause of fatigue and serves to create a somewhat dismal atmosphere in the office. One requirement of proper lighting is that it be of an appropriate intensity. Intensity is measured in foot-candles. According to the Illuminating Engineering Society of New York, for casual seeing tasks such as in reception rooms, inactive file rooms, and other service areas, it is recommending that the amount of light be 30 foot-candle. For ordinary seeing tasks such as reading, work in active file rooms, and in mailrooms, the recommended lighting is 100 foot-candles. For very difficult seeing tasks such as accounting, transcribing, and business machine use, the recommended lighting is 150 foot-candles.

Lighting intensity is only one requirement. Shadows and glare are to be avoided. For example, the larger the proportion of a ceiling filled with lighting units, the more glare-free and comfortable the lighting will be. Natural lighting from window is not too dependable because on dark wintry days, windows yield little usable light, and on sunny afternoons, the glare from windows may be very distracting. Desks should not face the windows. Finally, the main lighting source ought to be overhead and to the left of the user.

11. According to the above passage, insufficient light in the office may cause 11.____
    A. glare   B. tiredness   C. shadows   D. distraction

12. Based on the above passage, which of the following must be considered when planning lighting arrangements? The 12.____
    A. amount of natural light present
    B. amount of work to be done
    C. level of difficulty of work to be done
    D. type of activity to be carried out

13. It can be inferred from the above passage that a well-coordinated lighting scheme is LIKELY to result in 13.____
    A. greater employee productivity   B. elimination of light reflection
    C. lower lighting cost   D. more use of natural light

14. Of the following, the BEST title for the above passage is 14.____
    A. Characteristics of Light
    B. Light Measurement Devices
    C. Factors to Consider When Planning Lighting Systems
    D. comfort vs. Cost When Devising Lighting Arrangements

15. According to the above passage, a foot-candle is a measurement of the 15.____
    A. number of bulbs used
    B. strength of the light
    C. contrast between glare and shadow
    D. proportion of the ceiling filled with lighting units

16. According to the above passage, the number of foot-candles of light that would be needed to copy figures onto a payroll is _____ foot-candles. 16.____
    A. less than 30   B. 100   C. 30   D. 140

Questions 17-23.

DIRECTIONS: Questions 17 through 23 are to be answered SOLELY on the basis of the following passage.

FEE SCHEDULE

1. A candidate for any baccalaureate degree is not required to pay tuition fees for undergraduate courses until he exceeds 128 credits. Candidates exceeding 128 credits in undergraduate courses are charged at the rate of $100 a credit for each credit of undergraduate course work in excess of 128. Candidates for a baccalaureate degree who are taking graduate courses must pay the same fee as any other student taking graduate courses.

B. Non-degree students and college graduates are charged tuition fees for courses, whether undergraduate or graduate, at the rate of $180 a credit. For such students, there is an additional charge of $150 for each class hour per week in excess of the number of course credits. For example, if a three-credit course meets five hours a week, there is an additional charge for the extra two hours. Graduate courses are shown with a (G) before the course number.

C. All students are required to pay the laboratory fees indicated after the number of credits given for that course.

D. All students must pay a $250 general fee each semester.

E. Candidates for a baccalaureate degree are charged a $150 medical insurance fee for each semester. All other students are charged a $100 medical insurance fee each semester.

17. Miss Burton is not a candidate for a degree. She registers for the following courses in the spring semester: Economics 12, 4 hours a week, 3 credits; History (G 23, 4 hours a week, 3 credits; English 1, 2 hours a week, 2 credits. The TOTAL amount in fees that Miss Burton must pay is
   A. less than $2,000
   B. at least $2,000 but less than $2,100
   C. at least $2,100 but less than $2,200
   D. $2,200 or over

17._____

18. Miss Gray is not a candidate for a degree. She registers for the following courses in the fall semester: History 3, 3 hours a week, 3 credits; English 5, 3 hours a week, 2 credits; Physics 5, 6 hours a week, 3 credits, laboratory fee $60; Mathematics 7, 4 hours a week, 3 credits. The TOTAL amount in fees that Miss Gray must pay is
   A. less than $3,150
   B. at least $3,150 but less than $3,250
   C. at least $3,250 but less than $3,350
   D. $3,350 or over

18._____

19. Mr. Wall is a candidate for the Bachelor of Arts degree and has completed 126 credits. He registers for the following courses in the spring semester, his final semester at college; French 4, 3 hours a week, 3 credits; Physics (G) 15, 6 hours a week, 3 credits, laboratory fee $80; History (G) 33, 4 hours a week, 3 credits. The TOTAL amount in fees that this candidate must pay is
   A. less than $2,100
   B. at least $2,100 but less than $2,300
   C. at least $2,300 but less than $2,500
   D. $2,500

19._____

6 (#3)

20. Mr. Tindall, a candidate for the B.A. degree, has completed 122 credits of undergraduate courses. He registers for the following courses in his final semester: English 31, 3 hours a week, 3 credits; Philosophy 12, 4 hours a week, 4 credits; Anthropology 15, 3 hours a week, 3 credits; Economics (G) 68, 3 hours a week, 3 credits.
The TOTAL amount in fees that Mr. Tindall must pay in his final semester is
   A. less than $1,200
   B. at least $1,200 but less than $1,400
   C. at least $1,400 but less than $1,600
   D. $1,600

20._____

21. Mr. Cantrell, who was graduated from the college a year ago, registers for graduate courses in the fall semester. Each course for which he register carries the same number of credits as the number of hours a week it meets. If he pays a total of $1,530, including a $100 laboratory fee, the number of credits for which he is registered is
   A. 4   B. 5   C. 6   D. 7

21._____

22. Miss Jayson, who is not a candidate for a degree, has registered for several courses including a lecture course in History. She withdraws from the course in History for which she had paid the required course fee of $690.
The number of hours that this course is scheduled to meet is
   A. 4   B. 5   C. 2   D. 3

22._____

23. Mr. Van Arsdale, a graduate of a college in Iowa, registers for the following courses in one semester: Chemistry 35, 5 hours a week, 3 credits; Biology 14, 4 hours a week, 3 credits, laboratory fee $150; Mathematics (G) 179, 3 hours a week, 3 credits.
The TOTAL amount in fees that Mr. Van Arsdale must pay is
   A. less than $2,400
   B. at least $2,400 but less than $2,500
   C. at least $2,500 but less than $2,600
   D. at least $2,600 or over

23._____

Questions 24-25.

DIRECTIONS: Questions 24 and 25 are to be answered SOLELY on the basis of the following passage.

A duplex envelope is an envelope composed of two sections securely fastened together so that they become one mailing piece. This type of envelope makes it possible for a first class letter to be delivered simultaneously with third or fourth class matter and yet not require payment of the much higher first class postage rate on the entire mailing. First class postage is paid only on the letter which goes in the small compartment, third or fourth class postage being paid on the contents of the larger compartment. The larger compartment generally has an ungummed flap or clasp for sealing. The first class or smaller compartment has a gummed flap for sealing. Postal regulations require that the exact amount of postage applicable to each compartment be separately attached to it.

24. On the basis of the above passage, it is MOST accurate to state that
    A. the smaller compartment is placed inside the larger compartment before mailing
    B. the two compartments may be detached and mailed separately
    C. two classes of mailing matter may be mailed as a unit at two different postage rates
    D. the more expensive postage rate is paid on the matter in the larger compartment

25. When a duplex envelope is used, the
    A. first class compartment may be sealed with a clasp
    B. correct amount of postage must be placed on each compartment
    C. compartment containing third or fourth class mail requires a gummed flap for sealing
    D. full amount of postage for both compartments may be placed on the larger compartment

KEY (CORRECT ANSWERS)

1.	A	11.	C
2.	D	12.	D
3.	B	13.	A
4.	B	14.	C
5.	C	15.	B
6.	A	16.	D
7.	C	17.	B
8.	B	18.	A
9.	C	19.	B
10.	D	20.	B

21.	C
22.	A
23.	C
24.	C
25.	B

SPELLING

EXAMINATION SECTION

TEST 1

DIRECTIONS: In each of the following tests in this part, select the letter of the one MISSPELLED word in each of the following groups of words. *PRINT THE LETTER OF THE CORRECT ANSWER IN THE SPACE AT THE RIGHT.*

1. A. grateful   B. fundimental   C. census   D. analysis   1._____
2. A. installment   B. retrieve   C. concede   D. dissapear   2._____
3. A. accidentaly   B. dismissal   C. conscientious D. indelible   3._____
4. A. perceive   B. carreer   C. anticipate   D. acquire   4._____
5. A. facillity   B. reimburse   C. assortment   D. guidance   5._____
6. A. plentiful   B. across   C. advantagous   D. similar   6._____
7. A. omission   B. pamphlet   C. guarrantee   D. repel   7._____
8. A. maintenance   B. always   C. liable   D. anouncement   8._____
9. A. exaggerate   B. sieze   C. condemn   D. commit   9._____
10. A. pospone   B. altogether   C. grievance   D. excessive   10._____
11. A. banana   B. trafic   C. spectacle   D. boundary   11._____
12. A. commentator B. abbreviation   C. battaries   D. monastery   12._____
13. A. practically B. advise   C. pursuade   D. laboratory   13._____
14. A. fatigueing   B. invincible   C. strenuous   D. ceiling   14._____
15. A. propeller   B. reverence   C. piecemeal   D. underneth   15._____
16. A. annonymous   B. envelope   C. transit   D. variable   16._____
17. A. petroleum   B. bigoted   C. meager   D. resistence   17._____

2 (#1)

18. A. permissible   B. indictment   C. fundemental   D. nowadays   18.____

19. A. thief   B. bargin   C. nuisance   D. vacant   19.____

20. A. technique   B. vengeance   C. aquatic   D. heighth   20.____

KEY (CORRECT ANSWERS)

1. B. fundamental
2. D. disappear
3. A. accidentally
4. B. career
5. A. facility

6. C. advantageous
7. C. guarantee
8. D. announcement
9. B. seize
10. A. postpone

11. B. traffic
12. C. batteries
13. C. persuade
14. A. fatiguing
15. D. underneath

16. A. anonymous
17. D. resistance
18. C. fundamental
19. B. bargain
20. D. height

TEST 2

DIRECTIONS: In each of the following tests in this part, select the letter of the one MISSPELLED word in each of the following groups of words. *PRINT THE LETTER OF THE CORRECT ANSWER IN THE SPACE AT THE RIGHT.*

1. A. apparent   B. superintendent   C. relieve   D. calendar   1.____
2. A. foreign   B. negotiate   C. typical   D. disipline   2.____
3. A. posponed   B. argument   C. susceptible   D. deficit   3.____
4. A. preferred   B. column   C. peculiar   D. equiped   4.____
5. A. exaggerate   B. disatisfied   C. repetition   D. already   5.____
6. A. livelihood   B. physician   C. obsticle   D. strategy   6.____
7. A. courageous   B. ommission   C. ridiculous   D. awkward   7.____
8. A. sincerely   B. abundance   C. negligable   D. elementary   8.____
9. A. obsolete   B. mischievous   C. enumerate   D. atheletic   9.____
10. A. fiscel   B. beneficiary   C. concede   D. translate   10.____
11. A. segregate   B. excessivly   C. territory   D. obstacle   11.____
12. A. unnecessary   B. monopolys   C. harmonious   D. privilege   12.____
13. A. sinthetic   B. intellectual   C. gracious   D. archaic   13.____
14. A. beneficial   B. fulfill   C. sarcastic   D. disolve   14.____
15. A. umbrella   B. sentimental   C. inefficent   D. psychiatrist   15.____
16. A. noticable   B. knapsack   C. librarian   D. meant   16.____
17. A. conference   B. upheaval   C. vulger   D. odor   17.____
18. A. surmount   B. pentagon   C. calorie   D. inumerable   18.____
19. A. classifiable B. moisturize   C. monitor   D. assesment   19.____
20. A. thermastat   B. corrupting   C. approach   D. thinness   20.____

KEY (CORRECT ANSWERS)

1. C. relieve
2. D. discipline
3. A. postponed
4. D. equipped
5. B. dissatisfied

6. C. obstacle
7. B. omission
8. C. negligible
9. D. athletic
10. A. fiscal

11. B. excessively
12. B. monopolies
13. A. synthetic
14. D. dissolve
15. C. inefficient

16. A. noticeable
17. C. vulgar
18. D. innumerable
19. D. assessment
20. A. thermostat

TEST 3

DIRECTIONS: In each of the following tests in this part, select the letter of the one MISSPELLED word in each of the following groups of words. *PRINT THE LETTER OF THE CORRECT ANSWER IN THE SPACE AT THE RIGHT.*

1. A. typical B. descend C. summarize D. continuel 1._____
2. A. courageous B. recomend C. omission D. eliminate 2._____
3. A. compliment B. illuminate C. auxilary D. installation 3._____
4. A. preliminary B. aquainted C. syllable D. analysis 4._____
5. A. accustomed B. negligible C. interupted D. bulletin 5._____
6. A. summoned B. managment C. mechanism D. sequence 6._____
7. A. commitee B. surprise C. noticeable D. emphasize 7._____
8. A. occurrance B. likely C. accumulate D. grievance 8._____
9. A. obstacle B. particuliar C. baggage D. fascinating 9._____
10. A. innumerable B. seize C. applicant D. dictionery 10._____
11. A. monkeys B. rigid C. unnatural D. roomate 11._____
12. A. surveying B. figurative C. famous D. curiosety 12._____
13. A. rodeo B. inconcievable C. calendar D. magnificence 13._____
14. A. handicaped B. glacier C. defiance D. emperor 14._____
15. A. schedule B. scrawl C. seclusion D. sissors 15._____
16. A. tissues B. tomatos C. tyrants D. tragedies 16._____
17. A. casette B. graceful C. penicillin D. probably 17._____
18. A. gnawed B. microphone C. clinicle D. batch 18._____
19. A. amateur B. altitude C. laborer D. expence 19._____
20. A. mandate B. flexable C. despise D. verify 20._____

KEY (CORRECT ANSWERS)

1. D. continual
2. B. recommend
3. C. auxiliary
4. B. acquainted
5. C. interrupted

6. B. management
7. A. committee
8. A. occurrence
9. B. particular
10. D. dictionary

11. D. roommate
12. D. curiosity
13. B. inconceivable
14. A. handicapped
15. D. scissors

16. B. tomatoes
17. A. cassette
18. C. clinical
19. D. expense
20. B. flexible

TEST 4

DIRECTIONS: In each of the following tests in this part, select the letter of the one MISSPELLED word in each of the following groups of words. *PRINT THE LETTER OF THE CORRECT ANSWER IN THE SPACE AT THE RIGHT.*

1. A. primery   B. mechanic   C. referred   D. admissible   1.____
2. A. cessation   B. beleif   C. aggressive   D. allowance   2.____
3. A. leisure   B. authentic   C. familiar   D. contemtable   3.____
4. A. volume   B. forty   C. dilemma   D. seldum   4.____
5. A. discrepancy   B. aquisition   C. exorbitant   D. lenient   5.____
6. A. simultanous   B. penetrate   C. revision   D. conspicuous   6.____
7. A. ilegible   B. gracious   C. profitable   D. obedience   7.____
8. A. manufacturer   B. authorize   C. compelling   D. pecular   8.____
9. A. anxious   B. rehearsal   C. handicaped   D. tendency   9.____
10. A. meticulous   B. accompaning   C. initiative   D. shelves   10.____
11. A. hammaring   B. insecticide   C. capacity   D. illogical   11.____
12. A. budget   B. luminous   C. aviation   D. lunchon   12.____
13. A. moniter   B. bachelor   C. pleasurable   D. omitted   13.____
14. A. monstrous   B. transistor   C. narrative   D. anziety   14.____
15. A. engagement   B. judical   C. pasteurize   D. tried   15.____
16. A. fundimental   B. innovation   C. perpendicular D. extravagant   16.____
17. A. bookkeeper   B. brutality   C. gymnaseum   D. cemetery   17.____
18. A. sturdily   B. pretentious   C. gourmet   D. enterance   18.____
19. A. resturant   B. tyranny   C. kindergarten   D. ancestry   19.____
20. A. benefit   B. possess   C. speciman   D. noticing   20.____

KEY (CORRECT ANSWERS)

1.	A. primary		11.	A. hammering
2.	B. belief		12.	D. luncheon
3.	D. contemptible		13.	A. monitor
4.	D. seldom		14.	D. anxiety
5.	B. acquisition		15.	B. judicial
6.	A. simultaneous		16.	A. fundamental
7.	A. illegible		17.	C. gymnasium
8.	D. peculiar		18.	D. entrance
9.	C. handicapped		19.	A. restaurant
10.	B. accompanying		20.	C. specimen

TEST 5

DIRECTIONS: In each of the following tests in this part, select the letter of the one MISSPELLED word in each of the following groups of words. *PRINT THE LETTER OF THE CORRECT ANSWER IN THE SPACE AT THE RIGHT.*

1. A. arguing   B. correspondance   1.____
    C. forfeit   D. dissension

2. A. occasion   B. description   C. prejudice   D. elegible   2.____

3. A. accomodate   B. initiative   C. changeable   D. enroll   3.____

4. A. temporary   B. insistent   C. benificial   D. separate   4.____

5. A. achieve   B. dissappoint   C. unanimous   D. judgment   5.____

6. A. procede   B. publicly   C. sincerity   D. successful   6.____

7. A. deceive   B. goverment   C. preferable   D. repetitive   7.____

8. A. emphasis   B. skillful   C. advisible   D. optimistic   8.____

9. A. tendency   B. rescind   C. crucial   D. noticable   9.____

10. A. privelege   B. abbreviate   C. simplify   D. divisible   10.____

11. A. irresistible B. varius   C. mutual   D. refrigerator   11.____

12. A. amateur   B. distinguish   C. rehearsal   D. poision   12.____

13. A. biased   B. ommission   C. precious   D. coordinate   13.____

14. A. calculated   B. enthusiasm   C. sincerely   D. parashute   14.____

15. A. sentry   B. materials   C. incredable   D. budget   15.____

16. A. chocolate   B. instrument   C. volcanoe   D. shoulder   16.____

17. A. ancestry   B. obscure   C. intention   D. ninty   17.____

18. A. artical   B. bracelet   C. beggar   D. hopeful   18.____

19. A. tournament   B. sponsor   C. perpendiclar D. dissolve   19.____

20. A. yeild   B. physician   C. greasiest   D. admitting   20.____

KEY (CORRECT ANSWERS)

1. B. correspondence
2. D. eligible
3. A. accommodate
4. C. beneficial
5. B. disappoint

6. A. proceed
7. B. government
8. C. advisable
9. D. noticeable
10. A. privilege

11. B. various
12. D. poison
13. B. omission
14. D. parachute
15. C. incredible

16. C. volcano
17. D. ninety
18. A. article
19. C. perpendicular
20. A. yield

TEST 6

DIRECTIONS: In each of the following tests in this part, select the letter of the one MISSPELLED word in each of the following groups of words. *PRINT THE LETTER OF THE CORRECT ANSWER IN THE SPACE AT THE RIGHT.*

1. A. achievment B. maintenance C. questionnaire D. all are correct 1._____
2. A. prevelant B. pronunciation C. separate D. all are correct 2._____
3. A. permissible B. relevant C. seize D. all are correct 3._____
4. A. corroborate B. desparate C. eighth D. all are correct 4._____
5. A. exceed B. feasibility C. psycological D. all are correct 5._____
6. A. parallel B. aluminum C. calendar D. eigty 6._____
7. A. microbe B. ancient C. autograph D. existance 7._____
8. A. plentiful B. skillful C. amoung D. capsule 8._____
9. A. erupt B. quanity C. opinion D. competent 9._____
10. A. excitement B. discipline C. luncheon D. regreting 10._____
11. A. magazine B. expository C. imitation D. permenent 11._____
12. A. ferosious B. machinery C. precise D. magnificent 12._____
13. A. conceive B. narritive C. separation D. management 13._____
14. A. muscular B. witholding C. pickle D. glacier 14._____
15. A. vehicel B. mismanage C. correspondence D. dissatisfy 15._____
16. A. sentince B. bulletin C. notice D. definition 16._____
17. A. appointment B. exactly C. typest D. light 17._____
18. A. penalty B. suparvise C. consider D. division 18._____
19. A. schedule B. accurate C. corect D. simple 19._____
20. A. suggestion B. installed C. proper D. agincy 20._____

KEY (CORRECT ANSWERS)

1.	A. achievement		11.	D. permanent
2.	B. prevalent		12.	A. ferocious
3.	D. all are correct		13.	B. narrative
4.	B. desperate		14.	B. withholding
5.	C. psychological		15.	A. vehicle
6.	D. eighty		16.	A. sentence
7.	D. existence		17.	C. typist
8.	C. among		18.	B. supervise
9.	B. quantity		19.	C. correct
10.	D. regretting		20.	D. agency

TEST 7

DIRECTIONS: In each of the following tests in this part, select the letter of the one MISSPELLED word in each of the following groups of words. *PRINT THE LETTER OF THE CORRECT ANSWER IN THE SPACE AT THE RIGHT.*

1. A. symtom   B. serum   B. antiseptic   D. aromatic   1.____
2. A. register   B. registrar   C. purser   D. burser   2.____
3. A. athletic   B. tragedy   C. batallion   D. sophomore   3.____
4. A. latent   B. godess   C. aisle   D. whose   4.____
5. A. rhyme   B. rhythm   C. thime   D. thine   5.____
6. A. eighth   B. exaggerate   C. electoral   D. villain   6.____
7. A. statute   B. superintendent   7.____
    C. iresistible   D. colleague
8. A. sieze   B. therefor   C. auxiliary   D. changeable   8.____
9. A. siege   B. knowledge   C. lieutenent   D. weird   9.____
10. A. acquitted   B. polititian   C. professor   D. conqueror   10.____
11. A. changeable   B. chargeable   C. salable   D. useable   11.____
12. A. promissory   B. prisoner   C. excellent   D. tyrrany   12.____
13. A. conspicuous   B. essance   C. comparative   D. brilliant   13.____
14. A. notefying   B. accentuate   C. adhesive   D. primarily   14.____
15. A. exercise   B. sublime   C. stuborn   D. shameful   15.____
16. A. presume   B. transcript   C. strech   D. wizard   16.____
17. A. specify   B. regional   C. arbitrary   D. segragation   17.____
18. A. requirement   B. happiness   C. achievement   D. gently   18.____
19. A. endurance   B. fusion   C. balloon   D. enormus   19.____
20. A. luckily   B. schedule   C. simplicity   D. sanwich   20.____

KEY (CORRECT ANSWERS)

1. A. symptom
2. D. bursar
3. C. battalion
4. B. goddess
5. C. thyme

6. C. electoral
7. C. irresistible
8. A. seize
9. C. lieutenant
10. B. politician

11. D. usable
12. D. tyranny
13. B. essence
14. A. notifying
15. C. stubborn

16. C. stretch
17. D. segregation
18. D. gently
19. D. enormous
20. D. sandwich

TEST 8

DIRECTIONS: In each of the following tests in this part, select the letter of the one MISSPELLED word in each of the following groups of words. *PRINT THE LETTER OF THE CORRECT ANSWER IN THE SPACE AT THE RIGHT.*

1. A. maintain   B. maintainance   1.____
   C. sustain   D. sustenance

2. A. portend   B. portentious   C. pretend   D. pretentious   2.____

3. A. prophesize   B. prophesies   C. farinaceous   D. spaceous   3.____

4. A. choose   B. chose   C. choosen   D. chasten   4.____

5. A. censure   B. censorious   C. pleasure   D. pleasurable   5.____

6. A. cover   B. coverage   C. adder   D. adage   6.____

7. A. balloon   B. diregible   C. direct   D. descent   7.____

8. A. whemsy   B. crazy   C. flimsy   D. lazy   8.____

9. A. derision   B. pretention   C. sustention   D. contention   9.____

10. A. question   B. questionaire   C. legion   D. legionary   10.____

11. A. chattle   B. cattle   C. dismantle   D. kindle   11.____

12. A. canal   B. cannel   C. chanel   D. colonel   12.____

13. A. hemorrage   B. storage   C. manage   D. foliage   13.____

14. A. surgeon   B. sturgeon   C. luncheon   D. stancheon   14.____

15. A. diploma   B. commission   C. dependent   D. luminious   15.____

16. A. likelihood   B. blizzard   C. machanical   D. suppress   16.____

17. A. commercial   B. releif   C. disposal   D. endeavor   17.____

18. A. operate   B. bronco   C. excaping   D. grammar   18.____

19. A. orchard   B. collar   C. embarass   D. distant   19.____

20. A. sincerly   B. possessive   C. weighed   D. waist   20.____

KEY (CORRECT ANSWERS)

1. B. maintenance
2. B. portentous
3. D. spacious
4. C. chosen
5. D. pleasurable

6. D. adage
7. B. dirigible
8. A. whimsy
9. B. pretension
10. B. questionnaire

11. A. chattel
12. C. channel
13. A. hemorrhage
14. D. stanchion
15. D. luminous

16. C. mechanical
17. B. relief
18. C. escaping
19. C. embarrass
20. A. sincerely

TEST 9

DIRECTIONS: In each of the following tests in this part, select the letter of the one MISSPELLED word in each of the following groups of words. *PRINT THE LETTER OF THE CORRECT ANSWER IN THE SPACE AT THE RIGHT.*

1. A. statute B. stationary C. staturesque D. stature 1.____
2. A. practicible B. practical C. particle D. reticule 2.____
3. A. plague B. plaque C. ague D. aigrete 3.____
4. A. theology B. idealogy C. psychology D. philology 4.____
5. A. dilema B. stamina C. feminine D. strychnine 5.____
6. A. deceit B. benefit C. grieve D. hienous 6.____
7. A. commensurable B. measurable C. duteable D. salable 7.____
8. A. homogeneous B. heterogeneous C. advantageous D. religeous 8.____
9. A. criticize B. dramatise C. exorcise D. exercise 9.____
10. A. ridiculous B. comparable C. merciful D. cotten 10.____
11. A. antebiotic B. stitches C. pitiful D. sneaky 11.____
12. A. amendment B. candadate C. accountable D. recommendation 12.____
13. A. avocado B. recruit C. tripping D. probally 13.____
14. A. calendar B. desirable C. familar D. vacuum 14.____
15. A. deteriorate B. elligible C. liable D. missile 15.____
16. A. amateur B. competent C. mischeivous D. occasion 16.____
17. A. friendliness B. saleries C. cruelty D. ammunition 17.____
18. A. wholesome B. cieling C. stupidity D. eligible 18.____
19. A. comptroller B. traveled C. accede D. procede 19.____
20. A. Britain B. Brittainica C. conductor D. vendor 20.____

KEY (CORRECT ANSWERS)

1. C. statuesque
2. A. practicable
3. D. aigrette
4. B. ideology
5. A. dilemma

6. D. heinous
7. C. dutiable
8. D. religious
9. B. dramatize
10. D. cotton

11. A. antibiotic
12. B. candidate
13. D. probably
14. C. familiar
15. B. eligible

16. C. mischievous
17. B. salaries
18. B. ceiling
19. D. proceed
20. B. Brittanica

TEST 10

DIRECTIONS: In each of the following tests in this part, select the letter of the one MISSPELLED word in each of the following groups of words. *PRINT THE LETTER OF THE CORRECT ANSWER IN THE SPACE AT THE RIGHT.*

1. A. lengthen   B. region   C. gases   D. inspecter   1.____
2. A. imediately   B. forbidden   2.____
    C. complimentary   D. aeronautics
3. A. continuous   B. paralel   C. opposite   D. definite   3.____
4. A. Antarctic   B. Wednesday   C. Febuary   D. Hungary   4.____
5. A. transmission   B. exposure   C. pistol   D. customery   5.____
6. A. juvinile   B. martyr   C. deceive   D. collaborate   6.____
7. A. unnecessary   B. repetitive   C. cancellation   D. airey   7.____
8. A. transit   B. availible   C. objection   D. galaxy   8.____
9. A. ineffective   B. believeable   C. arrangement   D. aggravate   9.____
10. A. possession   B. progress   C. reception   D. predjudice   10.____
11. A. congradulate   B. percolate   C. major   D. leisure   11.____
12. A. convenience   B. privilige   C. emerge   D. immerse   12.____
13. A. erasable   B. inflammable   C. audable   D. laudable   13.____
14. A. final   B. fines   C. finis   D. Finish   14.____
15. A. emitted   B. representative   15.____
    C. discipline   D. insistance
16. A. diphthong   B. rarified   C. library   D. recommend   16.____
17. A. compel   B. belligerent   C. successful   D. sergeant   17.____
18. A. dispatch   B. dispise   C. dispose   D. dispute   18.____
19. A. administrator   B. adviser   C. diner   D celluler   19.____
20. A. ignite   B. ignision   C. igneous   D. ignited   20.____

101

KEY (CORRECT ANSWERS)

1. D. inspector
2. A. immediately
3. B. parallel
4. C. February
5. D. customary

6. A. juvenile
7. D. airy
8. B. available
9. B. believable
10. D. prejudice

11. A. congratulate
12. B. privilege
13. C. audible
14. D. Finnish
15. D. insistence

16. B. rarefied
17. D. sergeant
18. B. despise
19. D. cellular
20. B. ignition

TEST 11

DIRECTIONS: In each of the following tests in this part, select the letter of the one MISSPELLED word in each of the following groups of words. *PRINT THE LETTER OF THE CORRECT ANSWER IN THE SPACE AT THE RIGHT.*

1. A. repellent   B. secession   C. sebaceous   D. saxaphone   1.____
2. A. navel   B. counteresolution   2.____
    C. marginalia   D. perceptible
3. A. Hammerskjold B. Nehru   C. U Thamt   D. Krushchev   3.____
4. A. perculate   B. periwinkle   C. perigee   D. retrogression   4.____
5. A. buccaneer   B. tobacco   C. buffalo   D. oscilate   5.____
6. A. siege   B. wierd   C. seize   D. cemetery   6.____
7. A. equaled   B. bigoted   C. benefited   D. kaleideoscope   7.____
8. A. blamable   B. bullrush   C. questionnaire D. irascible   8.____
9. A. tobogganed   B. acquiline   C. capillary   D. cretonne   9.____
10. A. daguerrotype B. elegiacal   C. iridescent   D. inchoate   10.____
11. A. bayonet   B. braggadocio C. corollary   D. connoiseur   11.____
12. A. equinoctial B. fusillade   C. fricassee   D. potpouri   12.____
13. A. octameter   B. impressario C. hyetology   D. hieroglyphics   13.____
14. A. innanity   B. idyllic   C. fylfot   D. inimical   14.____
15. A. liquefy   B. rarefy   C. putrify   D. sapphire   15.____
16. A. canonical   B. stupified   C. millennium   D. memorabilia   16.____
17. A. paraphenalia   B. odyssey   17.____
    C. onomatopoeia   D. osseous
18. A. peregrinate B. pecadillo   C. reptilian   D. uxorious   18.____
19. A. pharisaical B. vicissitude C. puissance   D. wainright   19.____
20. A. holocaust   B. tesselate   C. scintilla   D. staccato   20.____

KEY (CORRECT ANSWERS)

1. D. saxophone
2. B. counterresolution
3. C. U Thant
4. A. percolate
5. D. oscillate

6. B. weird
7. D. kaleidoscope
8. B. bulrush
9. B. aquiline
10. A. daguerreotype

11. D. connoisseur
12. D. potpourri
13. B. impresario
14. A. inanity
15. C. putrefy

16. B. stupefied
17. A. paraphernalia
18. B. peccadillo
19. D. wainwright
20. B. tessellate

TEST 12

DIRECTIONS: In each of the following tests in this part, select the letter of the one MISSPELLED word in each of the following groups of words. *PRINT THE LETTER OF THE CORRECT ANSWER IN THE SPACE AT THE RIGHT.*

1. A. questionnaire B. gondoleer C. chandelier D. acquiescence 1.____
2. A. surveilance B. surfeit C. vaccinate D. belligerent 2.____
3. A. occassionally B. recurrence C. silhouette D. incessant 3.____
4. A. transferral B. benefical C. descendant D. dependent 4.____
5. A. separately B. flouresence C. deterrent D. parallel 5.____
6. A. acquittal B. enforceable C. counterfeit D. indispensible 6.____
7. A. susceptible B. accelarate C. exhilarate D. accommodation 7.____
8. A. impedimenta B. collateral C. liason D. epistolary 8.____
9. A. inveigle B. panegyric C. reservoir D. manuver 9.____
10. A. synopsis B. paraphernalia C. affidavit D. subpoena 10.____
11. A. grosgrain B. vermilion C. abbatoir D. connoiseur 11.____
12. A. gabardine B. camoflage C. hemorrhage D. contraband 12.____
13. A. opprobrious B. defalcate C. fiduciery D. recommendations 13.____
14. A. nebulous B. necessitate C. impricate D. discrepancy 14.____
15. A. discrete B. condescension C. condign D. condiment 15.____
16. A. cavalier B. effigy C. legitimatly D. misalliance 16.____
17. A. rheumatism B. vaporous C. cannister D. hallucinations 17.____
18. A. paleonthology B. octogenarian C. gradient D. impingement 18.____
19. A. fusilade B. fusilage C. ensilage D. desiccate 19.____
20. A. rationale B. raspberry C. reprobate D. varigated 20.____

KEY (CORRECT ANSWERS)

1. B. gondolier
2. A. surveillance
3. A. occasionally
4. B. beneficial
5. B. fluorescence

6. D. indispensable
7. B. accelerate
8. C. liaison
9. D. maneuver
10. B. paraphernalia

11. D. connoisseur
12. B. camouflage
13. C. fiduciary
14. C. imprecate
15. B. condescension

16. C. legitimately
17. C. canister
18. A. paleontology
19. A. fusillade
20. D. variegated

ENGLISH EXPRESSION
CHOICE OF EXPRESSION
COMMENTARY

One special form of the English Expression multiple-choice question in current use requires the candidate to select from among five (5) versions of a particular part of a sentence (or of an entire sentence), the one version that expresses the idea of the sentence most clearly, effectively, and accurately. Thus, the candidate is required not only to recognize errors, but also to choose the best way of phrasing a particular part of the sentence.

This is a test of choice of expression, which assays the candidate's ability to express himself correctly and effectively, including his sensitivity to the subtleties and nuances of the language.

SAMPLE QUESTIONS

DIRECTIONS: In each of the following sentences, some part of the sentence or the entire sentence is underlined. The underlined part presents a problem in the appropriate use of language. Beneath each sentence you will find five ways of writing the underlined part. The first of these indicates no change (that is, it repeats the original), but the other four are all different. If you think the original sentence is better than any of the suggested changes, you should choose answer A; otherwise you should mark one of the other choices. Select the BEST answer and print the letter in the space at the right.

This is a test of correctness and effectiveness of expression. In choosing answers, follow the requirements of standard written English; that is, pay attention to acceptable usage in grammar, diction (choice of words), sentence construction, and punctuation. Choose the answer that produces the most effective sentence—clear and exact, without awkwardness or ambiguity. Do not make a choice that changes the meaning of the original sentence.

SAMPLE QUESTION 1

Although these states now trade actively with the West, and although they are willing to exchange technological information, their arts and thoughts and social structure <u>remains substantially similar to what it has always been</u>.
- A. remains substantially similar to what it has always been
- B. remain substantially unchanged
- C. remains substantially unchanged
- D. remain substantially similar to what they have always been
- E. remain substantially without being changed

The purpose of questions of this type is to determine the candidate's ability to select the clearest and most effective means of expressing what the statement attempts to say. In this example, the phrasing in the statement, which is repeated in A, presents a problem of agreement between a subject and its verb (<u>their arts and thought and social structure</u> and <u>remains</u>), a problem of agreement between a pronoun and its antecedent (<u>their arts and thought and social structure</u> and <u>it</u>), an a problem of precise and concise phrasing (<u>remains</u>

substantially similar to what it has always been for remains substantially unchanged). Each of the four remaining choices in some way corrects one or more of the faults in the sentence, but only one deals with all three problems satisfactorily. Although C presents a more careful and concise wording of the phrasing of the statement and, in the process, eliminates the problem of agreement between pronoun and antecedent, it fails to correct the problem of agreement between the subject and its verb. In D, the subject agrees with its verb and the pronoun agrees with its antecedent, but the phrasing is not so accurate as it should be. The same difficulty persists in E. Only in B are all the problems presented corrected satisfactory. The question is not difficult.

SAMPLE QUESTION 2

Her latest novel is the largest in scope, the most accomplished in technique, and <u>it is more significant in theme than anything</u> she has written.
- A. it is more significant in theme than anything
- B. It is most significant in theme of anything
- C. more significant in theme than anything
- D. the most significant in theme than anything
- E. the most significant in theme of anything

This question is of greater difficulty than the preceding one. The problem posed in the sentence and repeated in A is essentially one of parallelism; Does the underlined portion of the sentence follow the pattern established by the first two elements of the series (<u>the largest…the most accomplished</u>)? It does not, for it introduces a pronoun and verb (<u>it is</u>) that the second term of the series indicates should be omitted and a degree of comparison (<u>more significant</u>) that is not in keeping with the superlatives used earlier in the sentence. B uses the superlative degree of <u>significant</u> but retains the unnecessary <u>it is</u>; C removes the <u>it is</u>, but retains the faulty comparative form of the adjective. D corrects both errors in parallelism, but introduces an error in idiom (<u>the most</u>…<u>than</u>). Only E corrects all the problems without introducing another fault.

SAMPLE QUESTION 3

Desiring to insure the continuity of their knowledge, <u>magical lore is transmitted by the chiefs</u> to their descendants.
- A. magical lore is transmitted by the chiefs
- B. transmission of magical lore is made by the chiefs
- C. the chiefs' magical lore is transmitted
- D. the chiefs transmit magical lore
- E. the chiefs make transmission of magical lore

The CORRECT answer is D.

SAMPLE QUESTION 4

<u>As Malcolm walks quickly and confident</u> into the purser's office, the rest of the crew wondered whether he would be charged with the theft.
- A. As Malcolm walks quickly and confident
- B. As Malcolm was walking quick and confident
- C. As Malcom walked quickly and confident

D. As Malcolm walked quickly and confidently
E. As Malcolm walks quickly and confidently
The CORRECT answer is D.

SAMPLE QUESTION 5

The chairman, <u>granted the power to assign any duties to whoever he</u> wished, was still unable to prevent bickering.
A. granted the power to assign any duties to whoever he wished
B. granting the power to assign any duties to whoever he wished
C. being granted the power to assign any duties to whoever he wished
D. having been granted the power to assign any duties to whosoever he wished
E. granted the power to assign any duties to whomever he wished
The CORRECT answer is E.

SAMPLE QUESTION 6

Certainly, well-seasoned products are more expensive, <u>but those kinds prove chaper</u> in the end.
A. but those kinds prove cheaper
B. but these kinds prove cheaper
C. but that kind proves cheaper
D. but those kind prove cheaper
E. but this kind proves cheaper
The CORRECT answer is A.

SAMPLE QUESTION 7

"We shall not," he shouted, "whatever the <u>difficulties." "lose faith in the success of our plan!!"</u>
A. difficulties," "lose faith in the success of our plan!"
B. difficulties, "lose faith in the success of our plan"!
C. "difficulties, lose faith in the success of our plan!"
D. difficulties, lose faith in the success of our plan"!
E. difficulties, lose faith in the success of our plan!"

SAMPLE QUESTION 8

<u>Climb up the tree</u>, the lush foliage obscured the chattering monkeys.
A. Climbing up the tree
B. Having climbed up the tree
C. Clambering up the tree
D. After we had climbed up the tree
E. As we climbed up the tree
The CORRECT answer is E.

EXAMINATION SECTION
TEST 1

DIRECTIONS: See DIRECTIONS for Sample Questions on Page 1. *PRINT THE LETTER OF THE CORRECT ANSWER IN THE SPACE AT THE RIGHT.*

1. At the opening of the story, Charles Gilbert has just come to make his home with his two unmarried aunts.
   A. No change
   B. hadn't hardly come
   C. has just came
   D. had just come
   E. has hardly came

   1.____

2. The sisters, who are no longer young, are use to living quiet lives.
   A. No change
   B. are used to live
   C. are use'd to living
   D. are used to living
   E. are use to live

   2.____

3. They willingly except the child.
   A. No change
   B. willingly eccepted
   C. willingly accepted
   D. willingly acepted
   E. willingly accept

   3.____

4. As the months pass, Charles' presence affects many changes in their household.
   A. No change
   B. affect many changes
   C. effects many changes
   D. effect many changes
   E. affected many changes

   4.____

5. These changes is not all together to their liking.
   A. No change
   B. is not altogether
   C. are not all together
   D. are not altogether
   E. is not alltogether

   5.____

6. In fact, they have some difficulty in adapting theirselves to these changes
   A. No change
   B. in adopting theirselves
   C. in adopting themselves
   D. in adapting theirselves
   E. in adapting themselves

   6.____

7. That is the man whom I believe was the driver of the car.
   A. No change
   B. who I believed
   C. whom I believed
   D. who to believe
   E. who I believe

   7.____

8. John's climb to fame was more rapid than his brother's.
   A. No change
   B. than his brother
   C. than that of his brother's
   D. than for his brother
   E. than the brother

   8.____

111

9. We knew that he had formerly swam on an Olympic team.
   - A. No change
   - B. has formerly swum
   - C. did formerly swum
   - D. had formerly swum
   - E. has formerly swam

10. Not one of us loyal supporters ever get a pass to a game.
    - A. No change
    - B. ever did got a pass
    - C. ever has get a pass
    - D. ever had get a pass
    - E. ever gets a pass

11. He was complemented on having done a fine job.
    - A. No change
    - B. was compliminted
    - C. was compleminted
    - D. was complimented
    - E. did get complimented

12. This play is different from the one we had seen last night.
    - A. No change
    - B. have seen
    - C. had saw
    - D. have saw
    - E. saw

13. A row of trees was planted in front of the house.
    - A. No change
    - B. was to be planted
    - C. were planted
    - D. were to be planted
    - E. are planted

14. The house looked its age in spite of our attempts to beautify it.
    - A. No change
    - B. looks its age
    - C. looked its' age
    - D. looked it's age
    - E. looked it age

15. I do not know what to council in this case.
    - A. No change
    - B. where to council
    - C. when to councel
    - D. what to counsel
    - E. what to counsil

16. She is more capable than any other girl in the office.
    - A. No change
    - B. than any girl
    - C. than any other girls
    - D. than other girl
    - E. than other girls

17. At the picnic the young children behaved very good.
    - A. No change
    - B. behave very good
    - C. behaved better
    - D. behave very well
    - E. behaved very well

18. I resolved to go irregardless of the consequences.
    - A. No change
    - B. to depart irregardless of
    - C. to go regarding of
    - D. to go regardingly of
    - E. to go regardless of

19. The new movie has a number of actors which have been famous on Broadway.
    A. No change
    B. which had been famous
    C. who had been famous
    D. that are famous
    E. who have been famous

20. I am certain that these books are not our's.
    A. No change
    B. have not been ours'
    C. have not been our's
    D. are not ours
    E. are not ours'

21. Each of your papers is filed for future reference.
    A. No change
    B. Each of your papers are filed
    C. Each of your papers have been filed
    D. Each of your papers are to be filed
    E. Each of your paper is filed

22. I wish that he would take his work more serious.
    A. No change
    B. he took his work more serious
    C. he will take his work more serious
    D. he shall take his work more seriously
    E. he would take his work more seriously

23. After the treasurer report had been read, the chairman called for the reports of the committees.
    A. No change
    B. After the treasure's report had been read
    C. After the treasurers' report had been read
    D. After the treasurerer's report had been read
    E. After the treasurer's report had been read

24. Last night the stranger lead us down the mountain.
    A. No change
    B. leaded us down the mountain
    C. let us down the mountain
    D. led us down the mountain
    E. had led us down the mountain

25. It would not be safe for either you or I to travel in Viet Nam.
    A. No change
    B. for either you or me
    C. for either I or you
    D. for either of you or I
    E. for either of I or you

KEY (CORRECT ANSWERS)

1.	A	11.	D
2.	D	12.	E
3.	E	13.	A
4.	C	14.	A
5.	D	15.	D
6.	E	16.	A
7.	E	17.	E
8.	A	18.	E
9.	D	19.	E
10.	E	20.	D

21. A
22. E
23. E
24. D
25. B

TEST 2

DIRECTIONS: See DIRECTIONS for Sample Questions on Page 1. *PRINT THE LETTER OF THE CORRECT ANSWER IN THE SPACE AT THE RIGHT.*

1. Both the body and the mind <u>needs exercise</u>. 1.____
   - A. No change
   - B. have needs of exercise
   - C. is needful of exercise
   - D. needed exercise
   - E. need exercise

2. <u>It's paw injured</u>, the animal limped down the road. 2.____
   - A. No change
   - B. It's paw injured
   - C. Its paw injured
   - D. Its' paw injured
   - E. Its paw injure

3. The butter <u>tastes rancidly</u>. 3.____
   - A. No change
   - B. tastes rancid
   - C. tasted rancidly
   - D. taste rancidly
   - E. taste rancid

4. <u>Who do you think</u> has sent me a letter? 4.____
   - A. No change
   - B. Whom do you think
   - C. Whome do you think
   - D. Who did you think
   - E. Whom can you think

5. If more nations <u>would have fought</u> against tyranny, the course of history would have been different. 5.____
   - A. No change
   - B. would fight
   - C. could have fought
   - D. fought
   - E. had fought

6. Radio and television programs, along with other media of communication, <u>helps us to appreciate the arts and to keep informed</u>. 6.____
   - A. No change
   - B. helps us to appreciate the arts and to be informed
   - C. helps us to be appreciative of the arts and to keep informed
   - D. helps us to be appreciative of the arts and to be informed
   - E. help us to appreciate the arts and to keep informed

7. Music, <u>for example most always</u> has listening and viewing audiences numbering in the hundreds of thousands. 7.____
   - A. No change
   - B. for example, most always
   - C. for example, almost always
   - D. for example nearly always
   - E. for example, near always

8. When operas are performed on radio or television, <u>they effect the listener</u>. 8.____
   - A. No change
   - B. they inflict the listener
   - C. these effect the listeners
   - D. they affects the listeners
   - E. they affect the listener

9. After hearing then the listener wants to buy recordings of the music.
   A. No change
   B. After hearing them, the listener wants
   C. After hearing them, the listener want
   D. By hearing them the listener wants
   E. By hearing them, the listener wants

10. To we Americans the daily news program has become important.
    A. No change
    B. To we the Americans
    C. To us Americans
    D. To us the Americans
    E. To we and us Americans

11. This has resulted from it's coverage of a days' events.
    A. No change
    B. from its coverage of a days' events
    C. from it's coverage of a day's events
    D. from its' coverage of a day's events
    E. from its coverage of a day's events

12. In schools, teachers advice their students to listen to or to view certain programs.
    A. No change
    B. teachers advise there students
    C. teachers advise their students
    D. the teacher advises their students
    E. teachers advise his students

13. In these ways we are preceding toward the goal of an educated and an informed public.
    A. No change
    B. we are preeceding toward the goal
    C. we are proceeding toward the goal
    D. we are preceding toward the goal
    E. we are proceeding toward the goal

14. The cost of living is raising again.
    A. No change
    B. are raising again
    C. is rising again
    D. are rising again
    E. is risen again

15. We did not realize that the boys' father had forbidden them to keep there puppy.
    A. No change
    B. had forbade them to keep there puppy
    C. had forbade them to keep their puppy
    D. has forbidden them to keep their puppy
    E. had forbidden them to keep their puppy

16. Her willingness to help others' was her outstanding characteristic. 16.____
    A. No change
    B. Her willingness to help other's,
    C. Her willingness to help others's
    D. Her willingness to help others
    E. Her willingness to help each other

17. Because he did not have an invitation, the girls objected to him going. 17.____
    A. No change
    B. the girls object to him going
    C. the girls objected to him's going
    D. the girls objected to his going
    E. the girls object to his going

18. Weekly dances have become a popular accepted feature of the summer schedule. 18.____
    A. No change
    B. have become a popular accepted feature
    C. have become a popular excepted feature
    D. have become a popularly excepted feature
    E. have become a popularly accepted feature

19. I couldn't hardly believe that he would desert our party. 19.____
    A. No change
    B. would hardly believe
    C. didn't hardly believe
    D. should hardly believe
    E. could hardly believe

20. I found the place in the book more readily than she. 20.____
    A. No change
    B. more readily than her
    C. more ready than she
    D. more quickly than her
    E. more ready than her

21. A good example of American outdoor activities are sports. 21.____
    A. No change
    B. is sports
    C. are sport
    D. are sports events
    E. are to be found in sports

22. My point of view is much different from your's. 22.____
    A. No change
    B. much different from your's
    C. much different than yours
    D. much different from yours
    E. much different than yours'

23. The cook was suppose to use two spoonfuls of dressing for each serving. 23.____
    A. No change
    B. was supposed to use two spoonsful
    C. was suppose to use two spoonsful
    D. was supposed to use two spoonsfuls
    E. was supposed to use two spoonfuls

24. If anyone has any doubt about the values of the tour, <u>refer him to me</u>.   24.____
    A. No change
    B. refer him to I
    C. refer me to he
    D. refer them to me
    E. refer he to I

25. We expect that the affects of <u>the trip will be neneficial</u>.   25.____
    A. No change
    B. the effects of the trip will be beneficial
    C. the effects of the trip should be beneficial
    D. the affects of the trip would be beneficial
    E. the effects of the trip will be benificial

KEY (CORRECT ANSWERS)

1.	E		11.	E
2.	C		12.	C
3.	B		13.	E
4.	A		14.	C
5.	E		15.	E
6.	E		16.	D
7.	C		17.	D
8.	E		18.	E
9.	B		19.	E
10.	C		20.	A

21. B
22. D
23. E
24. A
25. B

TEST 3

DIRECTIONS: See DIRECTIONS for Sample Questions on Page 1. *PRINT THE LETTER OF THE CORRECT ANSWER IN THE SPACE AT THE RIGHT.*

1. That, my friend is not the proper attitude.
    - A. No change
    - B. That my friend
    - C. That my fried,
    - D. That—my friend
    - E. That, my friend,

    1.____

2. The girl refused to admit that the note was her's.
    - A. No change
    - B. that the note were her's
    - C. that the note was hers'
    - D. that the note was hers
    - E. that the note might be hers

    2.____

3. There were fewer candidates that we had been lead to expect
    - A. No change
    - B. was fewer candidates than we had been lead
    - C. were fewer candidates than we had been lead
    - D. was fewer candidates than we had been led
    - E. were fewer candidates than we had been led

    3.____

4. When I first saw the car, its steering wheel was broke.
    - A. No change
    - B. its' steering wheel was broken
    - C. it's steering wheel had been broken
    - D. its steering wheel were broken
    - E. its steering wheel was broken

    4.____

5. I find that the essential spirit for we beginners is missing.
    - A. No change
    - B. we who begin are missing
    - C. us beginners are missing
    - D. us beginners is missing
    - E. we beginners are missing

    5.____

6. I believe that you had ought to study harder.
    - A. No change
    - B. you should have ought
    - C. you had better
    - D. you ought to have
    - E. you ought

    6.____

7. This is Tom, whom I am sure, will be glad to help you.
    - A. No change
    - B. Tom whom, I am sure,
    - C. Tom, whom I am sure
    - D. Tom who I am sure,
    - E. Tom, who, I am sure,

    7.____

8. His father or his mother has read to him every night since he was very small.
    - A. No change
    - B. did read to him
    - C. have been reading to him
    - D. had read to him
    - E. have read to him

    8.____

9. He become an authority
   A. No change
   B. becomed an authority
   C. become the authority
   D. became an authority
   E. becamed an authority

10. I know of no other reason in the club who is more kind-hearted than her.
    A. No change
    B. who are more kind-hearted than they
    C. who are more kind-hearted than them
    D. whom are more kind-hearted than she
    E. who is more kind-hearted than she

11. After Bill had ran the mile, he was breathless.
    A. No change
    B. had runned the mile
    C. has ran the mile
    D. had ranned the mile
    E. had run the mile

12. Wilson has scarcely no equal as a pitcher.
    A. No change
    B. has scarcely an equal
    C. has hardly no equal
    D. had scarcely no equal
    E. has scarcely any equals

13. It was the worse storm that the inhabitants of the island could remember.
    A. No change
    B. were the worse storm
    C. was the worst storm
    D. was the worsest storm
    E. was the most worse storm

14. If only we had began before it was too late.
    A. No change
    B. we had began
    C. we would have begun
    D. we had begun
    E. we had beginned

15. Lets evaluate our year's work.
    A. No change
    B. Let us' evaluate
    C. Lets' evaluate
    D. Lets' us evaluate
    E. Let's evaluate

16. This is an organization with which I wouldn't want to be associated with.
    A. No change
    B. with whom I wouldn't want to be associated with
    C. that I wouldn't want to be associated
    D. with which I would want not to be associated with
    E. with which I wouldn't want to be associated

17. The enemy fled in many directions, leaving there weapons on the field.
    A. No change
    B. leaving its weapons
    C. letting their weapons
    D. leaving alone there weapons
    E. leaving their weapons

18. I hoped that John could effect a compromise between the approved forces.   18.____
    A. No change
    B. could accept a compromise between
    C. could except a compromise between
    D. would have effected a compromise among
    E. could effect a compromise among

19. I was surprised to learn that he has not always spoke English fluently.   19.____
    A. No change
    B. that he had not always spoke English
    C. that he did not always speak English
    D. that he has not always spoken English
    E. that he could not always speak English

20. The lawyer promised to notify my father and I of his plans for a new trial.   20.____
    A. No change   B. to notify I and my father
    C. to notify me and our father   D. to notify my father and me
    E. to notify mine father and me

21. The most important feature of the series of tennis lessons were the large amount of strokes taught.   21.____
    A. No change   B. were the large number
    C. was the large amount   D. was the largeness of the amount
    E. was the large number

22. That the prize proved to be beyond her reach did not surprise him.   22.____
    A. No change
    B. has not surprised him
    C. had not ought to have surprised him
    D. should not surprise him
    E. would not have surprised him

23. I am not all together in agreement with the author's point of view.   23.____
    A. No change   B. all together of agreement
    C. all together for agreement   D. altogether with agreement
    E. altogether in agreement

24. Windstorms have recently established a record which meteorologists hope will not be equal for many years to come.   24.____
    A. No change   B. will be equal
    C. will not be equalized   D. will be equaled
    E. will not be equaled

25. A large number of Shakespeare's soliloquies must be considered <u>as representing thought</u>, not speech.
    A. No change
    B. as representative of speech, not thought
    C. as represented by thought, not speech
    D. as indicating thought, not speech
    E. as representative of thought, more than speech

25.____

KEY (CORRECT ANSWERS)

1. E
2. D
3. E
4. E
5. D

6. E
7. E
8. A
9. D
10. E

11. E
12. B
13. C
14. D
15. E

16. E
17. E
18. A
19. D
20. D

21. E
22. A
23. E
24. E
25. A

TEST 4

DIRECTIONS: See DIRECTIONS for Sample Questions on Page 1. *PRINT THE LETTER OF THE CORRECT ANSWER IN THE SPACE AT THE RIGHT.*

1. A sight to inspire fear <u>are wild animals on the lose</u>. 1.____
   A. No change
   B. are wild animals on the loose
   C. is wild animals on the loose
   D. is wild animals on the lose
   E. are wild animals loose

2. For many years, the settlers <u>had been seeking to workship as they please</u>. 2.____
   A. No change
   B. had seeked to workship as they pleased
   C. sought to workship as they please
   D. sought to have worshiped as they pleased
   E. had been seeking to worship as they pleased

3. The girls stated that the dresses were <u>their's</u>. 3.____
   A. No change   B. there's   C. theirs
   D. theirs'   E. there own

4. <u>Please fellows</u> don't drop the ball. 4.____
   A. No change   B. Please, fellows
   C. Please fellows;   D. Please, fellows,
   E. Please! fellows

5. Your sweater <u>has laid</u> on the floor for a week. 5.____
   A. No change   B. has been laying
   C. has been lying   D. laid
   E. has been lain

6. I wonder whether <u>you're sure that scheme of yours'</u> will work. 6.____
   A. No change
   B. your sure that scheme of your's
   C. you're sure that scheme of yours
   D. your sure that scheme of yours
   E. you're sure that your scheme's

7. Please let <u>her and me</u> do it. 7.____
   A. No change   B. she and I
   C. she and me   D. her and I
   E. her and him

8. I expected him to be angry <u>and to scold</u> her. 8.____
   A. No change   B. and that he would scold
   C. and that he might scold D. and that he should scold
   E. , scolding

9. Knowing little about algebra, <u>it was difficult to solve the equation</u>.   9.____
    A. No change
    B. the equation was difficult to solve
    C. the solution to the equation was difficult to find
    D. I found it difficult to solve the equation
    E. it being difficult to solve the equation

10. He <u>worked more diligent</u> now that he had become vice president of the company.   10.____
    A. No change
    B. works more diligent
    C. works more diligently
    D. began to work more diligent
    E. worked more diligently

11. <u>Flinging himself at the barricade he</u> pounded on it furiously.   11.____
    A. No change
    B. Flinging himself at the barricade: he
    C. Flinging himself at the barricade—he
    D. Flinging himself at the barricade; he
    E. Flinging himself at the barricade, he

12. When he <u>begun to give us advise</u>, we stopped listening.   12.____
    A. No change
    B. began to give us advise
    C. begun to give us advice
    D. began to give us advice
    E. begin to give us advice

13. John was only one of the boys <u>whom as you know was</u> not eligible.   13.____
    A. No change
    B. who as you know were
    C. whom as you know were
    D. who as you know was
    E. who as you know is

14. <u>Why was Jane and he</u> permitted to go?   14.____
    A. No change
    B. was Jane and him
    C. were Jane and he
    D. were Jane and him
    E. weren't Jane and he

15. <u>Take courage Tom: we</u> all make mistakes.   15.____
    A. No change
    B. Take courage Tom—we
    C. Take courage, Tom; we
    D. Take courage, Tom we
    E. Take courage! Tom: we

16. Henderson, the president of the class and <u>who is also captain of the team</u>, will lead the rally.   16.____
    A. No change
    B. since he is captain of the team
    C. captain of the team
    D. also being captain of the team
    E. who be also captain of the team

17. Our car has always <u>run good</u> on that kind of gasoline.   17.____
    A. No change
    B. run well
    C. ran good
    D. ran well
    E. done good

18. There was a serious difference of opinion among her and I.
    A. No change
    B. among she and I
    C. between her and I
    D. between her and me
    E. among her and me

19. "This is most unusual," said Helen, "the mailman has never been this late before."
    A. No change
    B. Helen, "The
    C. Helen—"The
    D. Helen; "The
    E. Helen." The

20. The three main characters in the story are Johnny Hobart a teenager, his mother a widow, and the local druggist.
    A. No change
    B. teenager; his mother, a widow; and
    C. teenager; his mother a widow; and
    D. teenager, his mother, a widow and
    E. teenager, his mother, a widow; and

21. How much has food costs raised during the past year?
    A. No change
    B. have food costs rose
    C. have food costs risen
    D. has food costs risen
    E. have food costs been raised

22. "Will you come too" she pleaded?
    A. No change
    B. too,?"she pleaded
    C. too?" she pleaded
    D. too," she pleaded?
    E. too, she pleaded?"

23. If he would have drank more milk, his health would have been better.
    A. No change
    B. would drink
    C. had drank
    D. had he drunk
    E. had drunk

24. Jack had no sooner laid down and fallen asleep when the alarm sounded.
    A. No change
    B. no sooner lain down and fallen asleep than
    C. no sooner lay down and fell asleep when
    D. no sooner laid down and fell asleep than
    E. no sooner lain down than he fell asleep when

25. Jackson is one of the few Sophomores, who has ever made the varsity team.
    A. No change
    B. one of the few Sophomores, who have
    C. one of the few sophomores, who has
    D. one of the few sophomores who have
    E. one of the few sophomores who has

KEY (CORRECT ANSWERS)

1. C
2. E
3. C
4. D
5. C

6. C
7. A
8. A
9. D
10. E

11. E
12. D
13. B
14. C
15. C

16. C
17. B
18. D
19. E
20. B

21. C
22. C
23. E
24. B
25. D

TEST 5

DIRECTIONS: See DIRECTIONS for Sample Questions on Page 1. *PRINT THE LETTER OF THE CORRECT ANSWER IN THE SPACE AT THE RIGHT.*

1. The lieutenant had ridden almost a kilometer when the scattering shells <u>begin landing</u> uncomfortably close.
   A. No change
   B. beginning to land
   C. began to land
   D. having begun to land
   E. begin to land

1.____

2. <u>Having studied eight weeks</u>, he now feels sufficiently prepared for the examination.
   A. No change
   B. For eight weeks he studies so
   C. Due to eight weeks of study
   D. After eight weeks of studying
   E. Since he's been spending the last eight weeks in study

2.____

3. <u>Coming from the Greek, and the word "democracy" means government by the people</u>.
   A. No change
   B. "Democracy," the word which comes from the Greek, means government by the people.
   C. Meaning government by the people, the word "democracy" comes from the Greek.
   D. Its meaning being government by the people in Greek, the word is "democracy."
   E. The word "democracy" comes from the Greek and means government by the people.

3.____

4. Moslem universities were one of the chief agencies <u>in the development</u> and spreading Arabic civilization.
   A. No change
   B. in the development of
   C. to develop
   D. in developing
   E. for the developing of

4.____

5. The water of Bering Strait <u>were closing</u> to navigation by ice early in the fall.
   A. No change
   B. has closed
   C. have closed
   D. had been closed
   E. closed

5.____

6. The man, <u>since he grew up</u> on the block, felt sentimental when returning to it.
   A. No change
   B. having grown up
   C. growing up
   D. since he had grown up
   E. whose growth had been

6.____

7. Jack and Jill watched the canoe to take their parents out of sight round the bend of the creek.
   A. No change
   B. The canoe, taking their parents out of sight, rounds the bend as Jack and Jill watch.
   C. Jack and Jill watched the canoe round the bend of the creek, taking their parents out of sight,
   D. The canoe rounded the bend of the creek as it took their parents out of sight, Jack and Jill watching.
   E. Jack and Jill watching, the canoe is rounding the bend of the creek to take their parents out of sight.

8. Chaucer's best-known work is THE CANTERBURY TALES, a collection of stories which he tells with a group of pilgrims as they travel to the town of Canterbury.
   A. No change
   B. which he tells through
   C. who tell
   D. told by
   E. told through

9. The Estates-General, the old feudal assembly of France, had not met for one hundred and seventy-five years when it convened in 1789.
   A. No change
   B. has not met
   C. has not been meeting
   D. had no meeting
   E. has no meeting

10. Just forty years ago, there had been fewer than one hundred symphony orchestras in the United States.
    A. No change
    B. there had
    C. there were
    D. there was
    E. there existed

11. Mrs. Smith complained that her son's temper tantrums aggravated her and caused her to have a headache.
    A. No change
    B. gave her aggravation
    C. were aggravating to her
    D. aggravated her condition
    E. instigated

12. A girl like I would never be seen in a place like that.
    A. No change   B. as I   C. as me
    D. like I am   E. like me

13. Between you and me, my opinion is that this room is certainly nicer than the first one we saw.
    A. No change
    B. between you and I
    C. among you and me
    D. betwixt you and I
    E. between we

14. It is important to know for <u>what kind of a person you are working</u>. 14.____
    A. No change
    B. what kind of a person for whom you are working
    C. what kind of person you are working
    D. what kind of person you are working for
    E. what kind of a person you are working for

15. I had <u>all ready</u> finished the book before you came in. 15.____
    A. No change   B. already   C. previously
    D. allready   E. all

16. <u>Ask not for who the bell tolls, it tolls for thee</u>. 16.____
    A. No change
    B. Ask not for whom the bell tolls, it tolls for thee.
    C. Ask not whom the bell tolls for; it tolls for thee.
    D. Ask not for whom the bell tolls; it tolls for thee.
    E. As not who the bell tolls for: It tolls for thee.

17. It is a far better thing I do, than <u>ever I did</u> before. 17.____
    A. No change   B. never I did
    C. I have ever did   D. I have ever been done
    E. ever have I done

18. <u>Ending a sentence with a preposition is something up with which I will not put</u>. 18.____
    A. No change
    B. Ending a sentence with a preposition is something with which I will not put up.
    C. To end a sentence with a preposition is that which I will not put up with.
    D. Ending a sentence with a preposition is something of which I will not put up.
    E. Something I will not put up with is ending a sentence with a preposition.

19. Everyone <u>took off their hats and stand up</u> to sing the national anthem. 19.____
    A. No change
    B. took off their hats and stood up
    C. take off their hats and stand up
    D. took off his hat and stood up
    E. have taken off their hats and standing up

20. <u>She promised me that if she had the opportunity she would have came irregardless of the weather</u>. 20.____
    A. No change
    B. She promised me that if she had the opportunity she would have come regardless of the weather.
    C. She assured me that had she had the opportunity he would have come regardless of the weather.
    D. She assured me that if she would have had the opportunity she would have come regardless of the weather.

E. She promised me that if she had had the opportunity she would have came irregardless of the weather.

21. The man decided it would be advisable to marry a girl <u>somewhat younger than him</u>.
    A. No change
    B. somehow younger than him
    C. some younger than him
    D. somewhat younger from him
    E. somewhat younger than he

21.____

22. Sitting near the campfire, the old man told <u>John and I about many exciting adventures he had had</u>.
    A. No change
    B. John and me about many exciting adventures he had,
    C. John and I about much exciting adventure which he'd had
    D. John and me about many exciting adventures he had had
    E. John and me about many exciting adventures he has had.

22.____

23. <u>If you had stood at home and done your homework</u>, you would not have failed the course.
    A. No change
    B. If you had stood at home and done you're homework,
    C. If you had staid at home and done your homework,
    D. Had you stayed at home and done your homework,
    E. Had you stood at home and done your homework,

23.____

24. The children didn't, as a rule, <u>do anything beyond</u> what they were told to do.
    A. No change
    B. do hardly anything beyond
    C. do anything except
    D. do hardly anything except for
    E. do nothing beyond

24.____

25. <u>Either the girls or him is</u> right.
    A. No change
    B. Either the girls or he is
    C. Either the girls or him are
    D. Either the girls or he are
    E. Either the girls nor he is

25.____

KEY (CORRECT ANSWERS)

1.	C	11.	D
2.	A	12.	E
3.	E	13.	A
4.	D	14.	C
5.	D	15.	B
6.	B	16.	D
7.	C	17.	E
8.	D	18.	E
9.	A	19.	D
10.	C	20.	C

21.	E
22.	D
23.	D
24.	A
25.	B

WRITTEN ENGLISH EXPRESSION
EXAMINATION SECTION
TEST 1

DIRECTIONS: In each of the sentences below, four portions are underlined and lettered. Read each sentence and decide whether any of the UNDERLINED parts contains an error in spelling, punctuation, or capitalization, or employs grammatical usage which would be inappropriate for carefully written English. If so, note the letter printed under the unacceptable form and indicate this choice in the space at the right. If all four of the underlined portions are acceptable as they stand, select the answer E. (No sentence contains more than ONE unacceptable form.)

1. The revised <u>procedure</u> was <u>quite</u> different <u>than</u> the one which <u>was</u> employed up
                  A   B   C   D
to that time. <u>No error</u>
              E

1._____

2. <u>Blinded</u> by the storm that <u>surrounded</u> him, his plane <u>kept going</u> in <u>circles</u>.
   A   B   C   D
<u>No error</u>
  E

2._____

3. They <u>should</u> give the book to <u>whoever</u> <u>they</u> think deserves <u>it</u>. <u>No error</u>
        A   B   C   D E

3._____

4. The <u>government</u> will not consent to your <u>firm</u> <u>sending</u> that package as
      A   B   C
<u>second class</u> matter. <u>No error</u>
   D   E

4._____

5. She <u>would have</u> avoided all the trouble <u>that</u> followed if she <u>would have</u> waited
       A   B   C
ten minutes <u>longer</u>. <u>No error</u>
           D   E

5._____

6. <u>His</u> poetry, <u>when</u> it was carefully examined, showed <u>characteristics</u> not unlike
   A   B   C
<u>Wordsworth</u>. <u>No error</u>
    D   E

6._____

7. <u>In my opinion</u>, based upon long years of research, <u>I think</u> the plan offered by
       A   B
my opponent is <u>unsound</u>, because it is not <u>founded</u> on true facts. <u>No error</u>
                C   D   E

7._____

8. The soldiers of <u>Washington's</u> army at Valley Forge <u>were</u> men ragged in
                       A   B
   <u>appearance</u> but <u>who were</u> noble in character. <u>No error</u>
      C   D   E

9. Rabbits <u>have a distrust</u> of man <u>due to</u> the fact <u>that</u> they are <u>so often</u> shot.
                 A   B   C   D
   <u>No error</u>
     E

10. <u>This</u> is the man <u>who</u> I believe <u>is</u> best <u>qualified</u> for the position. <u>No error</u>
      A   B   C   D   E

11. Her voice was <u>not only</u> <u>good</u>, but <u>she</u> also very clearly <u>enunciated</u>.
                      A   B   C   D
    <u>No error</u>
      E

12. <u>Today he</u> is wearing a <u>different</u> suit <u>than</u> the <u>one</u> he wore yesterday. <u>No error</u>
        A   B   C   D   E

13. Our work <u>is</u> to improve the club; if anybody <u>must</u> resign, let it <u>not</u> be you or <u>I</u>.
               A   B   C   D
    <u>No error</u>
      E

14. There was so much talking <u>in back of</u> me <u>as</u> I <u>could</u> not <u>enjoy</u> the music.
                                        A   B   C   D
    <u>No error</u>
      E

15. <u>Being that</u> he is that <u>kind of</u> <u>boy</u>, he cannot be blamed <u>for</u> the mistake.
         A   B   C   D
    <u>No error</u>
      E

16. <u>The king, having read</u> the speech, <u>he</u> and the <u>queen</u> <u>departed</u>. <u>No error</u>
                A   B   C   D   E

17. I <u>am</u> <u>so tired</u> I <u>can't</u> <u>scarcely</u> stand. <u>No error</u>
      A B   C   D   E

18. We are <u>mailing bills</u> to our customers <u>in Canada</u>, and, <u>being</u> eager to
                    A   B   C
    clear our books before the new season opens, it is <u>to be hoped</u> they will
                                                                     D
    send their remittances promptly. <u>No error</u>
                                         E

3 (#1)

19. I reluctantly acquiesced to the proposal. No error
    A   B   C   D   E   19._____

20. It had lain out in the rain all night. No error
    A B   C   D   E   20._____

21. If he would have gone there, he would have seen a marvelous sight.   21._____
          A   B   C   D
    No error
    E

22. The climate of Asia Minor is somewhat like Utah. No error   22._____
                  A   B   C   D   E

23. If everybody did unto others as they would wish others to do unto them, this   23._____
       A   B   C   D
    world would be a paradise. No error
                               E

24. This was the jockey whom I saw was most likely to win the race. No error   24._____
    A   B   C   D   E

25. The only food the general demanded was potatoes. No error   25._____
        A   B   C   D   E

KEY (CORRECT ANSWERS)

1.	C		11.	C
2.	A		12.	C
3.	B		13.	D
4.	B		14.	B
5.	C		15.	A
6.	D		16.	A
7.	B		17.	C
8.	D		18.	C
9.	B		19.	E
10.	E		20.	E

21. A
22. D
23. D
24. B
25. E

135

TEST 2

DIRECTIONS: In each of the sentences below, four portions are underlined and lettered. Read each sentence and decide whether any of the UNDERLINED parts contains an error in spelling, punctuation, or capitalization, or employs grammatical usage which would be inappropriate for carefully written English. If so, note the letter printed under the unacceptable form and indicate this choice in the space at the right. If all four of the underlined portions are acceptable as they stand, select the answer E. (No sentence contains more than ONE unacceptable form.)

1. A party <u>like</u> <u>that</u> <u>only</u> <u>comes</u> once a year. <u>No error</u>
         A   B   C   D   E

    1.____

2. <u>Our's</u> <u>is</u> <u>a</u> <u>swift moving</u> age. <u>No error</u>
    A   BC   D   E

    2.____

3. The <u>healthy</u> climate soon <u>restored</u> him <u>to</u> his <u>accustomed</u> vigor. <u>No error</u>
         A   B   C   D   E

    3.____

4. <u>They</u> needed six typists and hoped that <u>only</u> that <u>many</u> <u>would</u> apply for the position. <u>No error</u>
   A   B   C   D
                  E

    4.____

5. He <u>interviewed</u> people <u>whom</u> he thought had <u>something</u> <u>to impart</u>. <u>No error</u>
           A   B   C   D   E

    5.____

6. <u>Neither</u> of his three sisters <u>is</u> older <u>than</u> <u>he</u>. <u>No error</u>
    A   B   CD   E

    6.____

7. <u>Since</u> he is <u>that</u> <u>kind</u> of <u>a</u> boy, he cannot be expected to cooperate with us. <u>No error</u>
   A   B   C   D   E

    7.____

8. <u>When passing</u> <u>through</u> the tunnel, the air pressure <u>affected</u> <u>our</u> years. <u>No error</u>
        A   B   C   D   E

    8,____

9. <u>The story having</u> a sad ending, <u>it</u> never <u>achieved</u> popularity <u>among</u> the students. <u>No error</u>
      A   B   C   D
         E

    9.____

10. <u>Since</u> we are both hungry, <u>shall</u> we go <u>somewhere</u> for lunch? <u>No error</u>
    A   B   C   D   E

    10.____

2 (#2)

11. <u>Will</u> you please <u>bring</u> this book <u>down to</u> the library and give it to my friend<u>,</u>   11.____
    A   B   C   D
    who is waiting for it? <u>No error</u>
                              E

12. You <u>may</u> <u>have</u> the book; I <u>am</u> finished <u>with</u> it. <u>No error</u>   12.____
         A   B   C   D   E

13. I <u>don't</u> know <u>if</u> I <u>should</u> mention <u>it</u> to her or not. <u>No error</u>   13.____
       A   B   C   D   E

14. Philosophy is not <u>a subject</u> <u>which</u> <u>has to do</u> with philosophers and   14.____
                         A   B   C
    mathematics <u>only</u>. <u>No error</u>
                    D   E

15. The thoughts of the scholar <u>in his library</u> are little different <u>than</u> the old woman   15.____
                                    A   B
    who first said, <u>"It's</u> no use crying over spilt milk." <u>No error</u>
                      C   D   E

16. A complete <u>system</u> of philosophical ideas <u>are</u> <u>implied</u> in many simple   16.____
                  A   B   C
    <u>utterances.</u> <u>No error</u>
        D   E

17. Even <u>if</u> one has never put <u>them</u> into words, <u>his</u> ideas <u>compose</u> a kind of a   17.____
            A   B   C   D
    philosophy. <u>No error</u>
                    E

18. Perhaps it <u>is</u> <u>well enough</u> that most <u>people</u> do not attempt this <u>formulation.</u>   18.____
                 A   B   C   D
    <u>No error</u>
        E

19. <u>Leading their</u> ordered lives, this <u>confused</u> <u>body</u> of ideas and feelings <u>is</u>   19.____
        A   B   C   D
    sufficient. <u>No error</u>
                    E

20. Why <u>should</u> we <u>insist upon</u> <u>them</u> <u>formulating</u> it? <u>No error</u>   20.____
           A   B   C   D   E

21. <u>Since</u> it includes <u>something</u> of the wisdom of the ages, it is <u>adequate</u> for the   21.____
        A   B   C
    <u>purposes</u> of ordinary life. <u>No error</u>
        D   E

137

22. Therefore, I <u>have sought</u> to make a pattern <u>of mine,</u> <u>and so</u> there were, early
        A   B   C
moments of <u>my trying</u> to find out what were the elements with which I had to
                  D
deal. <u>No error</u>
             E   22.____

23. I <u>wanted</u> <u>to get</u> <u>what</u> knowledge I <u>could</u> about the general structure of the
       A   B   C   D
universe. <u>No error</u>
                  E   23.____

24. I wanted to <u>know</u> <u>if</u> life <u>per se</u> had any meaning or <u>whether</u> I must strive to give
                  A   B   C   D
it one. <u>No error</u>
              E   24.____

25. <u>So,</u> in a <u>desultory</u> way, I <u>began</u> <u>to read</u>. <u>No error</u>
     A   B   C   D   E   25.____

KEY (CORRECT ANSWERS)

1.	C		11.	B
2.	A		12.	C
3.	A		13.	B
4.	C		14.	D
5.	B		15.	B
6.	A		16.	B
7.	D		17.	A
8.	A		18.	C
9.	A		19.	A
10.	E		20.	D

21. E
22. C
23. C
24. B
25. E

EXAMINATION SECTION
TEST 1

DIRECTIONS: In each of the following questions, only one of the four sentences conforms to standards of correct usage. The other three contain errors in grammar, diction, or punctuation. Select the choice in each question which BEST conforms to standards of correct usage. Consider a choice correct if it contains none of the errors mentioned above, even though there may be other ways of expressing the same thought. *PRINT THE LETTER OF THE CORRECT ANSWER IN THE SPACE AT THE RIGHT.*

1.
   A. Because he was ill was no excuse for his behavior
   B. I insist that he see a lawyer before he goes to trial.
   C. He said "that he had not intended to go."
   D. He wasn't out of the office only three days.

2.
   A. He came to the station and pays a porter to carry his bags into the train.
   B. I should have liked to live in medieval times.
   C. My father was born in Linville. A little country town where everybody knows everyone else.
   D. The car, which is parked across the street, is disabled.

3.
   A. He asked the desk clerk for a clean, quiet, room.
   B. I expected James to be lonesome and that he would want to go home.
   C. I have stopped worrying because I have heard nothing further on the subject.
   D. If the board of directors controls the company, they may take actions which are disapproved by the stockholders.

4.
   A. Each of the players knew their place.
   B. He whom you saw on the stage is the son of an actor.
   C. Susan is the smartest of the twin sisters.
   D. Who ever thought of him winning both prizes?

5.
   A. An outstanding trait of early man was their reliance on omens.
   B. Because I had never been there before.
   C. Neither Mr. Jones nor Mr. Smith has completed his work.
   D. While eating my dinner, a dog came to the window.

6.
   A. A copy of the lease, in addition to the Rules and Regulations, are to be given to each tenant.
   B. The Rules and Regulations and a copy of the lease is being given to each tenant.
   C. A copy of the lease, in addition to the Rules and Regulations, is to be given to each tenant.
   D. A copy of the lease, in addition to the Rules and Regulations, are being given to each tenant.

7. A. Although we understood that for him music was a passion, we were disturbed by the fact that he was addicted to sing along with the soloists.
    B. Do you believe that Steven is liable to win a scholarship?
    C. Give the picture to whomever is a connoisseur of art.
    D. Whom do you believe to be the most efficient worker in the office?

8. A. Each adult who is sure they know all the answers will some day realize their mistake.
    B. Even the most hardhearted villain would have to feel bad about so horrible a tragedy.
    C. Neither being licensed teachers, both aspirants had to pass rigorous tests before being appointed.
    D. The principal reason why he wanted to be designated was because he had never before been to a convention.

9. A. Being that the weather was so inclement, the party has been postponed for at least a month.
    B. He is in New York City only three weeks and he has already seen all the thrilling sights in Manhattan and in the other four boroughs.
    C. If you will look it up in the official directory, which can be consulted in the library during specified hours, you will discover that the chairman and director are Mr. T. Henry Long.
    D. Working hard at college during the day and at the post office during the night, he appeared to his family to be indefatigable.

10. A. I would have been happy to oblige you if you only asked me to do it.
    B. The cold weather, as well as the unceasing wind and rain, have made us decide to spend the winter in Florida.
    C. The politician would have been more successful in winning office if he would have been less dogmatic.
    D. These trousers are expensive; however, they will wear well.

11. A. All except him wore formal attire at the reception for the ambassador.
    B. If that chair were to be blown off of the balcony, it might injure someone below.
    C. Not a passenger, who was in the crash, survived the impact.
    D. To borrow money off friends is the best way to lose them.

12. A. Approaching Manhattan on the ferry boat from Staten Island, an unforgettable sight of the skyscrapers is seen.
    B. Did you see the exhibit of modernistic paintings as yet?
    C. Gesticulating wildly and ranting in stentorian tones, the speaker was the sinecure of all eyes.
    D. The airplane with crew and passengers was lost somewhere in the Pacific Ocean.

13. A. If one has consistently had that kind of training, it is certainly too late to change your entire method of swimming long distances.
    B. The captain would have been more impressed if you would have been more conscientious in evacuation drills.
    C. The passengers on the stricken ship were all ready to abandon it at the signal.
    D. The villainous shark lashed at the lifeboat with it's tail, trying to upset the rocking boat in order to partake of it's contents.

13.____

14. A. As one whose been certified as a professional engineer, I believe that the decision to build a bridge over that harbor is unsound.
    B. Between you and me, this project ought to be completed long before winter arrives.
    C. He fervently hoped that the men would be back at camp and to find them busy at their usual chores.
    D. Much to his surprise, he discovered that the climate of Korea was like his home town.

14.____

15. A. An industrious executive is aided, not impeded, by having a hobby which gives him a fresh point of view on life and its problems.
    B. Frequent absence during the calendar year will surely mitigate against the chances of promotion.
    C. He was unable to go to the committee meeting because he was very ill.
    D. Mr. Brown expressed his disapproval so emphatically that his associates were embarassed

15.____

16. A. At our next session, the office manager will have told you something about his duties and responsibilities.
    B. In general, the book is absorbing and original and have no hesitation about recommending it.
    C. The procedures followed by private industry in dealing with lateness and absence are different from ours.
    D We shall treat confidentially any information about Mr. Doe, to whom we understand you have sent reports to for many years.

16.____

17. A. I talked to one official, whom I knew was fully impartial.
    B. Everyone signed the petition but him.
    C. He proved not only to be a good student but also a good athlete.
    D. All are incorrect.

17.____

18. A. Every year a large amount of tenants are admitted to housing projects.
    B. Henry Ford owned around a billion dollars in industrial equipment.
    C. He was aggravated by the child's poor behavior.
    D. All are incorrect.

18.____

19. A. Before he was committed to the asylum he suffered from the illusion that he was Napoleon.
    B. Besides stocks, there were also bonds in the safe.
    C. We bet the other team easily.
    D. All are incorrect.

19.____

20. A. Bring this report to your supervisory.
    B. He set the chair down near the table.
    C. The capitol of New York is Albany.
    D. All are incorrect.

20.____

21. A. He was chosen to arbitrate the dispute because everyone knew he would be disinterested.
    B. It is advisable to obtain the best council before making an important decision.
    C. Less college students are interested in teaching than ever before.
    D. All are incorrect.

21.____

22. A. She, hearing a signal, the source lamp flashed.
    B. While hearing a signal, the source lamp flashed.
    C. In hearing a signal, the source lamp flashed.
    D. As she heard a signal, the source lamp flashed.

22.____

23. A. Every one of the time records have been initialed in the designated spaces.
    B. All of the time records has been initialed in the designated spaces.
    C. Each one of the time records was initialed in the designated spaces.
    D. The time records all been initialed in the designated spaces.

23.____

24. A. If there is no one else to answer the phone, you will have to answer it.
    B. You will have to answer it yourself if no one else answers the phone.
    C. If no one else is not around to pick up the phone, you will have to do it.
    D. You will have to answer the phone when nobodys here to do it.

24.____

25. A. Dr. Barnes not in his office. What could I do for you?
    B. Dr. Barnes is not in his office. Is there something I can do for you?
    C. Since Dr. Barnes is not in his office, might there be something I may do for you?
    D. Is there any ways I can assist you since Dr. Barnes is not in his office?

25.____

26. A. She do not understand how the new console works.
    B. The way the new console works, she doesn't understand.
    C. She doesn't understand how the new console works.
    D. The new console works, so that she doesn't understand.

26.____

27. A. Certain changes in my family income must be reported as they occur.
    B. When certain changes in family income occur, it must be reported.
    C. Certain family income change must be reported as they occur.
    D. Certain changes in family income must be reported as they have been occurring.

27.____

28. A. Each tenant has to complete the application themselves.
    B. Each of the tenants have to complete the application by himself.
    C. Each of the tenants has to complete the application himself.
    D. Each of the tenants has to complete the application by themselves.

28.____

29. A. Yours is the only building that the construction will effect.
    B. Your's is the only building affected by the construction.
    C. The construction will only effect your building.
    D. Yours is the only building that will be affected by the construction.

29.____

30. A. There is four tests left.
    B. The number of tests left are four.
    C. There are four tests left.
    D. Four of the tests remains.

30.____

31. A. Each of the applicants takes a test.
    B. Each of the applicant take a test.
    C. Each of the applicants take tests.
    D. Each of the applicants have taken tests.

31.____

32. A. The applicant, not the examiners, are ready.
    B. The applicants, not the examiners, is ready.
    C. The applicants, not the examiner, are ready.
    D. The applicant, not the examiner, are ready

32.____

33. A. You will not progress except you practice.
    B. You will not progress without you practicing.
    C. You will not progress unless you practice.
    D. You will not progress provided you do not practice.

33.____

34. A. Neither the director or the employees will be at the office tomorrow.
    B. Neither the director nor the employees will be at the office tomorrow.
    C. Neither the director, or the secretary nor the other employees will be at the office tomorrow.
    D. Neither the director, the secretary or the other employees will be at the office tomorrow.

34.____

35. A. In my absence, he and her will have to finish the assignment.
    B. In my absence he and she will have to finish the assignment.
    C. In my absence she and him, they will have to finish the assignment.
    D. In my absence he and her both will have to finish the assignment.

35.____

KEY (CORRECT ANSWERS)

1.	B	11.	A	21.	A	31.	A
2.	B	12.	D	22.	D	32.	C
3.	C	13.	C	23.	C	33.	C
4.	B	14.	B	24.	A	34.	B
5.	C	15.	A	25.	B	35.	B
6.	C	16.	C	26.	C		
7.	D	17.	B	27.	A		
8.	B	18.	D	28.	C		
9.	D	19.	B	29.	D		
10.	D	20.	B	30.	C		

TEST 2

DIRECTIONS: Each question or incomplete statement is followed by several suggested answers or completions. Select the one that BEST answers the question or completes the statement. *PRINT THE LETTER OF THE CORRECT ANSWER IN THE SPACE AT THE RIGHT.*

Questions 1-4.

DIRECTIONS: Questions 1 through 4 consist of three sentences each. For each question, select the sentence which contains NO error in grammar or usage.

1. A. Be sure that everybody brings his notes to the conference.
   B. He looked like he meant to hit the boy.
   C. Mr. Jones is one of the clients who was chosen to represent the district.
   D. All are incorrect.

   1.____

2. A. He is taller than I.
   B. I'll have nothing to do with these kind of people.
   C. The reason why he will not buy the house is because it is too expensive.
   D. All are incorrect.

   2.____

3. A. Aren't I eligible for this apartment.
   B. Have you seen him anywheres?
   C. He should of come earlier.
   D. All are incorrect.

   3.____

4. A. He graduated college in 2022.
   B. He hadn't but one more line to write.
   C. Who do you think is the author of this report?
   D. All are incorrect.

   4.____

Questions 5-35.

DIRECTIONS: In each of the following questions, only one of the four sentences conforms to standards of correct usage. The other three contain errors in grammar, diction, or punctuation. Select the choice in each question which BEST conforms to standards of correct usage. Consider a choice correct if it contains none of the errors mentioned above, even though there may be other ways of expressing the same thought.

5. A. It is obvious that no one wants to be a kill-joy if they can help it.
   B. It is not always possible, and perhaps it never ispossible, to judge a person's character by just looking at him.
   C. When Yogi Berra of the New York Yankees hit an immortal grandslam home run, everybody in the huge stadium including Pittsburgh fans, rose to his feet.
   D. Every one of us students must pay tuition today.

   5.____

6. A. The physician told the young mother that if the baby is not able to digest its milk, it should be boiled.   6.____
   B. There is no doubt whatsoever that he felt deeply hurt because John Smith had betrayed the trust.
   C. Having partaken of a most delicious repast prepared by Tessie Breen, the hostess, the horses were driven home immediately thereafter.
   D. The attorney asked my wife and myself several questions.

7. A. Despite all denials, there is no doubt in my mind that   7.____
   B. At this time everyone must deprecate the demogogic attack made by one of our Senators on one of our most revered statesmen.
   C. In the first game of a crucial two-game series, Ted Williams, got two singles, both of them driving in a run.
   D. Our visitor brought good news to John and I.

8. A. If he would have told me, I should have been glad to help him in his dire financial emergency.   8.____
   B. Newspaper men have often asserted that diplomats or so-called official spokesmen sometimes employ equivocation in attempts to deceive.
   C. I think someones coming to collect money for the Red Cross.
   D. In a masterly summation, the young attorney expressed his belief that the facts clearly militate against this opinion.

9. A. We have seen most all the exhibits.   9.____
   B. Without in the least underestimating your advice, in my opinion the situation has grown immeasurably worse in the past few days.
   C. I wrote to the box office treasurer of the hit show that a pair of orchestra seats would be preferable.
   D. As the grim story of Pearl Harbor was broadcast on that fateful December 7, it was the general opinion that war was inevitable.

10. A. Without a moment's hesitation, Casey Stengel said that Larry Berra works harder than any player on the team.   10.____
    B. There is ample evidence to indicate that many animals can run faster than any human being.
    C. No one saw the accident but I.
    D. Example of courage is the heroic defense put up by the paratroopers against overwhelming odds.

11. A. If you prefer these kind, Mrs. Grey, we shall be more than willing to let you have them reasonably.   11.____
    B. If you like these here, Mrs. Grey, we shall be more than willing to let you have them reasonably.
    C. If you like these, Mrs. Grey, we shall be more than willing to let you have them.
    D. Who shall we appoint?

12. A. The number of errors are greater in speech than in writing.
    B. The doctor rather than the nurse was to blame for his being neglected.
    C. Because the demand for these books have been so great, we reduced the price.
    D. John Galsworthy, the English novelist, could not have survived a serious illness; had it not been for loving care.

    12._____

13. A. Our activities this year have seldom ever been as interesting as they have been this month.
    B. Our activities this month have been more interesting, or at least as interesting as those of any month this year.
    C. Our activities this month has been more interesting than those of any other month this year.
    D. Neither Jean nor her sister was at home.

    13._____

14. A. George B. Shaw's view of common morality, as well as his wit sparkling with a dash of perverse humor here and there, have led critics to term him "The Incurable Rebel."
    B. The President's program was not always received with the wholehearted endorsement of his own party, which is why the party faces difficulty in drawing up a platform for the coming election.
    C. The reason why they wanted to travel was because they had never been away from home.
    D. Facing a barrage of cameras, the visiting celebrity found it extremely difficult to express his opinions clearly.

    14._____

15. A. When we calmed down, we all agreed that our anger had been kind of unnecessary and had not helped the situation.
    B. Without him going into all the details, he made us realize the horror of the accident.
    C. Like one girl, for example, who applied for two positions.
    D. Do not think that you have to be so talented as he is in order to play in the school orchestra.

    15._____

16. A. He looked very peculiarly to me.
    B. He certainly looked at me peculiar.
    C. Due to the train's being late, we had to wait an hour.
    D. The reason for the poor attendance is that it is raining.

    16._____

17. A. About one out of four own an automobile.
    B. The collapse of the old Mitchell Bridge was caused by defective construction in the central pier.
    C. Brooks Atkinson was well acquainted with the best literature, thus helping him to become an able critic.
    D. He has to stand still until the relief man comes up, thus giving him no chance to move about and keep warm.

    17._____

18. A. He is sensitive to confusion and withdraws from people whom he feels are too noisy.
    B. Do you know whether the data is statistically correct?
    C. Neither the mayor or the aldermen are to blame.
    D. Of those who were graduated from high school, a goodly percentage went to college.

18.____

19. A. Acting on orders, the offices were searched by a designated committee.
    B. The answer probably is nothing.
    C. I thought it to be all right to excuse them from class.
    D. I think that he is as successful a singer, if not more successful, than Mary.

19.____

20. A. $360,000 is really very little to pay for such a wellbuilt house.
    B. The creatures looked like they had come from outer space.
    C. It was her, he knew!
    D. Nobody but me knows what to do.

20.____

21. A. Mrs. Smith looked good in her new suit.
    B. New York may be compared with Chicago.
    C. I will not go to the meeting except you go with me.
    D. I agree with this editorial.

21.____

22. A. My opinions are different from his.
    B. There will be less students in class now.
    C. Helen was real glad to find her watch.
    D. It had been pushed off of her dresser.

22.____

23. A. Almost everyone, who has been to California, returns with glowing reports.
    B. George Washington, John Adams, and Thomas Jefferson, were our first presidents.
    C. Mr. Walters, whom we met at the bank yesterday, is the man, who gave me my first job.
    D. One should study his lessons as carefully as he can.

23.____

24. A. We had such a good time yesterday.
    B. When the bell rang, the boys and girls went in the schoolhouse.
    C. John had the worst headache when he got up this morning.
    D. Today's assignment is somewhat longer than yesterday's.

24.____

25. A. Neither the mayor nor the city clerk are willing to talk.
    B. Neither the mayor nor the city clerk is willing to talk.
    C. Neither the mayor or the city clerk are willing to talk.
    D Neither the mayor or the city clerk is willing to talk.

25.____

26. A. Being that he is that kind of boy, cooperation cannot be expected.
    B. He interviewed people who he thought had something to say.
    C. Stop whomever enters the building regardless of rank or office held.
    D. Passing through the countryside, the scenery pleased us.

26.____

27. A. The childrens' shoes were in their closet.
    B. The children's shoes were in their closet.
    C. The childs' shoes were in their closet.
    D. The childs' shoes were in his closet.

27.____

28. A. An agreement was reached between the defendant, the plaintiff, the plaintiff's attorney and the insurance company as to the amount of the settlement.
    B. Everybody was asked to give their versions of the accident.
    C. The consensus of opinion was that the evidence was inconclusive.
    D. The witness stated that if he was rich, he wouldn't have had to loan the money.

28.____

29. A. Before beginning the investigation, all the materials related to the case were carefully assembled.
    B. The reason for his inability to keep the appointment is because of his injury in the accident.
    C. This here evidence tends to support the claim of the defendant.
    D. We interviewed all the witnesses who, according to the driver, were still in town.

29.____

30. A. Each claimant was allowed the full amount of their medical expenses.
    B. Either of the three witnesses is available.
    C. Every one of the witnesses was asked to tell his story.
    D. Neither of the witnesses are right.

30.____

31. A. The commissioner, as well as his deputy and various bureau heads, were present.
    B. A new organization of employers and employees have been formed.
    C. One or the other of these men have been selected.
    D. The number of pages in the book is enough to discourage a reader.

31.____

32. A. Between you and me, I think he is the better man.
    B. He was believed to be me.
    C. Is it us that you wish to see?
    D. The winners are him and her.

32.____

33. A. Beside the statement to the police, the witness spoke to no one.
    B. He made no statement other than to the police and I.
    C. He made no statement to any one else, aside from the police.
    D. The witness spoke to no one but me.

33.____

34. A. The claimant has no one to blame but himself.
    B. The boss sent us, he and I, to deliver the packages.
    C. The lights come from mine and not his car.
    D. There was room on the stairs for him and myself.

34.____

35. A. Admission to this clinic is limited to patients' inability to pay for medical care.
     B. Patients who can pay little or nothing for medical care are treated in this clinic.
     C. The patient's ability to pay for medical care is the determining factor in his admission to this clinic.
     D. This clinic is for the patient's that cannot afford to pay or that can pay a little for medical care.

35.____

KEY (CORRECT ANSWERS)

1.	A	11.	C	21.	A	31.	D
2.	A	12.	B	22.	A	32.	A
3.	D	13.	D	23.	D	33.	D
4.	C	14.	D	24.	D	34.	A
5.	D	15.	D	25.	B	35.	B
6.	D	16.	D	26.	B		
7.	B	17.	B	27.	B		
8.	B	18.	D	28.	C		
9.	D	19.	B	29.	D		
10.	B	20.	D	30.	C		

ENGLISH EXPRESSION
EXAMINATION SECTION
TEST 1

DIRECTIONS: Each question or incomplete statement is followed by several suggested answers or completions. Select the one that BEST answers the question or completes the statement. *PRINT THE LETTER OF THE CORRECT ANSWER IN THE SPACE AT THE RIGHT.*

Questions 1-9.

DIRECTIONS: The following sentences contain problems in grammar, usage diction (choice of words), and idiom. Some sentences are correct. No sentence contains more than one error. You will find that the error, if there is one, is underlined and lettered. Assume that all other elements of the sentence are correct and cannot be changed. In choosing answers, follow the requirements of standard written English. If there is an error, select the *one underlined* part that must be changed in order to make the sentence correct. If there is no error, mark E.

1. <u>In planning</u> your future, <u>one must be</u> as honest with yourself as possible, make careful   1.____
       A   B
   decisions about the best course <u>to follow to achieve</u> a particular purpose, and, above all,
                                           C
   have the courage <u>to stand by those</u> decisions. <u>No error</u>
                       D   E

2. <u>Even though</u> history does not actually repeat itself, knowledge <u>of</u> history <u>can give</u>   2.____
       A   B   C
   current problems a familiar, <u>less</u> formidable look. <u>No error</u>
                            D   E

3. The Curies <u>had almost exhausted</u> their resources, and <u>for a time it seemed</u>   3.____
                       A   B
   <u>unlikely that they ever</u> would find the <u>solvent to their financial problems</u>. <u>No error</u>
       C   D   E

4. <u>If the rumors are</u> correct, Deane <u>will not be convicted</u>, for each of the officers   4.____
       A   B
   on the court realizes that Colson and Holdman may be <u>the real culprit and</u> that
                                                       C
   <u>their</u> testimony is not completely trustworthy. <u>No error</u>
    D   E

5. The citizens of Washington, <u>like Los Angeles</u>, prefer to commute by automobile,
                                                A
   even though motor vehicles contribute <u>nearly as many</u> contaminants to the air
                                                        B
   <u>as do all other</u> sources <u>combined</u>. <u>No error</u>
        C   D   E

   5.____

6. <u>By the time Robert Vasco completes</u> his testimony, every major executive of our
                    A
   company but Ray Ashurst <u>and I</u> <u>will have been</u> <u>accused of</u> complicity in the stock
                          B   C   D
   swindle. <u>No error</u>
          E

   6.____

7. <u>Within six months</u> the store was operating <u>profitably and efficient</u>; shelves
       A   B
   <u>were well stocked</u>, goods were selling rapidly, and the cash register
    C
   <u>was ringing constantly</u>. <u>No error</u>
       D   E

   7.____

8. Shakespeare's comedies have an advantage <u>over Shaw</u> <u>in that Shakespeare's</u> were
                                       A   B
   <u>written primarily</u> to entertain and <u>not to</u> argue for a cause. <u>No error</u>
       C   D   E

   8.____

9. Any true insomniac <u>is well aware of</u> the futility of <u>such measures as</u> drinking
                 A   B
   hot milk, <u>regular hours, deep breathing</u>, counting sheep, and <u>concentrating on</u>
              C   D
   black velvet. <u>No error</u>
          E

   9.____

Questions 10-15.

DIRECTIONS: In each of the following sentences, some part of the sentence or the entire sentence is underlined. Beneath each sentence you will find five ways of phrasing the underlined part. The first of these repeats the original; the other four are different. If you think the original is better than any of the alternatives, choose answer A; otherwise choose one of the others. In choosing answers, follow the requirements of standard written English; that is, pay attention to grammar, choice of words, sentence construction, and punctuation. Choose the answer that produces the most effective sentence—clear and exact, without awkwardness or ambiguity. Do not make a choice that changes the meaning of the original sentence.

10. The tribe of warriors believed that boys and girls should be <u>reared separate, and, as soon as he was weaned, the boys were taken from their mothers.</u>

    A. reared separate, and, as soon as he was weaned, the boys were taken from their mothers

10.____

B. reared separate, and, as soon as he was weaned, a boy was taken from his mother
C. reared separate, and, as soon as he was weaned, the boys were taken from their mothers
D. reared separately, and, as soon as a boy was weaned, they were taken from their mothers
E. reared separately, and, as soon as a boy was weaned, he was taken from his mother

11. <u>Despite Vesta being only the third largest, it is by far the brightest of the known asteroids.</u>
    A. Despite Vesta being only the third largest, it is by far the brightest of the known asteroids.
    B. Vesta, though only the third largest asteroid, is by far the brightest of the known ones.
    C. Being only the third largest, yet Vesta is by far the brightest of the known asteroids.
    D. Vesta, though only the third largest of the known asteroids, is by far the brightest.
    E. Vesta is only the third largest of the asteroids, it being, however, the brightest one.

12. As a result of the discovery of the Dead Sea Scrolls, our understanding of the roots of Christianity <u>has had to be revised considerably.</u>
    A. has had to be revised considerably
    B. have had to be revised considerably
    C. has had to undergo revision to a considerable degree
    D. have had to be subjected to considerable revision
    E. has had to be revised in a considerable way

13. Because <u>it is imminently suitable to</u> dry climates, adobe has been a traditional building material throughout the southwestern states.
    A. it is imminently suitable to
    B. it is eminently suitable for
    C. It is eminently suitable when in
    D. of its eminent suitability with
    E. of being imminently suitable in

14. <u>Martell is more concerned with demonstrating that racial prejudice exists than preventing it from doing harm, which explains</u> why his work is not always highly regarded.
    A. Martell is more concerned with demonstrating that racial prejudice exists than preventing it from doing harm, which explains
    B. Martell is more concerned with demonstrating that racial prejudice exists than with preventing it from doing harm, and this explains
    C. Martell is more concerned with demonstrating that racial prejudice exists than with preventing it from doing harm, an explanation of
    D. Martell's greater concern for demonstrating that racial prejudice exists than preventing it from doing harm—this explains
    E. Martell's greater concern for demonstrating that racial prejudice exists than for preventing it from doing harm explains

15. <u>Throughout this history of the American West there runs a steady commentary on the deception and mistreatment of the Indians.</u> 15._____
    A. Throughout this history of the American West there runs a steady commentary on the deception and mistreatment of the Indians.
    B. There is a steady commentary provided on the deception and mistreatment of the Indians and it runs throughout this history of the American West.
    C. The deception and mistreatment of the Indians provide a steady comment that runs throughout this history of the American West.
    D. Comment on the deception and mistreatment of the Indians is steadily provided and runs throughout this history of the American West.
    E. Running throughout this history of the American West is a steady commentary that is provided on the deception and mistreatment of the Indians.

Questions 16-20.

DIRECTIONS: In each of the following questions you are given a complete sentence to be rephrased according to the directions which follow it. You should rephrase the sentence mentally to save time, although you may make notes in your test book if you wish. Below each sentence and its directions are listed words or phrases that may occur in your revised sentence. When you have thought out a good sentence, look in the choices A through E for the word or entire phrase that is included in your revised sentence, and print the letter of the correct answer in the space at the right. The word or phrase you choose should be the most accurate and most nearly complete of all the choices given, and should be part of a sentence that meets the requirements of standard written English. Of course, a number of different sentences can be obtained if the sentence is revised according to directions, and not all of these possibilities can be included in only five choices. If you should find that you have thought of a sentence that contains none of the words or phrases listed in the choices, you should attempt to rephrase the sentence again so that it includes a word or phrase that is listed. Although the directions may at times require you to change the relationship between parts of the sentence or to make slight changes in meaning in other ways, <u>make only those changes that the directions require</u>; that is, keep the meaning the same, or as nearly the same as the directions permit. If you think that more than one good sentence can be made according to the directions, select the sentence that is most exact, effective, and natural in phrasing and construction.

EXAMPLES

I. <u>Sentence</u>: Coming to the city as a young man, he found a job as a newspaper reporter.
<u>Directions</u>: Substitute <u>He came</u> for <u>Coming</u>.
   A. and so he found   B. and found
   C. and there he had found   D. and then finding
   E. and had found

5 (#1)

Your rephrased sentence will probably read: "He came to the city as a young man and found a job as a newspaper reporter." This sentence contains the correct answer: <u>B. and found</u>. A sentence which used one of the alternate phrases would <u>change the</u> meaning or <u>intention</u> of the original sentence, would be a <u>poorly written sentence</u>, or would be <u>less effective</u> than another possible revision.

II. <u>Sentence</u>: Owing to her wealth, Sarah had many suitors.
<u>Directions</u>: Begin with <u>Many men courted</u>.
    A. so   B. while   C. although   D. because   E. and

Your rephrased sentence will probably read: "Many men courted Sarah because she was wealthy." This new sentence contains only choice D, which is the correct answer. None of the other choices will fit into an effective, correct sentence that retains the original meaning.

16. The archaeologists could only mark out the burial site, for then winter came.
 Begin with <u>Winter came before</u>.
    A. could do nothing more   B. could not do anything
    C. could only do   D. could do something
    E. could do anything more

16.____

17. The white reader often receives some insight into the reasons why black men are angry from descriptions by a black writer of the injustice they encounter in a white society.
 Begin with <u>A black writer often gives</u>.
    A. when describing   B. by describing
    C. he has described   D. in the descriptions
    E. because of describing

17.____

18. The agreement between the university officials and the dissident students provides for student representation on every university committee and on the board of trustees.
 Substitute <u>provides that</u> for <u>provides for</u>.
    A. be   B. are   C. would have
    D. would be   E. is to be

18.____

19. English Romanticism had its roots in German idealist philosophy, first described in England by Samuel Coleridge.
 Begin with <u>Samuel Coleridge was the first in</u>.
    A. in which English   B. and from it English
    C. where English   D. the source of English
    E. the birth of English

19.____

20. Four months have passed since his dismissal, during which time Alan has looked for work daily.
 Begin with <u>Each day</u>.
    A. will have passed   B. that have passed   C. that passed
    D. were to pass   E. had passed

20.____

KEY (CORRECT ANSWERS)

1.	B	11.	D
2.	E	12.	A
3.	D	13.	B
4.	C	14.	E
5.	A	15.	A
6.	B	16.	E
7.	B	17.	B
8.	A	18.	A
9.	C	19.	D
10.	E	20.	B

ARITHMETICAL REASONING
EXAMINATION SECTION
TEST 1

DIRECTIONS: Each question or incomplete statement is followed by several suggested answers or completions. Select the one that BEST answers the question or completes the statement. *PRINT THE LETTER OF THE CORRECT ANSWER IN THE SPACE AT THE RIGHT.*

1. If a secretary answered 28 phone calls and typed the addresses for 112 credit statements in one morning, what is the RATIO of phone calls answered to credit statements typed for that period of time?

    A. 1:4   B. 1:7   C. 2:3   D. 3:5

2. According to a suggested filing system, no more than 10 folders should be filed behind any one file guide and from 15 to 25 file guides should be used in each file drawer for easy finding and filing.
   The MAXIMUM number of folders that a five-drawer file cabinet can hold to allow easy finding and filing is

    A. 550   B. 750   C. 1,100   D. 1,250

3. An employee had a starting salary of $19,353. He received a salary increase at the end of each year, and at the end of the seventh year his salary was $25,107.
   What was his AVERAGE annual increase in salary over these seven years?

    A. $765   B. $807   C. $822   D. $858

4. The 55 typists and 28 senior clerks in a certain agency were paid a total of $1,457,400 in salaries in 2005.
   If the average annual salary of a typist was $16,800, the average annual salary of a senior clerk was

    A. $19,050   B. $19,950   C. $20,100   D. $20,250

5. A typist has been given a three-page report to type. She has finished typing the first two pages. The first page has 283 words, and the second page has 366 words.
   If the total report consists of 954 words, how many words will she have to type on the third page of the report?

    A. 202   B. 287   C. 305   D. 313

6. In one day, Clerk A processed 30% more forms than Clerk B, and Clerk C processed 1 1/4 as many forms as Clerk A.
   If Clerk B processed 40 forms, how many more forms were processed by Clerk C than Clerk B?

    A. 12   B. 13   C. 21   D. 25

7. A clerk who earns a gross salary of $678 every 2 weeks has the following deductions taken from her paycheck: 15% for city, state, and federal taxes; 2 1/2% for Social Security; $1.95 for health insurance; and $9.00 for union dues.
The amount of her take-home pay is

   A. $429.60   B. $468.60   C. $497.40   D. $548.40

8. In 2002, an agency spent $400 to buy pencils at a cost of $1.00 a dozen.
If the agency used 3/4 of these pencils in 2002 and used the same number of pencils in 2003, how many more pencils did it have to buy to have enough pencils for all of 2003?

   A. 1,200   B. 2,400   C. 3,600   D. 4,800

9. A clerk who worked in Agency X earned the following salaries: $15,105 the first year, $15,750 the second year, and $16,440 the third year. Another clerk who worked in Agency Y for three years earned $15,825 a year for two years and $16,086 the third year.
The DIFFERENCE between the average salaries received by both clerks over a three-year period is

   A. $147   B. $153   C. $261   D. $423

10. An employee who works more than 40 hours in any week receives overtime payment for the extra hours at time and one-half (1 1/2 times) his hourly rate of pay. An employee who earns $13.60 an hour works a total of 45 hours during a certain week.
His TOTAL pay for that week would be

   A. $564.40   B. $612.00   C. $646.00   D. $824.00

11. Suppose that the amount of money spent for supplies in 2006 for a division in a city department was $156,500. This represented an increase of 12% over the amount spent for supplies for this division in 2005.
The amount of money spent for supplies for this division in 2005 was MOST NEARLY

   A. $139,730   B. $137,720   C. $143,460   D. $138,720

12. Suppose that a group of five clerks have been assigned to insert 24,000 letters into envelopes. The clerks perform this work at the following rates of speed: Clerk A, 1,100 letters an hour; Clerk B, 1,450 letters an hour; Clerk C, 1,200 letters an hour; Clerk D, 1,300 letters an hour; Clerk E, 1,250 letters an hour. At the end of two hours of work, Clerks C and D are assigned to another task.
From the time that Clerks C and D were taken off the assignment, the number of hours required for the remaining clerks to complete this assignment is

   A. less than 3 hours
   B. 3 hours
   C. more than 3 hours, but less than 4 hours
   D. more than 4 hours

13. The number 60 is 40% of

   A. 24   B. 84   C. 96   D. 150

14. If 3/8 of a number is 96, the number is

   A. 132   B. 36   C. 256   D. 156

15. A city department uses an average of 25 20-cent, 35 30-cent, and 350 40-cent postage stamps each day.
The TOTAL cost of stamps used by the department in a five-day period is

    A. $29.50   B. $155.50   C. $290.50   D. $777.50

16. A city department issued 12,000 applications in 2000. The number of applications that the department issued in 1998 was 25% greater than the number it issued in 2000.
If the department issued 10% fewer applications in 1996 than it did in 1998, the number it issued in 1996 was

    A. 16,500   B. 13,500   C. 9,900   D. 8,100

17. A clerk can add 40 columns of figures an hour by using an adding machine and 20 columns of figures an hour without using an adding machine.
The TOTAL number of hours it would take him to add 200 columns if he does 3/5 of the work by machine and the rest without the machine is

    A. 6   B. 7   C. 8   D. 9

18. In 1997, a city department bought 500 dozen pencils at $1.20 per dozen. In 2000, only 75 percent as many pencils were bought as were bought in 1997, but the price was 20 percent higher than the 1997 price. The TOTAL cost of the pencils bought in 2000 was

    A. $540   B. $562.50   C. $720   D. $750

19. A clerk is assigned to check the accuracy of the entries on 490 forms. He checks 40 forms an hour. After working one hour on this task, he is joined by another clerk, who checks these forms at the rate of 35 an hour.
The TOTAL number of hours required to do the entire assignment is

    A. 5   B. 6   C. 7   D. 8

20. Assume that there are a total of 420 employees in a city agency. Thirty percent of the employees are clerks, and 1/7 are typists.
The DIFFERENCE between the number of clerks and the number of typists is

    A. 126   B. 66   C. 186   D. 80

21. Assume that a duplicating machine produces copies of a bulletin at a cost of 2 cents per copy. The machine produces 120 copies of the bulletin per minute.
If the cost of producing a certain number of copies was $12, how many minutes of operation did it take the machine to produce this number of copies?

    A. 5   B. 2   C. 10   D. 6

22. An assignment is completed by 32 clerks in 22 days. Assuming that all the clerks work at the same rate of speed, the number of clerks that would be needed to complete this assignment in 16 days is

    A. 27   B. 38   C. 44   D. 52

23. A department head hired a total of 60 temporary employees to handle a seasonal increase in the department's workload. The following lists the number of temporary employees hired, their rates of pay, and the duration of their employment:
    One-third of the total were hired as clerks, each at the rate of $27,500 a year, for two months.
    30 percent of the total were hired as office machine operators, each at the rate of $31,500 a year, for four months.
    22 stenographers were hired, each at the rate of $30,000 a year, for three months.
    The total amount paid to these temporary employees was MOST NEARLY

    A. $1,780,000 B. $450,000
    C. $650,000   D. $390,000

24. Assume that there are 2,300 employees in a city agency. Also, assume that five percent of these employees are accountants, that 80 percent of the accountants have college degrees, and that one-half of the accountants who have college degrees have five years of experience. Then, the number of employees in the agency who are accountants with college degrees and five years of experience is

    A. 46   B. 51   C. 460   D. 920

25. Assume that the regular 8-hour working day of a laborer is from 8 A.M. to 5 P.M., with an hour off for lunch. He earns a regular hourly rate of pay for these 8 hours and is paid at the rate of time-and-a-half for each hour worked after his regular working day.
    If, on a certain day, he works from 8 A.M. to 6 P.M., with an hour off for lunch, and earns $171, his regular hourly rate of pay is

    A. $16.30   B. $17.10   C. $18.00   D. $19.00

KEY (CORRECT ANSWERS)

1. A	11. A
2. D	12. B
3. C	13. D
4. A	14. C
5. C	15. D
6. D	16. B
7. D	17. B
8. B	18. A
9. A	19. C
10. C	20. B

21. A
22. C
23. B
24. A
25. C

SOLUTIONS TO PROBLEMS

1. 28/112 is equivalent to 1:4

2. Maximum number of folders = (10)(25)(5) = 1250

3. Average annual increase = ($25,107-19,353) ÷ 7 = $822

4. $1,457,400 - (55)($16,800) = $533,400 = total amount paid to senior clerks. Average senior clerk's salary = $533,400 ÷ 28 = $19,050

5. Number of words on 3rd page = 954 - 283 - 366 = 305

6. Clerk A processed (40)(1.30) = 52 forms and clerk C processed (52)(1.25) = 65 forms. Finally, 65 - 40 = 25

7. Take-home pay = $678 - (.15)($678) - (.025)($678) - $1.95 - $9.00 = $548.40

8. (400)(12) = 4800 pencils. In 2002, (3/4)(4800) = 3600 were used, so that 1200 pencils were available at the beginning of 2003. Since 3600 pencils were also used in 2003, the agency had to buy 3600 - 1200 = 2400 pencils.

9. Average salary for clerk in Agency X = ($15,105+$15,750+$16,440)/3 = $15,765. Average salary for clerk in Agency Y = ($15,825+ $15,825+$16,086) ÷ 3 = $15,912. Difference in average salaries = $147.

10. Total pay = ($13.60)(40) + ($20.40)(5) = $646.00

11. In 2005, amount spent = $156,500 ÷ 1.12 ≈ $139,730 (Actual value = $139,732.1429)

12. At the end of 2 hours, (1100)(2) + (1450)(2) + (1200)(2) + (1300X2) + (1250X2) = 12,600 letters have been inserted into envelopes. The remaining 11,400 letters done by clerks A, B, and C will require 11,400 ÷ (1100+1450+1250) = 3 hours.

13. 60 ÷ .40 = 150

14. 96 ÷ 3/8 = (96)(8/3) = 256

15. Total cost = (5)[(25)(.20)+(35)(.30)+(350)(.40)]= $777.50

16. In 1998, (12,000) (1.25) = 15,000 applications were issued In 1996, (15,000)(.90) = 13,500 applications were issued

17. Total number of hours = $\frac{120}{40} + \frac{80}{20} = 7$

18. (.75)(500 dozen) = 375 dozen purchased in 2000 at a cost of ($1.20)(1.20) = $1.44 per dozen. Total cost for 2000 = ($1.44) (375) = $540

19. Total time = 1 hour + 450/75 hrs. = 7 hours

20. (.30)(420) - (1/7)(420) = 126 - 60 = 66

21. Cost per minute = (120)(.02) = $2.40. Then, $12 ÷ $2.40 = 5 minutes

22. (32)(22) ÷ 16 = 44 clerks

23. Total amount paid = (20)($27,500)(2/12) + (18)($31,500)(4/12) + (22)($30,000)(3/12) = $445,666.$\overline{6}$ ≈ $450,000

24. Number of accountants with college degrees and five years of experience = (2300)(.05)(.80)(1/2) = 46

25. Let x = regular hourly pay. Then, (8)(x) + (1)(1.5x) = $1.71 So, 9.5x = 171. Solving, x = $18

TEST 2

DIRECTIONS: Each question or incomplete statement is followed by several suggested answers or completions. Select the one that BEST answers the question or completes the statement. *PRINT THE LETTER OF THE CORRECT ANSWER IN THE SPACE AT THE RIGHT.*

1. Assume that you know the capacity of a filing cabinet, the extent of which it is filled, and the daily rate at which material is being added to the file.
   In order to estimate how many more days it will take for the cabinet to be filled to capacity, you should

   A. divide the extent to which the cabinet is filled by the daily rate
   B. take the difference between the capacity of the cabinet and the material in it, and multiply the result by the daily rate of adding material
   C. divide the daily rate of adding material by the difference between the capacity of the cabinet and the material in it
   D. take the difference between the capacity of the cabinet and the material in it, and divide the result by the daily rate of adding material

   1.____

2. Suppose you have been asked to compute the average salary earned in your department during the past year. For each of the divisions of the department, you are given the number of employees and the average salary.
   In order to find the requested overall average salary for the department, you should

   A. add the average salaries of the various divisions and divide the total by the number of divisions
   B. multiply the number of employees in each division by the corresponding average salary, add the results and divide the total by the number of employees in the department
   C. add the average salaries of the various divisions and divide the total by the total number of employees in the department
   D. multiply the sum of the average salaries of the various divisions by the total number of divisions and divide the resulting product by the total number of employees in the department

   2.____

3. Suppose that a group of six clerks has been assigned to assemble the duplicated pages of a report into completed copies. After four hours of work, they have been able to complete one-third of the job.
   In order to assemble all the remaining copies in three more hours of work, the number of clerks which will have to be added to the original six, assuming that all the clerks assigned to this task work at the same rate of speed, is

   A. 10   B. 16   C. 2   D. 6

   3.____

4. A study of the grades of students in a certain college revealed that in 2005, 15% fewer students received a passing grade in mathematics than in 2004, whereas in 2006 the number of students passing mathematics increased 15% over 2005.
   On the basis of this study, it would be MOST accurate to conclude that

   A. the same percentage of students passed mathematics in 2004 as in 2006
   B. of the three years studied, the greatest percentage of students passed mathematics in 2006

   4.____

163

C. the percentage of students who passed mathematics in 2006 was less than the percentage passing this subject in 2004
D. the percentage of students passing mathematics in 2004 was 15% greater than the percentage of students passing this subject in 2006

5. A city department employs 1,400 people, of whom 35% are clerks and 1/8 are stenographers.
   The number of employees in the department who are neither clerks nor stenographers is

   A. 640   B. 665   C. 735   D. 760

6. Assume that there are 190 papers to be filed and that Clerk A and Clerk B are assigned to file these papers. If Clerk A files 40 papers more than Clerk B, then the number of papers that Clerk A files is

   A. 75   B. 110   C. 115   D. 150

7. A stock clerk had on hand the following items:
   500 pads, each worth 16 cents
   130 pencils, each worth 12 cents
   50 dozen rubber bands, worth 8 cents a dozen
   If, from this stock, he issued 125 pads, 45 pencils, and 48 rubber bands, the value of the remaining stock would be

   A. $25.72   B. $27.80   C. $70.52   D. $73.88

8. In a particular agency, there were 160 accidents in 2002. Of these accidents, 75% were due to unsafe acts and the rest were due to unsafe conditions. In the following year, a special safety program was established. The number of accidents in 2004 due to unsafe acts was reduced to 35% of what it had been in 2002.
   How many accidents due to unsafe acts were there in 2004?

   A. 20   B. 36   C. 42   D. 56

9. At the end of every month, the petty cash fund of Agency A is reimbursed for payments made from the fund during the month. During the month of February, the amounts paid from the fund were entered on receipts as follows: 10 bus fares of $1.40 each and one taxi fare of $14.00. At the end of the month, the money left in the fund was in the following denominations: 60 one-dollar bills, 16 quarters, 40 dimes, and 80 nickels.
   If the petty cash fund is reduced by 20% for the following month, how much money will there be available in the petty cash fund for March?

   A. $44   B. $80   C. $86   D. $100

10. An employee worked on a job for 6 weeks, 5 days per week, and 8 hours per day. How many hours did he work on the job?

    A. 40   B. 48   C. 55   D. 240

11. Divide 35 by .7.

    A. 5   B. 42   C. 50   D. 245

12. .1% of 25 =

    A. .025　　B. .25　　C. 2.5　　D. 25

13. In a city agency, 80 percent of the total number of employees are more than 25 years of age and 65 percent of the total number of employees are high school graduates.
    The SMALLEST possible percent of employees who are both high school graduates and more than 25 years of age is

    A. 35%　　B. 45%　　C. 55%　　D. 65%

14. Two clerical units, X and Y, each having a different number of clerks, are assigned to file registration cards. It takes Unit X, which contains 8 clerks, 21 days to file the same number of cards that Unit Y can file in 28 days. It is also a fact that Unit X can file 174,528 cards in 72 days.
    Assuming that all the clerks in both units work at the same rate of speed, the number of cards which can be filed by Unit Y in 144 days, if 4 more clerks are added to the staff of Unit Y, is MOST NEARLY

    A. 392,000　　B. 436,000　　C. 523,000　　D. 669,000

15. Assume that two machines, each costing $14,750, were purchased for your office. Each machine requires the services of an operator at a salary of $2,000 per month. These machines are to replace six clerks, two of whom earn $1,550 per month each, and four of whom earn $1,700 per month each.
    The number of months it will take for the cost of the machines to be made up from the savings in salaries is

    A. less than four　　B. four
    C. five　　D. more than five

16. Suppose that the amount of stationery used by your department in August decreased by 16% as compared with the amount used in July, and that the amount used in September increased by 25% as compared with the amount used in August.
    The amount of stationery used in September as compared with the amount used in July is

    A. greater by 5 percent　　B. less by 5 percent
    C. greater by 9 percent　　D. the same

17. An employee earns $48 a day and works 5 days a week.
    He will earn $2,160 in _____ weeks.

    A. 5　　B. 7　　C. 8　　D. 9

18. In a certain bureau, the entire staff consists of 1 senior supervisor, 2 supervisors, 6 assistant supervisors, and 54 associate workers.
    The percent of the staff who are not associate workers is MOST NEARLY

    A. 14　　B. 21　　C. 27　　D. 32

19. In a certain bureau, five employees each earn $1,000 a month, another 3 employees each earn $2,200 a month, and another two employees each earn $1,400 a month.
    The monthly payroll for these employees is

    A. $3,600　　B. $8,800　　C. $11,400　　D. $14,400

20. An employee contributes 5% of his salary to the pension fund. 20.____
    If his salary is $1,200 a month, the amount of his contribution to the pension fund in a year is

    A. $480 B. $720 C. $960 D. $1,200

21. The number of square feet in an area that is 50 feet long and 30 feet wide is 21.____

    A. 80 B. 150 C. 800 D. 1,500

22. A farm hand was paid a weekly wage of $332.16 for a 48-hour work week. As a result of 22.____
    a new labor contract, he is paid $344.96 a week for a 44-hour work week with time and one-half pay for time worked in excess of 44 hours in any work week.
    If he continues to work 48 hours weekly under the new contract, the amount by which his average hourly rate for a 48-hour work week under the new contract exceeds the hourly rate previously paid him lies between _____ and _____ cents, inclusive.

    A. 91;100 B. 101;110 C. 111;120 D. 121;130

23. Each side of a square room, which is being used as an office, measures 66 feet. The 23.____
    floor of the room is divided by six traffic aisles, each aisle being six feet wide. Three of the aisles run parallel to the east and west sides of the room, and the other three run parallel to the north and south sides of the room, so that the remaining floor space is divided into 16 equal sections. If all of the floor space which is not being used for traffic aisles is occupied by desk and chair sets, and each set takes up 24 square feet of floor space, the number of desk and chair sets in the room is

    A. 80 B. 64 C. 36 D. 96

24. In 2005, a city agency bought 12,000 envelopes at $4.00 per hundred. In 2006, the price 24.____
    of envelopes purchased was 40 percent higher than the 2005 price, but only 60 percent as many envelopes were bought.
    The total cost of the envelopes purchased in 2006 was MOST NEARLY

    A. $250 B. $320 C. $400 D. $480

25. In a city agency, 25 percent of the women employees and 50 percent of the men employ- 25.____
    ees attended a general staff meeting.
    If 48 percent of all the employees in the agency are women, the percentage of all the employees who attended the meeting is

    A. 36% B. 37% C. 38% D. 75%

KEY (CORRECT ANSWERS)

1.	D	11.	C
2.	B	12.	A
3.	A	13.	B
4.	C	14.	A
5.	C	15.	C
6.	C	16.	A
7.	D	17.	D
8.	C	18.	A
9.	B	19.	D
10.	D	20.	B

21. D
22. D
23. D
24. C
25. C

SOLUTIONS TO PROBLEMS

1. To determine number of days required to fill cabinet to capacity, subtract material in it from capacity amount, then divide by daily rate of adding material. Example: A cabinet already has 10 folders in it, and the capacity is 100 folders. Suppose 5 folders per day are added. Number of days to fill to capacity = (100-10) ÷ 5 = 18

2. To determine overall average salary, multiply number of employees in each division by that division's average salary, add results, then divide by total number of employees. Example: Division A has 4 employees with average salary of $40,000; division B has 6 employees with average salary of $36,000; division C has 2 employees with average salary of $46,000. Average salary = [(4)($40,000)+(6)($36,000)+(2)($46,000)] / 12 = $39,000

3. (6)(4) = 24 clerk-hours. Since only one-third of work has been done, (24)(3) - 24 = 48 clerk-hours remain. Then, 48 3 = 16 clerks. Thus, 16 - 6 = 10 additional clerks.

4. The percentage of students passing math in 2006 was less than the percentage of those passing math in 2004. Example: Suppose 400 students passed math in 2004. Then, (400)(.85) = 340 passed in 2005. Finally, (340)(1.15) = 391 passed in 2006.

5. 1400 - (.35)(1400) - (1/8)(1400) = 735

6. Let x = number of papers filed by clerk A, x-40 = number of papers filed by clerk B. Then, x + (x-40) = 190 Solving, x = 115

7. (500-125)(.16) + (130-45)(.12) + (50 - 48/12)(.08) = $60.00 + $10.20 + $3.68 = $73.88

8. (160)(.75) = 120 accidents due to unsafe acts in 2002. In 2004, (120)(.35) = 42 accidents due to unsafe acts

9. Original amount at beginning of February in the fund = (10)($1.40) + (1)($14.00) + (60)($1) + (16)(.25) + (40)(.10) + (80)(.05) = $100. Finally, for March, ($100)(.80) = $80 will be available

10. Total hours = (6)(5)(8) = 240

11. 35 ÷ .7 = 50

12. .1% of 25 = (.001)(25) = .025

13. Let A = percent of employees who are at least 25 years old and B = percent of employees who are high school graduates. Also, let N = percent of employees who fit neither category and J = percent of employees who are in both categories.
Then, 100 = A + B + N - J. Substituting, 100 = 80 + 65 + N - J To minimize J, let N = 0. So, 100 = 80 + 65 + 0 - J. Solving, J = 45

14. Let Y = number of clerks in Unit Y. Then, (8)(21) = (4)(28), so Y = 6. Unit X has 8 clerks who can file 174,528 cards in 72 flays; thus, each clerk in Unit X can file 174,528 ÷ 72 ÷ 8 = 303 cards per day. Adding 4 clerks to Unit Y will yield 10 clerks in that unit. Since their rate is equal to that of Unit X, the clerks in Unit Y will file, in 144 days, is (303)(10)(144) = 436,320 ≈ 436,000 cards.

15. Let x = required number of months. The cost of the machines in x months = (2)(14,750) + (2)(2000)(x) = 29,500 + 4000x. The savings in salaries for the displaced clerks = x[(2)(1550) +(4)(1700)] = 9900x. Thus, 29,500 + 4000x = 9900x. Solving, x = 5. So, five months will elapse in order to achieve a savings in cost.

16. Let x = amount used in July, so that .84x = amount used in August. For September, the amount used = (.84x)(1.25) = 1.05x. This means the amount used in September is 5% more than the amount used in July.

17. Each week he earns ($48)(5) = $240. Then, $2160 ÷ $240 = 9 weeks

18. (1+2+6) ÷ 63 = 1/7 ≈ 14%

19. Monthly payroll = (5)($1000) + (3)($2200) + (2)($1400) = $14,400

20. Yearly contribution to pension fund = (12)($1200)(.05) = $720

21. (50')(30') = 1500 sq.ft.

22. Old rate = 332.16 ÷ 48 = 6.92 (48 hours)
    New rate = 344.96 (44 hours)
    Overtime rate = 344.96 ÷ 44 = 7.75/hr. x 1.5 x 4 = 46.48
    344.96 + 46.48 = 391.44
    391.44 ÷ 48 = 8.15
    815 - 692 = 123 cents an hour more

23. Each of the 16 sections is a square with side [66'-(3)(6')] ÷ 4 = 12'. So each section contains (12')(12') = 144 sq.ft.
    The number of desk and chair sets = (144 ÷ 24) (16) = 96

24. In 2006, (.60)(12,000) = 7200 envelopes were bought and the price per hundred was ($4.00)(1.40) = $5.60. The total cost = (5.60)(72) = $403.20 ≈ $400

25. (.25)(.48) + (.50)(.52) = .38 = 38%

TEST 3

DIRECTIONS: Each question or incomplete statement is followed by several suggested answers or completions. Select the one that BEST answers the question or completes the statement. *PRINT THE LETTER OF THE CORRECT ANSWER IN THE SPACE AT THE RIGHT.*

1. According to one suggested filing system, no more than 12 folders should be filed behind any one file guide and from 10 to 20 file guides should be used in each file drawer. Based on this filing system, the MAXIMUM number of folders that a four-drawer file cabinet can hold is

    A. 240 B. 480 C. 960 D. 1,200

    1.____

2. A certain office uses three different forms. Last year, it used 3,500 copies of Form L, 6,700 copies of Form M, and 10,500 copies of Form P. This year, the office expects to decrease the use of each of these forms by 5%. The TOTAL number of these three forms which the office expects to use this year is

    A. 10,350 B. 16,560 C. 19,665 D. 21,735

    2.____

3. The hourly rate of pay for a certain part-time employee is computed by dividing his yearly salary rate by the number of hours in the work year. The employee's yearly salary rate is $18,928, and there are 1,820 hours in the work year.
If this employee works 18 hours during one week, his TOTAL earnings for these 18 hours are

    A. $180.00 B. $183.60 C. $187.20 D. $190.80

    3.____

4. Assume that the regular work week of an employee is 35 hours and that the employee is paid for any extra hours worked according to the following schedule. For hours worked in excess of 35 hours, up to and including 40 hours, the employee receives his regular hourly rate of pay. For hours worked in excess of 40 hours, the employee receives 1 1/2 times his hourly rate of pay.
If the employee's hourly rate of pay is $11.20 and he works 43 hours during a certain week, his TOTAL pay for the week would be

    A. $481.60 B. $498.40 C. $556.00 D. $722.40

    4.____

5. A clerk divided his 35 hour work week as follows:
    1/5 of his time in sorting mail;
    1/2 of his time in filing letters; and
    1/7 of his time in reception work.
The rest of his time was devoted to messenger work. The percentage of time spent on messenger work by the clerk during the week was MOST NEARLY

    A. 6% B. 10% C. 14% D. 16%

    5.____

6. A city department has set up a computing unit and has rented 5 computing machines at a yearly rental of $700 per machine. In addition, the cost to the department for the maintenance and repair of each of these machines is $50 per year. Five computing machine operators, each receiving an annual salary of $15,000, and a supervisor, who receives $19,000 a year, have been assigned to this unit. This unit will perform the work previously performed by 10 employees whose combined salary was $162,000 a year.
On the basis of these facts, the savings that will result from the operation of this computing unit for 5 years will be MOST NEARLY

    A. $250,000 B. $320,000 C. $330,000 D. $475,000

    6.____

7. Twelve clerks are assigned to enter certain data on index cards. This number of clerks could perform the task in 18 days. After these clerks have worked on this assignment for 6 days, 4 more clerks are added to the staff to do this work.
Assuming that all the clerks work at the same rate of speed, the entire task, instead of taking 18 days, will be performed in _____ days.

    A. 9 B. 12 C. 15 D. 16

8. Suppose that a file cabinet, which has a capacity of 3,000 cards, now contains approximately 2,200 cards. Cards are added to the file at the average rate of 30 cards a day.
To find the number of days it will take to fill the cabinet to capacity,

    A. divide 3,000 by 30
    B. divide 2,200 by 3,000
    C. divide 800 by 30
    D. multiply 30 by the fraction 2,200 divided by 3,000

9. Six gross of special drawing pencils were purchased for use in a city department.
If the pencils were used at the rate of 24 a week, the MAXIMUM number of weeks that the six gross of pencils would last is _____ weeks.

    A. 6 B. 12 C. 24 D. 36

10. A stock clerk had 600 pads on hand. He then issued 3/8 of his supply of pads to Division X, 1/4 to Division Y, and 1/6 to Division Z.
The number of pads remaining in stock is

    A. 48 B. 125 C. 240 D. 475

11. If a certain job can be performed by 18 clerks in 26 days, the number of clerks needed to perform the job in 12 days is _____ clerks.

    A. 24 B. 30 C. 39 D. 52

12. In anticipation of a seasonal increase in the amount of work to be performed by his division, a division chief prepared the following list of additional temporary employees needed by his division and the amount of time they would be employed:
    26 cashiers, each at $24,000 a year, for 2 months
    15 laborers, each at $85.00 a day, for 50 days
    6 clerks, each at $21,000 a year, for 3 months
The total approximate cost for this additional personnel would be MOST NEARLY

    A. $200,000 B. $250,000 C. $500,000 D. $600,000

13. A copy machine company offered to sell a city agency 4 copy machines at a discount of 15% from the list price, and to allow the agency $850 for each of its two old machines.
The list price of the new machines is $6,250 per machine.
If the city agency accepts this offer, the amount of money it will have to provide for the purchase of these 4 machines is

    A. $17,350 B. $22,950 C. $19,550 D. $18,360

14. A stationery buyer was offered bond paper at the following price scale:
    $1.43 per ream for the first 1,000 reams
    $1.30 per ream for the next 4,000 reams
    $1.20 per ream for each additional ream beyond 5,000 reams
    If the buyer ordered 10,000 reams of paper, the average cost per ream, computed to the nearest cent, was

    A. $1.24   B. $1.26   C. $1.31   D. $1.36

15. A clerk has 5.70 percent of his salary deducted for his retirement pension. If this clerk's annual salary is $20,400, the monthly deduction for his retirement pension is

    A. $298.20   B. $357.90   C. $1,162.80   D. $96.90

16. In a certain bureau, two-thirds of the employees are clerks and the remainder are typists. If there are 90 clerks, then the number of typists in this bureau is

    A. 135   B. 45   C. 120   D. 30

17. The number of investigations conducted by an agency in 1999 was 3,600. In 2000, the number of investigations conducted was one-third more than in 1999. The number of investigations conducted in 2001 was three-fourths of the number conducted in 2000. It is anticipated that the number of investigations conducted in 2002 will be equal to the average of the three preceding years. On the basis of this information, the MOST accurate of the following statements is that the number of investigations conducted in

    A. 1999 is larger than the number anticipated for 2002
    B. 2000 is smaller than the number anticipated for 2002
    C. 2001 is equal to the number conducted in 1999
    D. 2001 is larger than the number anticipated in 2002

18. A city agency engaged in repair work uses a small part which the city purchases for 14 each. Assume that, in a certain year, the total expenditure of the city for this part was $700.
    How many of these parts were purchased that year?

    A. 50   B. 200   C. 2,000   D. 5,000

19. The work unit which you supervise is responsible for processing 15 reports per month. If your unit has 4 clerks and the best worker completes 40% of the reports himself, how many reports would each of the other clerks have to complete if they all do an equal number?

    A. 1   B. 2   C. 3   D. 4

20. Assume that the work unit in which you work has 24 clerks and 18 stenographers. In order to change the ratio of stenographers to clerks so that there is 1 stenographer for every 4 clerks, it would be necessary to REDUCE the number of stenographers by

    A. 3   B. 6   C. 9   D. 12

21. The arithmetic mean salary for five employees earning $18,500, $18,300, $18,600, $18,400, and $18,500, respectively, is

    A. $18,450   B. $18,460   C. $18,475   D. $18,500

22. Last year, a city department which is responsible for purchasing supplies ordered bond paper in equal quantities from 22 different companies. The price was exactly the same for each company, and the total cost for the 22 orders was $693,113.
    Assuming prices did not change during the year, the cost of each order was MOST NEARLY

    A. $31,490   B. $31,495   C. $31,500   D. $31,505

23. Suppose that a large bureau has 187 employees. On a particular day, approximately 14% of these employees are not available for work because of absences due to vacation, illness, or other reasons. Of the remaining employees, 1/7 are assigned to a special project while the balance are assigned to the normal work of the bureau. The number of employees assigned to the normal work of the bureau on that day is

    A. 112   B. 124   C. 138   D. 142

24. Suppose that you are in charge of a typing pool of 8 typists. Two typists type at the rate of 38 words per minute; three type at the rate of 40 words per minute; three type at the rate of 42 words per minute. The average typewritten page consists of 50 lines, 12 words per line. Each employee works from 9 to 5 with one hour off for lunch.
    The total number of pages typed by this pool in one day is, on the average, CLOSEST to _____ pages.

    A. 205   B. 225   C. 250   D. 275

25. Suppose that part-time workers are paid $7.20 an hour, prorated to the nearest half hour, with pay guaranteed for a minimum of four hours if services are required for less than four hours. In one operation, part-time workers signed the time sheet as follows:

Worker	In	Out
A	8:00 A.M.	11:35 A.M.
B	8:30 A.M.	3:20 P.M.
C	7:55 A.M.	11:00 A.M.
D	8:30 A.M.	2:25 P.M.

    How much would TOTAL payment to these part-time workers amount to for this operation, assuming that those who stayed after 12 Noon were not paid for one hour which they took off for lunch?

    A. $134.40   B. $136.80   C. $142.20   D. $148.80

KEY (CORRECT ANSWERS)

1. C
2. C
3. C
4. B
5. D

6. B
7. C
8. C
9. D
10. B

11. C
12. A
13. C
14. B
15. D

16. B
17. C
18. D
19. C
20. D

21. B
22. D
23. C
24. B
25. B

———

SOLUTIONS TO PROBLEMS

1. Maximum number of folders = (4)(12)(20) = 960

2. (3500+6700+10,500)(.95) = 19,665

3. Hourly rate = $18,928 ÷ 1820 = $10.40. Then, the pay for 18 hours = ($10.40)(18) = $187.20

4. Total pay = ($11.20)(40) + ($11.20)(1.5)(3) = $498.40

5. (1 - 1/5 - 1/2 - 1/7)(100)% ≈ 16%

6. Previous cost for five years = ($324,000)(5) = $1,620,000
   Present cost for five years = (5)(5)($1,400) + (5)(5)($100) + (5)(5)($30,000) + (1)(5)($38,000) = $977,500   The net savings = $642,500 ≈ $640,000

7. (12)(18) = 216 clerk-days. Then, 216 - (12)(6) = 144 clerk-days of work left when 4 more clerks are added. Now, 16 clerks will finish the task in 144 ÷ 16 = 9 more days. Finally, the task will require a total of 6 + 9 = 15 days.

8. Number of days needed = (3000-2200) ÷ 30 = 26.7, which is equivalent to dividing 800 by 30.

9. (6)(144) = 864 pencils purchased. Then, 864 ÷ 24 = 36 maximum number of weeks

10. Number of remaining pads = 600 - (1)(600) - (1/4)(600) - (1/6)(600) = 125

11. (18)(26) ÷ 12 = 39 clerks

12. Total cost = (26)($24,000)(2/12) + (15)($85)(50) + (6)($21,000)(3/12) = $199,250 $200,000

13. (4)($6250)(.85) - (2)($850) = $19,550

14. Total cost = ($1.43)(1000) + ($1.30)(4000) + ($1.20X5000) = $12,630. Average cost per ream = $12,630 10,000 ≈ $1.26

15. Monthly salary = $20,400 ÷ 12 = $1700. Thus, the monthly deduction for his pension = ($1700)(.057) + $96.90

16. Number of employees = 90 ÷ 2/3 = 135. Then, the number of typists = (1/3)(135) = 45

17. The number of investigations for each year is as follows:
    1999: 3600
    2000: (3600)(1 1/3) = 4800
    2001: (4800)(3/4) = 3600
    2002: (3600+4800+3600)/3 = 4000
    So, the number of investigations were equal for 1999 and 2001.

18. $700 ÷ .14 = 5000 parts

19. The best worker does (.40)(15) = 6 reports. The other 9 reports are divided equally among the other 3 clerks, so each clerk does 9 ÷ 3 = 3 reports.

20. 1:4 = 6:24 . Thus, the number of stenographers must be reduced by 18 - 6 = 12

21. Mean = ($18,500+$18,300+$18,400+$18,500) ÷ 5 = $18,460

22. The cost per order = $693,113 ÷ 22 ≈ $31,505

23. 187 - (.14) = 26. 187 - 26 = 161 - 1/7 (161) = 23
    161 - 23 = 138

24. Number of words typed in 1 min. = (2)(38) + (3)(40) + (3)(42) = 322. For 7 hours, the total number of words typed = (7)(60)(322) = 135,240. Each page contains (on the average) (50)(12) = 600 words. Finally, 135,240 ÷ 600 ≈ 225 pages

25. Worker A = ($7.20)(4) = $28.80
    Worker B = ($7.20)(3 1/2) + ($7.20)(2 1/2) = $43.20
    Worker C = ($7.20)(4) = $28.80
    Worker D = ($7.20)(3 1/2) + ($7.20)(1 1/2) = $36.00
    Total for all 4 workers = $136.80
    Note: Workers A and C received the guaranteed minimum 4 hours pay each.

STENOGRAPHER-TYPIST EXAMINATION
CONTENTS

	Page
THE TYPING TEST	1
How the Test is Given	1
How the Test is Rated	1
How to Construct Additional Tests	2
Exhibit No. 6 Copying From Plain Paper	3
Practice Exercise	3
Test Exercise	4
Exhibit No. 7 Line Key for 5-Minute Typing Test	5
Speed	5
Accuracy	5
Exhibit No. 8 Maximum Number of Errors Permitted on 5-Minute Tests	6
THE DICTATION TEST	7
How the Transcript Booklet Works	7
How the Test is Administered	8
How the Answer Sheet is Scored	8
How to Construct Additional Tests	9
Exhibit No. 9 Dictation Test	11
Practice Dictation	11
Exhibit No. 10 Practice Dictation Transcript Sheet	13
Alphabetic World List	13
Transcript	13
Exhibit No. 11 Transcript Booklet-Dictation Test	15
Directions for Completing the Transcript	15
Directions for Marking the Separate Answer Sheet	15
Word List	16
Transcript	16
Exhibit No. 12 Key (Correct Answers)	18

THE TYPING TEST

In the test of ability to type, the applicant meets a single task, that of copying material exactly as it is presented. He must demonstrate how rapidly he can do so and with what accuracy. A specimen of the typing test is shown as Exhibit No. 6.

How The Test is Given

In order to follow usual examination procedure in giving the test, each competitor will need a copy of the test and two sheets of typewriter paper. About 15 minutes will be needed for the complete typing test.

Three minutes are allowed for reading the instructions on the face of the test and 3 minutes for the practice typing. The practice exercise consists of typing instructions as to spacing, capitalization, etc., and contains a warning that any erasures will be penalized. The practice typing helps make sure that the typewriter is functioning properly.

After the 3 minutes' practice typing, instruct the competitors to put fresh paper in their machines, and to turn the test page over and read the test for 2 minutes. After the 2 minutes, they are instructed to start typing the test. Five minutes are allowed for the test proper.

How the Test is Rated

The exercise must have been typed about once to meet the speed requirement of 40 words a minute. If this speed is not attained, the test is not scored for accuracy. As shown in Exhibit No. 7, a test paper that contains 17 lines meets the minimum speed requirement. Applicants have been instructed to begin and end each line precisely as in the printed test copy. From Exhibit No. 7 it can be quickly determined whether a typing test is to be rated for accuracy and, if so, the greatest number of errors permitted for the lines typed.

The next step is to compare the test paper with the printed test exercise and to mark and charge errors. The basic principles in charging typing errors are as follows:

Charge 1 for each—
WORD or PUNCTUATION MARK incorrectly typed or in which there is an erasure. (An error in spacing which follows an incorrect word or punctuation mark is not further charged.)
SERIES of consecutive words omitted, repeated, inserted, transposed, or erased. Charge for errors within such series, but the total charge cannot exceed the number of words.
LINE or part of line typed over other material, typed with all capitals, or apparently typed with the fingers on the wrong keys.
Change from the MARGIN where most lines are begun by the applicant or from the PARAGRAPAH INDENTION most frequently used by the applicant.

The typing score used in the official examination reflects both speed and accuracy, with accuracy weighted twice as heavily as speed. Other methods of rating typing often used in schools are based on gross words per minute or net words per minute (usually with not more than a fixed number of errors). Exhibit No. 8 will enable teachers and applicants to calculate typing proficiency in terms of gross words per minute and errors, and to determine whether that proficiency meets the minimum standards of eligibility required in the regular Civil Service examination.

Exhibit No. 8 gives the maximum number of errors permitted at various speeds for three different levels of typing ability. For example, at the minimum acceptable speed of 17 lines, or 40 gross words per minute, 3 errors are permitted for eligibility as GS-2 Clerk Typist or GS-3 Clerk-Stenographer. For GS-3 Clerk-Typist and GS-4 Clerk-Stenographer, and for GS-4 Clerk-Typist and GS-5 Clerk-Stenographer, higher standards of accuracy in relation to speed are reqired.

How to Construct Additional Tests

Here are some of the principal points followed by the examining staff in constructing typing tests so that the various tests will be comparable.

A passage should be subject matter that might reasonably be given a new typist in a government office. All words must be in sufficiently common use to be understood by most high school seniors, and the more difficult words must be dispersed throughout the passage rather than concentrated in one or two sentences. Sentence structure is not complicated. The length of the test exercise in Exhibit No. 6 is typical—21 lines of about 60 strokes each, with a total of about 1,250 strokes.

EXHIBIT NO. 6: COPYING FROM PLAIN COPY
(Part of the Stenographer-Typist Examination)

Read these directions carefully.

A practice exercise appears at the bottom of this sheet, and the test exercise itself is on the following page. First study these directions. Then, when the signal is given, begin to practice by typing the practice exercise below on the paper that has been given you. The examiner will tell you when to stop typing the practice exercise.

In both the practice and the test exercises, *space, paragraph, spell, punctuate, capitalize,* and *begin and end each line* precisely as shown in the exercises.

The examiner will tell you the exact time you will have to make repeated copies of the test exercise. Each time you complete the exercise, simply double space and begin again. If you fill up one side of the paper, turn it over and continue typing on the other side. Keep on typing until told to stop.

Keep in mind that you must meet minimum standards in both speed and accuracy and that, above these standards, accuracy is twice as important as speed. Make no erasures, insertions, or other corrections in this plain-copy test. Since errors are penalized whether or not they are erased or otherwise "corrected," it is best to keep on typing even though you detect an error.

PRACTICE EXERCISE

This practice exercise is similar in form and in difficulty to the one that you will be required to typewriter for the plain-copy test. You are to space, capitalize, punctuate, spell, and begin and end each line precisely as in the copy. Make no erasures, insertions, or other changes in this test because errors will be penalized even if they are erased or otherwise corrected. Practice typewriting this material on scratch paper until the examiner tells you to stop, remembering that for this examination it is more important for you to typewrite accurately than to typewrite rapidly.

TEST EXERCISE

    Because they have often learned to know types of architecture by decoration, casual observers sometimes fail to realize that the significant part of a structure is not the ornamentation but the body itself. Architecture, because of its close contact with human lives, is peculiarly and intimately governed by climate. For instance, a home built for comfort in the cold and snow of the northern areas of this country would be unbearably warm in a country with weather such as that of Cuba. A Cuban house, with its open court, would prove impossible to heat in a northern winter.

    Since the purpose of architecture is the construction of shelters in which human beings may carry on their numerous activities, the designer must consider not only climatic conditions but also the function of a building. Thus, although the climate of a certain locality requires that an auditorium and a hospital have several features in common, the purposes for which they will be used demand some difference in structure. For centuries builders have first complied with these two requirements and later added whatever ornamentation they wished. Logically, we should see as mere additions, not as basic parts, the details by which we identify architecture.

EACH TIME YOU REACH THIS POINT, DOUBLE SPACE AND BEGIN AGAIN.

EXHIBIT NO. 7: LINE KEY FOR 5-MINUTE TYPING TEST SHOWING MAXIMUM NUMBER OF ERRORS PERMISSIBLE FOR VARIOUS TYPING SPEEDS, AT GRADES GS-2 TYPIST AND GS-3 STENOGRAPHER

SPEED: In the following example, more than 16 lines have been typed for any speed rating. This sample key is constructed on the premise that if the competitor made the first stroke in her final line (even if it was an error), she is given credit for that line in determining the gross words per minute.

ACCURACY: The gross words per minute typed, at any line is the number *outside* the parentheses opposite that line. The numbers *in* the parentheses show the maximum number of errors permitted for that number of gross words per minute typed. The number of errors permitted increases with the speed. (This sample key shows the requirements for GS-2 Typist and GS-3 Stenographer. Exhibit No. 8 shows the standards for higher grades.) If the number of strokes per line were different, this table would have to be altered accordingly.

	Maximum Number of Errors Per Gross Words Per Minute Typed	
	1st Typing of Exercise	2nd Typing of Exercise
Because they have often learned to know types of architec		52(7)
tecture by decoration, casual observers sometimes fail to		54(7)
realize that the significant part of a structure is not the		56(8)
ornamentation but the body itself. Architecture, because		59(8)
of its close contact with human lives, is peculiarly and		61(9)
intimately governed by climate. For instance, a home built		64(9)
for comfort in the cold and snow of the northern areas of		66(10)
this country would be unbearably warm in a country with		68(10)
weather such as that of Cuba. A Cuban house, with its open		71(11)
court, would prove impossible to heat in a northern winter.		73(11)
Since the purpose of architecture is the construction of		76(12)
shelters in which human beings may carry on their numerous		78(12)
activities, the designer must consider not only climatic con-		80(12)[2]
ditions, but also the function of a building. Thus, although		
the climate of a certain locality requires that an auditorium		
and a hospital have several features in common, the purposes		
for which they will be used demand some difference in struc-	40(3)[1]	
ture. For centuries builders have first complied with these	42(4)	
two requirements and later added whatever ornamentation they	44(5)	
wished. Logically, we should see as mere additions, not as	47(6)	
basic parts, the details by which we identify architecture.	49(6)	

[1] The minimum rated speed is 40 gross words per minute for typing from printed copy.

[2] Any material typed after 80 gross words per minute (which is considered 100 in speed) is *not* rated for accuracy.

Note: The number of errors shown above must be proportionately increased for tests which are longer than 5 minutes.

EXHIBIT NO. 8: MAXIMUM NUMBER OF ERRORS PERMITTED ON 5-MINUTE TESTS AT VARIOUS SPEEDS FOR TYPING SCORES REQUIRED FOR TYPIST AND STENOGRAPHER POSITIONS

SPEED	MAXIMUM NUMBER OF ERRORS PERMITTED		
Gross Words Per Minute	GS-2 Clerk-Typist GS-3 Clerk-Stenographer	GS-3 Clerk-Typist GS-4 Clerk-Stenographer	GS-4 Clerk-Typist GS-5 Clerk-Stenographer
Under 40	Ineligible	Ineligible	Ineligible
40	3	9	2
41-42	4	4	2
43-44	5	4	2
45-47	6	5	3
48-49	6	5	3
50-52	7	6	4
53-54	7	6	4
55-56	8	7	5
57-59	8	7	5
60-61	9	8	6
62-64	9	8	7
65-66	10	9	7
67-68	10	9	8
69-71	11	10	8
72-73	11	10	9
74-76	12	11	10
77-78	12	11	10
79-80	12	12	10

NOTE: The number of errors shown above must be proportionately increased for tests which are longer than 5 minutes.

THE DICTATION TEST

The dictation test includes a practice dictation and a test exercise, each consisting of 240 words. The rate of dictation is 80 words a minute.

The dictation passages are nontechnical subject matter that might be given a stenographer in a government office. Sentence structure is not complicated and sentences are not extremely long or short. The words average 1.5 syllables in length.

As shown in Exhibit No. 9, each dictation passage is printed with spacing to show the point that the dictator should reach at the end of each 10 seconds in order to maintain an even dictation rate of 80 words a minute. This indication of timing is one device for assisting all examiners to conform to the intended dictation rate. All examiners are also sent instructions for dictating and a sample passage to be used in practicing dictating before the day of the test. By using these devices for securing uniform dictating and by providing alternate dictation passages that are as nearly equal as possible, the Commission can give each applicant a test that is neither harder nor easier than those given others competing for the same jobs.

The test differs from the conventional dictation test in the method of transcribing the notes. The applicant is not required to type a transcript of the notes, but follows a procedure that permits machine scoring of the test. When typewritten transcripts were still required, examiners rated the test by comparing every word of a competitor's paper with the material dictated and charging errors. Fairness to those competing for employment required that comparable errors be penalized equally. Because of the variety of errors and combinations of error that can be made in transcripts, the scoring of typewritten transcripts required considerable training and consumed much time—many months for large nationwide examination. After years of experimentation, a transcript booklet procedure was devised that simplified and speeded the scoring procedure.

Today, rating is decentralized to U.S. Civil Service Commission area offices, and test scores can be furnished quickly and accurately. The transcript booklet makes these improvements possible.

How the Transcript Booklet Works

The transcript booklet (see Exhibit No. 11) gives the stenographer parts of the dictated passage, but leaves blank spaces where many of the words belong. With adequate shorthand notes, the stenographer can readily fit the correct words into the blank spaces, which are numbered 1 through 125. At the left of the printed partial transcript is a list of words, each word with a capital letter A, B, C, or D beside it. Knowing from the notes what word belongs in a blank space, the competitor looks for it among the words in the list. The letter beside the word or phrase in the list is the answer to be marked in the space on the transcript. In the list there are other words that a competitor with inadequate notes might guess belong in that space, but the capital letter beside these words would be an incorrect answer. (Some persons find it helpful to write the word or the shorthand symbol in the blank space before looking for it in the word list. There is no objection to doing this.)

Look, for example, at the Practice Dictation Transcript Sheet, Exhibit No. 10, question 10. The word dictated is "physical"; it is in the word list with a capital "D." In the transcript, blank number 10 should be answered "D."

None of the words in the list is marked "E." This is because the answer "E" is reserved for any question when the word dictated for that spot does not appear in the list. Every transcript booklet has spots for which the list does not include the correct words. This provision reduces the possibility that competitors may guess correct answers.

After the stenographer has written the letter of the missing word or phrase in each numbered blank of the transcript, he transfers the answers to the proper spaces on the answer sheet. Directions for marking the separate answer sheet are given on page 1 of Exhibit No. 11.

This transcription procedure should not cause any good stenographer to make a poor showing on the examination. To this end, illustrations of the procedure are included in a sheet of samples that is mailed to each applicant with the notice of when and where to report for examination. Again in the examination room, the applicant uses such a transcript on the practice dictation before the actual dictation is given. A major objective in preparing this publication is to further insure that each prospective competitor is made to feel at ease about using this method of handling how good the notes are.

Use of the transcript booklet and transfer of answers to the answer sheet are clerical tasks that are not part of transcribing by typewriter. Most stenographic positions involve clerical duties for some percentage of the time and it is reasonable, therefore, to include clerical tasks in the examination. Although some unsuccessful competitors for stenographic positions attribute their failure to the use of transcript booklets, analysis of many test papers, notes, and transcripts has shown the frequency of clerical error in this test to be negligible.

How the Test is Administered

Each competitor will need a copy of the Practice Dictation Transcript Sheet (Exhibit No. 10), a copy of the Transcript Booklet (Exhibit No. 11), and an answer sheet (Exhibit No. 2). These should be distributed at the times indicated below.

The Practice Dictation of Exhibit No. 9 should be dictated at the rate indicated by the 10 second divisions in which it is printed. This will be at the rate of 80 words a minute. Then each competitor should be given a copy of the Practice Dictation Transcript Sheet and allowed 7 minutes to study the instructions and to transcribe part of the practice dictation.

The text exercise (reverse of Exhibit No. 9) should also be dictated at the rate of 80 words a minute, for 3 minutes. Each competitor should be given a Transcript Booklet and an answer sheet. He should be told that he will have 3 minutes for reading the directions on the face page, followed by 30 minutes for writing answers in the blank spaces, and then 10 minutes for transferring his answers to the answer sheet. These time limits are those used in the official examination and have been found ample.

How the Answer Sheet is Scored

The correct answers for the test are given in Exhibit No. 12. A scoring stencil may be prepared by copying these answers on a blank answer sheet and then punching out the marked answer boxes. Directions for using the scoring stencil are given at the top of Exhibit No. 12.

In some rare instances where the typewritten transcript is still used, the passing standard on the total transcript is 24 or fewer errors for GS-3 Clerk-Stenographer, and 12 or fewer errors for GS-4. Comparable standards on the parts of the dictation measured by the machine-scored method of transcription are 14 or fewer errors for GS-3, and 6 or fewer errors for GS-4 positions.

A stenographer who can take dictation at 80 words a minute with this degree of accuracy is considered fully qualified. Positions such as Reporting Stenographer and Shorthand Reporter require ability to take dictation at much higher speeds. The test for Reporting Stenographer is dictated at 120 words a minute. Two rates of dictation, 160 and 175 words a minute, are used for the Shorthand Reporter tests for different grade levels.

How to Construct Additional Tests

A teacher who has examined students by the tests in this part may wish to re-examine some of them after a period of further training. For this purpose, it is desirable to use new tests rather than to repeat the same test too often. If additional test material is needed, it should be constructed in accordance with the following principles in order to keep alternative tests comparable.

As already indicated, the subject matter and the vocabulary should not be technical or too unusual; they should appear to be part of the day-to-day business of an efficient government office. In view of the broad range of activities of Federal agencies, this restriction still allows a wide range of subject matter.

For 3 minutes of dictation at 80 words a minute, the exercise should contain 240 words. The average number of syllables should be about 1.5. Sentences should be straightforward, rather than of complicated grammatical construction. At the same time, they should not be short and choppy.

Before the transcript booklet is made, a skeleton transcript should be prepared. One way of beginning is to choose words and groups of words that should be tested. A total of about 140 words of the complete dictation passage should be chosen for testing, since some of the 125 numbered blank spaces in the transcript booklet should represent more than one word. As shown in the transcripts in Exhibits No. 10 and 11, the words selected for testing are not chosen simply by taking every other word; rather, they are single words or series of words distributed throughout the dictation passage. The first word of any sentence should not be used as a test word.

The dictation passage should be divided into four sections of about equal length with a section always breaking at the end of a sentence. A worksheet similar to that shown below should be prepared for each section.

For illustration of the next steps, look at the reverse side of the Practice Dictation Transcript Sheet, Exhibit No. 10; let the two sentences at the bottom of that page represent the dictation. The words that have been chosen for testing are "bring," "about," "to visit," "their," and so on; these words or phrases have been numbered 16, 17, etc. For a convenient worksheet, ruled paper can be divided into columns headed A, B, C, D, and E. Now the words chosen for the blanks should be distributed at random in the various columns. At this point the worksheet for this part of the test will look like the following:

	A	B	C	D	E
16	bring				
17					about
18		to visit			
19				their	
20				to discuss	
21					treatment
22			correction		
23					value
24		see			
25	is not				

(and so on)

Next, think of several plausible errors for each of the blanks; that is, a word beginning with the same sound, a word that fits the preceding or the following word almost as a cliché, etc. Avoid any error that is too conspicuously wrong or too clearly a misfit with printed auxiliaries or articles to present any difficulty. Place each plausible error in column A, B, C, or D of the worksheet, *avoiding* the column that contains the *answer*. The worksheet will now look like the columns below.

Experience will bring out situations that must be avoided, such as use of the same word in more than one column.

Each word in columns A, B, C, and D takes the letter at the head of the column. The words in these columns are grouped in alphabetic order to become the "Word List" for the section of the transcript covered by this worksheet. Since instructions provide that E is to be selected when the exact answer is not listed, the words in column E are NOT included in the "Word List." The sentences are presented with numbered blanks as the "Transcript."

	A	B	C	D	E
16	bring	promote	discuss	understand	
17	all				about
18	visit	to visit	at	during	
19	(all)		young	their	
20	to discover	undertake	{to endorse {indicated	to discuss	
21	treatments				treatment
22	reducing	collection	correction	recognizing	
23	friend	volume		virtue	value
24	know	see	say	satisfied	
25	is not	is	soon	{knows {insisted	

(and so on)

EXHIBIT NO. 9: DICTATION TEST
(Part of the Stenographer-Typist Examination)

PRACTICE DICTATION

INSTRUCTIONS TO THE EXAMINER: This Practice Dictation and one exercise will be dictated at the rate of 80 words a minute. Do not dictate the punctuation except for periods, but dictate with the expression that the punctuation indicates. Use a watch with a second hand to enable you to read the exercises at the proper speed.

Exactly on a minute, start dictating.

Finish reading each two lines at the number of seconds indicated below.

Text	Time
I realize that this practice dictation is not a part of the examination	10
proper and is not to be scored. (Period) The work of preventing and correcting	20
physical defects in children is becoming more effective as a result of a change	30
in the attitude of many parents. (Period) In order to bring about this change	40
mothers have been invited to visit the schools when their children are being examined	50
and to discuss the treatment necessary for the correction of defects. (Period)	1 min.
There is a distinct value in having a mother see that her child is not the	10
only one who needs attention. (Period) Otherwise a few parents might feel that they	20
were being criticized by having the defects of their children singled out for medical	30
treatment. (Period) The special classes that have been set up have shown the value of	40
the scientific knowledge that has been applied in the treatment of children. (Period)	50
In these classes the children have been taught to exercise by a trained teacher	2 min.
under medical supervision. (Period) The hours of the school day have been divided	10
between school work and physical activity that helps not only to correct their defects	20
but also to improve their general physical condition. (Period) This method of treatment	30
has been found to be very effective except for those who have severe medical	40
defects. (Period) Most parents now see how desirable it is to have these classes	50
that have been set up in the regular school system to meet special needs. (Period)	3 min.

After dictating the practice, pause for 15 seconds to permit competitors to complete their notes. Then continue in accordance with the directions for conducting the examination.

After the Practice Dictation Transcript has been completed, dictate the test from the following.

Exactly on a minute, start dictating.

	Finish reading each two lines at the number of seconds indicated below.
The number enrolled in shorthand classes in the high schools has shown a marked increase. (Period)	10
Today this subject is one of the most popular offered in the field of	20
business education. (Period) When shorthand was first taught, educators claimed that it was of	30
value mainly in sharpening the powers of observation and discrimination. (Period)	40
However, with the growth of business and the increased demand for office workers,	50
educators have come to realize the importance of stenography as a vocational	1 min.
tool. (Period) With the differences in the aims of instruction came changes in	10
the grade placement of the subject. (Period) The prevailing thought has always been that it	20
should be offered in high school. (Period) When the junior high school first came into	30
being, shorthand was moved down to that level with little change in the manner in which	40
the subject was taught. (Period) It was soon realized that shorthand had no place there	50
because the training had lost its vocational utility by the time the student could	2 min.
graduate. (Period) Moreover, surveys of those with education only through junior	10
high school seldom found them at work as stenographers. (Period) For this reason, shorthand	20
was returned to the high school level and is offered as near as possible to the time	30
of graduation so that the skill will be retained when the student takes a job. (Period)	40
Because the age at which students enter office jobs has advanced, there is now	50
a tendency to upgrade business education into the junior college. (Period)	3 min.

After completing the dictation, pause of 15 seconds.
Give a Transcript to each competitor.

EXHIBIT NO. 10: PRACTICE DICTATION TRANSCRIPT SHEET
(Part of the Stenographer-Typist Examination)

The transcript below is part of the material that was dictated to you for practice, except that many of the words have been left out. From your notes, you are to tell what the missing words are. Proceed as follows:

Compare your notes with the transcript and, when you come to a blank in the transcript, decide what word or words belong there. For example, you will find that the word "practice" belongs in blank number 1. Look at the Word List to see whether you can find the same word there. Notice what letter (A, B, C, or D) is printed beside it, and write that letter in the blank. For example, the word "practice" is listed, followed by the letter "B." We have already written "B" in blank number 1 to show you how you are to record your choice. Now decide what belongs in each of the other blanks. (You may also write the word or words, or the shorthand for them, if you wish.) The same word may belong in more than one blank. If the exact answer is not listed, write "E" in the blank.

TRANSCRIPT

I realize that this __B__ dictation is _____
                       1   2
a _____ of the _____ _____ and is _____ _____
  3   4   5   6   7
scored.

    The work of _____ and _____ _____ defects in
                            8   9   10
_____ is becoming more _____ as a _____ a
 11   12   13
change in the _____ of many _____....
                14   15

ALPHABETIC WORD LIST	
about-B	paper-B
against-C	parents-B
attitude-A	part-C
being-D	physical-D
childhood-B	portion-D
children-A	practical-A
correcting-C	practice-B
doctors-B	preliminary-D
effective-D	preventing-B
efficient-A	procedure-A
examination-A	proper-C
examining-C	reason for-A
for-B	result-B
health-B	result of-C
mothers-C	schools-C
never-C	to be-C
not-D	to prevent-A

Each numbered blank in the Transcript is a question. You will be given a separate answer sheet like the sample here, to which you will transfer your answers. The answer sheet has a numbered row of boxes for each question. The answer for blank number 1 is "B." We have already transferred this to number 1 in the Sample Answer Sheet, by darkening the box under "B."

Now transfer your answer for each of questions 2 through 15 to the answer sheet. That is, beside each number on the answer sheet find the letter that is the same as the letter you wrote in the blank with the same number in the transcript, and darken the box below that letter.

After you have marked 15, continue with blank number 16 on the next page WITHOUT WAITING FOR A SIGNAL.

TRANSCRIPT (continued)

In order to _____ _____ this change, mothers
                16   17
have been invited _____ the schools when _____
                      18   19
children are being examined and _____ the _____
                                 20   21
necessary for the _____ of defects. There is a
                   22
distinct _____ in having a mother _____ that her
        23   24
child _____ the only one who needs attention....
       25

ALPHABETIC WORD LIST	
all-A	reducing-A
at-C	satisfied-D
bring-A	say-C
collection-B	see-B
correction-C	soon-C
discuss-C	their-D
during-D	to discover-A
friend-A	to discuss-D
indicated-C	to endorse-C
insisted-D	to visit-B
is-B	treatments-A
is not-A	understand-D
know-A	undertake-B
knows-D	virtue-D
needed-B	visit-A
promote-B	volume-B
recognizing-D	young-C

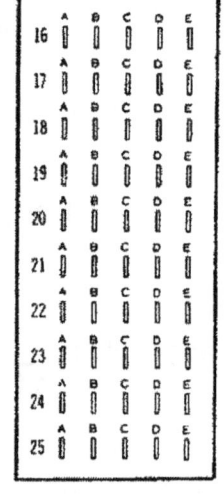

Your notes should show that the word "bring" goes in blank 16, and "about" in blank 17. But "about" is *not in the list*; so "E" should be your answer for Question 17.

The two words, "to visit-B," are needed for 18, and the one word "visit-A," would be an incorrect answer.

Fold this page so that the Correct Answers to Samples 1 through 8, below, will lie beside the Sample Answer Sheet you marked for those questions. Compare your answers with the correct answers. Then fold the page and compare the correct answers with your answers for 9 through 15. If one of your answers does not agree with the correct answer, again compare your notes with the samples and make certain you understand the instructions. The correct answers for 16 through 25 are as follows: 16-A, 17-E, 18-B, 19-D, 20-D, 21-E, 22-C, 23-E, 24-B, and 25-A.

For the actual test, you will use a separate answer sheet. As scoring will be done by an electronic scoring machine, it is important that you follow directions carefully. Use a medium No. 2 pencil. You must keep your mark for a question within the box. If you have to erase a mark, be sure to erase it completely. Mark only one answer for each question.

For any stenographer who missed the practice dictation, part of it is given below:

"I realize that this practice dictation is not a part of the examination proper and is not to be scored.

"The work of preventing and correcting physical defects in children is becoming more effective as a result of a change in the attitude of many parents. In order to bring about this change, mothers have been invited to visit the schools when their children are being examined and to discuss the treatment necessary for the correction of defects. There is a distinct value in having a mother see that her child is not the only one who needs attention..."

EXHIBIT NO. 11: TRANSCRIPT BOOKLET – DICTATION TEST
(Part of Stenographer-Typist Examination)

Directions for Completing the Transcript

A transcript of the dictation you have just taken is given on Pages 15 and 16. As in the transcript for the practice dictation, there are numbered blank spaces for many of the words that were dictated. You are to compare your notes with the transcript and, when you come to a blank, decide what word or words belong there. For most of the blanks the words are included in the list beside the transcript; each is followed by a letter, A, B, C, or D. To show that you know which word or words belong in each blank space, you are to write the letter in the blank. You are to write E if the exact answer is NOT listed. (In addition, you may write the word or words, or the shorthand for them, if you wish.) The same choice may belong in more than one blank.

After you have compared your notes with the transcript and have chosen the answer for each blank space, you will be given additional time to transfer your answers to a separate answer sheet.

Directions for Marking the Separate Answer Sheet

On the answer sheet, each question number stands for the blank with the same number in the transcript. For each number, you are to darken the box below the letter that is the same as the letter you wrote in the transcript. (The answers in this booklet will not be rated.) Be sure to use your pencil and record your answers on the separate answer sheet. You must keep your mark within the bod. If you have to erase a mark, be sure to erase it completely. Make only one mark for each question.

Work quickly so that you will be able to finish in the time allowed. First, you should darken the boxes on the answer sheet for the blanks you have lettered. You may continue to use your notes if you have not finished writing letters in the blanks in the transcript, or if you wish to make sure you have lettered them correctly.

TRANSCRIPT

The number _____ in shorthand _____ _____
    1   2   3
high schools has _____ a _____ _____. Today _____
                  4   5   6   7
_____ is one of the most _____ _____ _____ _____ of
  8   9   10   11   12
business _____. When _____ _____ _____ _____
          13   14   15   16   17
educators _____ that it _____ _____ _____ in _____
           18   19   20   21   22
_____ _____ of _____ and _____.
  23   24   25   26

...However, _____ the growth of _____ and the _____
              27   28   29
for _____ _____, _____ have _____ _____ the _____
     30   31   32   33   34   35
of _____ _____ _____ _____ in the _____ _____ of the
    36   37   38   39   40   41
_____. The _____ _____ _____ _____ that _____
  42   43   44   45   46   47
_____ _____ in _____.
  48   49   50

ALPHABETIC WORD LIST	
Write E if the answer is NOT listed	
administration-C	observation-B
along the-B	observing-A
area-A	offered-C
at first-A	of value-C
claimed-C	open-A
classes-B	popular-B
concluded-D	power-B
could be-D	powers-D
courses-C	practical-A
decrease-D	shaping-A
discriminating-C	sharpen-B
discrimination-D	shorthand-D
education-B	shown-C
enrolled-D	stenography-B
entering-A	study-C
field-D	subject-A
first-D	taught-D
given-B	that-C
great-C	the-D
increase-A	these-B
in the-D	this-A
known-D	thought-B
line-C	to be-A
mainly-B	training-D
marked-B	valuable-A
mostly-D	vast-A

ALPHABETIC WORD LIST	
Write E if the answer is NOT listed	
a change-D	offered-C
administration-C	office-A
aims-A	official-C
always been-A	often been-B
begun-D	ought to be-B
businesses-A	place-B
came-D	placement-D
changes-B	prevailing-B
come-C	rule-D
defects-B	schools-D
demand-B	shorthand-D
demands-A	should be-A
differences-D	significance-C
education-B	stenography-B
educators-D	study-A
for-D	subject-A
given-B	thinking-C
grade-C	this-A
grading-B	thought-B
has-C	tool-B
had-B	to realize-B
have come-A	to recognize-B
high school-B	valuable-A
increased-D	vocational-C
increasing-C	when the-D
institutions-D	with-A
instruction-C	without-C
it-B	workers-C

...When the _____ school _____ _____ _____ _____, _____
                57   58   59   60   61
was _____ to _____ _____ with _____ _____ in _____
       62   63   64   65   66   67
_____ _____ the _____ was _____. It was _____
  68   69   70   71   72
_____ that _____ _____ place _____ _____ the _____
  73   74   75   76   77   78
had _____ _____ _____ _____ by the _____ the
      79   80   81   82   83
_____ _____ _____.
  84   85   86

ALPHABETIC WORD LIST	
Write E if the answer is NOT listed	
became-B	moved-C
because-B	moved down-B
came-D	occupational-B
change-A	recognized-A
changed-C	shorthand-D
could-C	since-C
could be-D	soon-C
date-D	stenography-B
first-D	student-A
graduate-D	students-C
graduated-B	study-C
had little-C	subject-A
had no-A	taught-D
here-D	that-C
high-C	the-D
into being-A	their-B
into business-C	there-B
junior high-D	this-A
less-B	time-B
lessened-C	training-D
level-C	usefulness-B
little-A	utility-C
lost-D	vocational-C
manner-B	which-A
method-C	

...Moreover, _____ of _____ with _____ _____ _____
              87   88   89   90   91
_____ school _____ _____ them _____ as _____. For
  92   93   94   95   96
_____ _____, shorthand was _____ to the _____ _____
  97   98   99   100 101
and is _____ as _____ _____ to the _____ _____ _____
        102   103   104   105   106   107
_____ the skill _____ _____ _____ _____ the student
  108   109   110   111   112
_____ a _____. Because the _____ _____ students
  113   114   115   116
_____ office _____ _____ _____, there is _____ a
  117   118   119   120   121
_____ to _____ _____ education _____ the junior
  122   123   124   125
college.

ALPHABETIC WORD LIST	
Write E if the answer is NOT listed	
advanced-A	reason-B
age-A	reasons-D
as far as-C	retained-B
at which-D	school-A
at work-A	secretaries-D
be-B	secures-D
date-D	seldom-C
education-B	showed-A
enter-D	so-A
found-D	stenographers-C
graduating-A	studies-B
graduation-C	surveys-A
has-C	takes-A
high school-B	taught-D
in-A	tendency-B
in order-D	that-C
increased-D	there-B
into-B	this-A
job-B	through-D
junior high-D	time-B
level-C	training-D
may be-C	undertake-A
near as-A	until-A
nearly as-C	upgrade-D
offered-C	when-C
often-B	which-A
only-B	will-B
possible-D	would-D
rarely-D	working-B

KEY (CORRECT ANSWERS)

EXHIBIT NO. 12: SCORING STENCIL-RIGHT ANSWERS

If the competitor marked more than one answer to any question, draw a line through the answer boxes for the question. To make a stencil, punch out the answers on this page or on a separate answer sheet. Place this punched key over a competitor's sheet. Count the right answers. DO NOT GIVE CREDIT FOR DOUBLE ANSWERS.

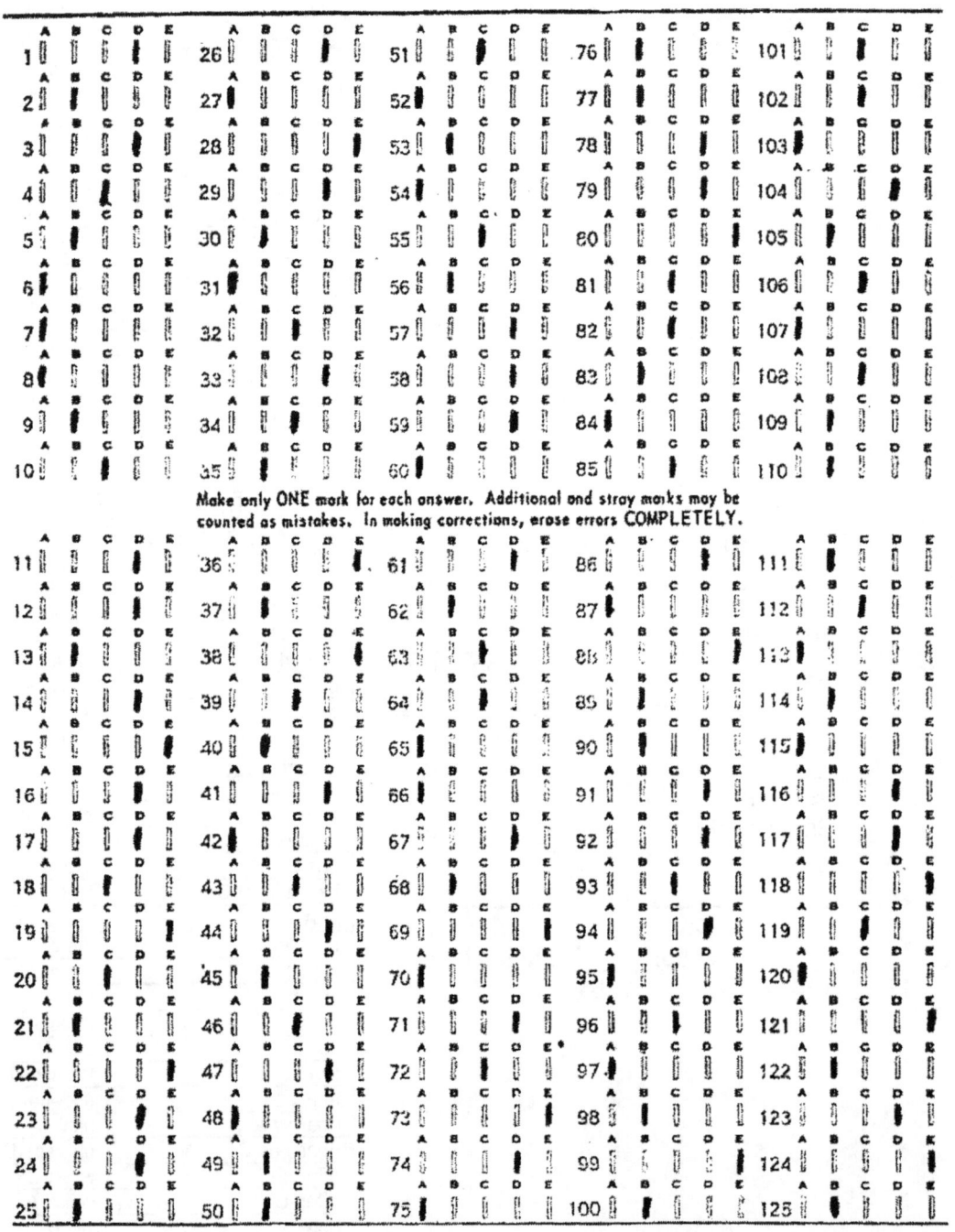

Make only ONE mark for each answer. Additional and stray marks may be counted as mistakes. In making corrections, erase errors COMPLETELY.

www.ingramcontent.com/pod-product-compliance
Lightning Source LLC
Chambersburg PA
CBHW080731230426
43665CB00020B/2694